I0418936

MEDITERRANEAN
TATTOOS

MEDITERRANEAN
TATTOOS

The History of Tattooing
Since Its Earliest Origins

Edited by Luisa Gnecchi Ruscone and Guido Guerzoni

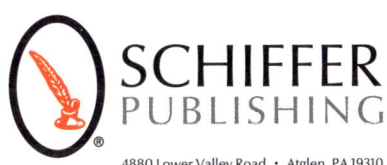

SCHIFFER
PUBLISHING

4880 Lower Valley Road · Atglen, PA 19310

MEDITERRANEAN
TATTOOS

28.03.2024
28.07.2024

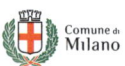

Mayor
Giuseppe Sala

Assessore alla Cultura
Tommaso Sacchi

Councillor for Culture
Domenico Piraina

Director of the Museum of Cultures, Intercultural Projects, and Art in Public Spaces
Marina Pugliese

MUDEC
Museo delle Culture

Coordination
Renato Rossetti

Administrative Office
Rossella Di Marco
Rosa Regine

Conservatory
Carolina Orsini
Sara Rizzo

Deputy Curator of Contemporary Art
Katya Inozemtseva

Technical Office
Giuseppe Braga

Secretariat
Susi Silvestre
Sonia Farano

Communication
Gaia D'Onofrio

INTERCULTURAL PROJECTS OFFICE, NETWORKS AND COOPERATION

Coordination
Bianca Aravecchia
Alessandra Cecchinato

Conservatory
Sara Chiesa
Anna Antonini

ART OFFICE IN PUBLIC SPACES

Coordination
Alice Cosmai
Franca Faragò
Aldo Marchesini

Conservatory
Alessandro Oldani

UNIVERSAL CIVIL SERVICE

Lorenzo Gandola
Giorgia Garuti
Giulia Longoni
Francesca Salemi

HERITAGE ENHANCEMENT AND HEADQUARTERS SECURITY AREAI

Director
Fabrizio Chirico

Management and Development Unit Museum Services
Organizational Position
Monica Chiapello

Area Command Office Modern Art Museums Director
Eugenio Maserati

Contact
Alessia De Pasquale
Elena Marchiol
Chiara Marina Nasti

Museum operators
Mudec

IL SOLE 24 ORE S.p.A.

President
Edoardo Garrone

Chief Executive Officer
Mirja Cartia d'Asero

24 ORE CULTURA S.r.l.

President
Mirja Cartia d'Asero

Chief Executive Officer
Federico Silvestri

SECTOR MANAGERS

Mudec, Ticketing, Education and Communications
Simona Serini

Exhibitions, Development and International Relations Office
Paola Cappitelli

Editorial Office and Bookshop
Chiara Savino

EXHIBITION OFFICE

Coordination
Francesca Calabretta

Coordination and foreign development
Francesca Cavola

Elena Calasso
Raffaella Ferraro
Lucia Frassoni
Roberta Pagani
Giuseppe Scandiani

Registrar
Sandra Serafini

MARKETING & EVENTS

Coordination
Daniela Piuzzi

Francesco Cassinari
Victoria Sara Kaspar

with the assistance of
Erica Kullmann
Alessia Rampoldi

Copyright © 2026 by Schiffer Publishing, Ltd.

Originally published as *Tatuaggio: Storie dal Mediterraneo* by 24 ORE Cultura srl © 2024 24 ORE Cultura Translated from the Italian by Liza Tripp

Library of Congress Control Number: 2025939858

All rights reserved. No part of this work may be reproduced or used in any form or by any means—graphic, electronic, or mechanical, including photocopying or information storage and retrieval systems—without written permission from the publisher.
    The scanning, uploading, and distribution of this book or any part thereof via the Internet or any other means without the permission of the publisher is illegal and punishable by law. Please purchase only authorized editions and do not participate in or encourage the electronic piracy of copyrighted materials.
    "Schiffer," "Schiffer Publishing, Ltd.," and the pen and inkwell logo are registered trademarks of Schiffer Publishing, Ltd.

Graphic design and layout by Davide Canesi / PEPE nymi

ISBN: 978-0-7643-7100-4

Printed in China
10 9 8 7 6 5 4 3 2 1

Published by Schiffer Publishing, Ltd.
4880 Lower Valley Road
Atglen, PA 19310
Phone: (610) 593-1777; Fax: (610) 593-2002
Email: info@schifferbooks.com
Web: www.schifferbooks.com

For our complete selection of fine books on this and related subjects, please visit our website at www.schifferbooks.com. You may also write for a free catalog.
    Schiffer Publishing's titles are available at special discounts for bulk purchases for sales promotions or premiums. Special editions, including personalized covers, corporate imprints, and excerpts, can be created in large quantities for special needs. For more information, contact the publisher.

Show

COMMUNICATION OFFICE

Coordination
Martina Amadessi

Rebecca Fabbri

with the assistance of
Claudia Bambacigno

*Digital communication
and social media*
Delfina Grassi

*Graphic and technical
coordination*
Maurizio Bartomioli

24 ORE Group Press Office
Ginevra Cozzi
Elettra Occhini

SERVICES

*Museum Services Operation
and Ticketing*
Giorgia Montagna

*Coordination of Museum
Services*
Cinzia Leccioli

Educational Services Specialist
Martina Fusaro

Groups and Ticketing Office
Davide Negri
Marco Nidasio
Elisabetta Palestra

EDITORIAL OFFICE

Coordination
Stefania Vadrucci

Gian Marco Sivieri
Giulia Vielmi

Marketing and Italian Bookstore
Monica Panciera

BOOKSHOP OFFICE

Verdiana Iannazzo
Marika Valbuzzi

*Editorial Operation and
Bookshop*
Monica Ricca
Ornella Fiorellinetto

GENERAL SECRETARIAT

Elisabetta Colombo

Curated by
Luisa Gnecchi Ruscone
Guido Guerzoni

With the collaboration of
Jurate Francesca Piacenti

*Exhibition design,
multimedia, graphics
and corporate identity*
Dotdotdot

Lighting design
Francesco Murano

Lights
Gigi Events

Graphic design and printing
Way srl

Hardwares & service
Neo Tech

*Transport and installation
of works*
Crown Fine Art

Condition report
Studio Fiori

Translations
Sylvia Notini

Insurance
Marsh S.p.A.

Audioguide
Orpheo Group

*Guided tours and
educational activities*
24 ORE Cultura Education

Display Security services
Natuna

Ticket office
Ticket 24 ORE

*Thanks for your valuable
assistance:*
Francesco Aquilanti
Anne Austin
Zohra Bensemra
Cristina Cilli
Gianmaurizio Fercioni
Olivia Fercioni
Aimen Finear
Elisabetta Gnecchi Ruscone
Cédric Gobeil
Jodi Hilton
Nataša Ilinčić
Lars Krutak
Vito Punzi

*For the iconographic
and textual research, we
thank:*
Beatrice Corti
Lucia Prennushi
Massimo Zanella

A special thanks to all
the tattoo artists who lent
their voices and their visual
narratives of tattooing today.

Exhibit Lenders

Collezione delle cere
anatomiche "Luigi
Cattaneo" – Alma Mater
Studiorum Università
di Bologna

Delegazione Pontificia
per il Santuario della Santa
Casa di Loreto

Mudec – Museo delle
Culture, Milan

Museo Archeologico
dell'Alto Adige, Bolzano

Museo delle Civiltà, Rome

Museo di Antropologia
Criminale Cesare Lombroso
– Università
di Torino

Parco Archeologico
di Cerveteri e Tarquinia

Rijksmuseum van
Oudheden, Leiden

Tattoo Museo Gianmaurizio
Fercioni, Milan

Wassim Razzouk Collection,
Jerusalem

Fondazione Gian Paolo
Barbieri, Milan

Catalog

A cura di
Luisa Gnecchi Ruscone
Guido Guerzoni

Testi di
Cristina Cilli
Cedric Gobeil
Katharina Hersel
Nataša Ilinčić
Luisa Gnecchi
Guido Guerzoni
Silvano Montaldo

*Coordinamento
e ricerca iconografica*
Massimo Zanella

Editing
Milanoedit srl;
Marco Torriani

*Progetto grafico
e impaginazione*
Davide Canesi / PEPE nymi

Si ringrazia
Walter Rocchetti per
la consulenza tecnica

Sponsor

INSTITUTIONAL PARTNER

**Fondazione
Deloitte**

Deloitte.

Deloitte Italy, under the patronage
of the Deloitte Foundation, is
partnering with 24 ORE Cultura for
projects to be implemented at Mudec. Culture is one of the key areas
on which the Deloitte Foundation
has chosen to focus its efforts,
both by promoting the protection
and enhancement of cultural
heritage and artistic assets and by
working alongside organizations
of excellence in Italy—such as 24
ORE Cultura—to disseminate and
disseminate knowledge of scientific and human knowledge.

OFFICIAL TRAIN SERVICE

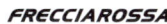

TECHNICAL SPONSOR

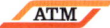

The *Mediterranean Tattoos* exhibition, masterfully curated by Luisa Gnecchi Ruscone and Guido Guerzoni, and with the extraordinary participation of Jurate Francesca Piacenti, invites viewers on a journey into the fascinating world of tattooing at the Museum of Cultures.

With an impressive 48 percent of the adult population tattooed, Italy stands as a world leader in this cultural phenomenon, and the exhibition project aims to probe the depths of tattooing, shedding light on essential questions regarding those who undergo this art form, what motivations drive them to do so, and what stories lie behind the indelible marks on the skin.

The itinerary, embellished with multimedia installations and documents from institutions such as the Archaeological Museum of South Tyrol, the "Cesare Lombroso" Museum of Criminal Anthropology of the University of Turin, the National Museum of Popular Arts and Traditions in Rome, the Pontifical Museum of the Sanctuary of the Holy House of Loreto, and the exclusive collections of the Gianmaurizio Fercioni Tattoo Museum in Milan, spans five thousand years of human history.

The exhibition explores the many functions of tattooing, from talisman to therapy and social practice, highlighting its crucial role in different eras, from the great explorations to the stigmatization of the nineteenth century, culminating in its current mass diffusion.

Through a compelling perspective, the *Mediterranean Tattoos* exhibition reveals how, over the centuries, tattooing has transformed from a personal symbol to a socially recognized and celebrated artistic expression.

Tommaso Sacchi
Councillor for Culture
Municipality of Milan

Organizing an exhibition on the history of tattooing in the vast area of the Mediterranean basin, moreover with insights into the very long-lasting Italian history, overturns the usual and often-preconceived reading of a millenary phenomenon in its diachronic ubiquity that is usually associated with other cultures and that instead has a lot to do with ours as well.

In the exhibition, lesser-known aspects of our deepest history have been reread and reinterpreted, which have remained hidden in the folds of an embarrassed historiographical silence. Speaking therefore of a local "primitivism" that intersects not only, as might seem obvious, with phenomena of deviance, marginality, and delinquency, but also with the aristocratic ethos, the devotional practices of the continental elites, and with popular cults and lesser-known forms of religious proselytism.

From cultural tattooing to tribal tattooing, to the serial tattoo of recent times, the exhibition intelligently interprets a complex and too-often-trivialized phenomenon against the light, shedding light on an identity practice that is very far from its massified homologation today.

Marina Pugliese
Director of the Museum of Cultures Area,
Intercultural Projects and Art in Public Space
Municipality of Milan

According to the latest published research, Italy is at the top of the list of countries with the highest number of tattooed people. It is a recent social and cultural phenomenon, but one that characterizes us significantly, also by virtue of an ancient tradition that few people know.

For a museum whose mission is to tell the cultures of the world and the material culture of peoples and to investigate the great themes of contemporaneity through the multifaceted gaze of art, a moment of reflection dedicated to this theme could not be missing, given the wide social relevance recorded for this phenomenon.

The result was a survey commissioned by 24 ORE Cultura, the results of which are the content of a very interesting and unprecedented exhibition on the evolution of tattooing in the Mediterranean basin.

After all, it is also in the DNA of our group to pay constant attention to social issues, analyzed with the objective gaze of those who publish investigations, articles, and reports every day that investigate reality through the analysis of numbers and facts.

This is also the added value of all our exhibitions: trying to find more gazes each time to interpret past and present society. The artistic one is never lacking, and from it we can often take inspiration to decipher the modern reality that surrounds us, using all the tools we have at our disposal, starting with an exhibition that is a kaleidoscope of stimuli for the visitor and an incubator of personal reflections.

Edoardo Garrone
President of 24 ORE Group

CONTENTS

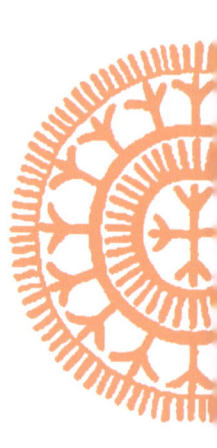

12

A Mediterranean History

Guido Guerzoni

18

Why a Book on Tattoos of
the Mediterranean Basin

Luisa Gnecchi

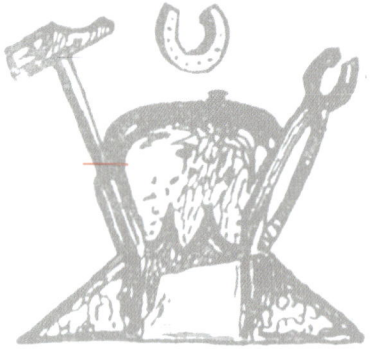

28

Ötzi, the Tattooed Iceman

Katharina Hersel

40

A Tattooed Female Mummy
in Deir el-Medina

Cedric Gobeil

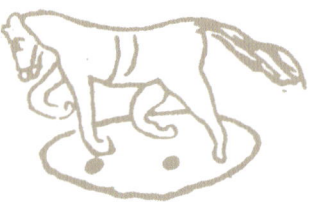

54

The Tattooing of Artisans in Italy
and Europe After the Fall of
the Roman Empire

Luisa Gnecchi

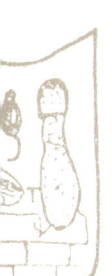

66

Devotional Tattoos in Italy: The Case of Loreto and the Connection to Jerusalem

Guido Guerzoni

96

Engraved Prison Pottery and Tattoos of the Museo di Antropologia Criminale "Cesare Lombroso" of the University of Turin

Cristina Cilli and Silvano Montaldo

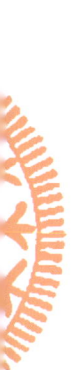

120

Traditional Tattoos of Women in the Balkans: Jajce, a Case Study in Bosnia and Herzegovina

Nataša Ilinčić

144

Tattoo Gallery

A Mediterranean History

—— Guido Guerzoni

I'm both honored and pleased to be writing this preface, because this book has managed (and I believe unquestionably so) to overcome strong and deep-rooted historiographic prejudices. In the past, most Italian authors have insisted on the nonnative and exotic origins of tattoos, de facto renouncing any form of historical continuity in Italy and across Europe.

Therefore, while not completely discounting the dissemination of tattoos across the Egyptian and Greco-Roman world, it was long considered that tattooing had quickly disappeared from the old continent, being a practice specific to pre- and protohistoric civilizations, "one of the peculiar features of primitive man, of man in a state of savageness," a shameful mark that would reveal with a

1. See, on this subject, R. S. Bianchi, "Tattoo in Ancient Egypt," in Rubin, *Marks of Civilisation*, 21–28 and ID.; "Tätowierung," in W. Helck and E. Otto, eds., *Lexicon der Ägyptologie* (Wiesbaden, Germany, 1986), 145–146; V. Burrus, "Macrina's Tattoo," *Journal of Medieval and Early Modern Studies* 33 (2003): 403–417; K. M. Coleman, "Fatal Charades: Roman Executions Staged as Mythological Enactments," *Journal of Roman Studies* 80 (1990): 44–73; F. J. Dölger, *Sphragis: Eine Altchristliche Tuafbezeichnung in ihren Beziehungen zur profanen und religiösen Kultur des Altertums* (Paderborn, Germany, 1911 and ID.; "Religiöser oder profaner Charakter der Stammestätowierung?" *Jahrbuch für Antike und Christentum* 2 (1930): 204–209 and ID.; "Beiträge zur Geschichte des Kreuzzeichens," *Jahrbuch für Antike und Christentum* 1 (1958): 5–19; S. Elm, "Pierced by Bronze Needles," *Journal of Early Christian Studies* 4 (1996): 409–439 and EAD.; "Sklave Gottes–Stigmata, Bischöfe und anti-häretische Propoganda im vierten Jahrhunder," *Historische Anthropologie* 8 (1999): 345–363 and EAD.; "Marking the Self in Late Antiquity. Inscriptions, Baptism and the Conversion of Mimes," in B. Menke and B. Vinken, eds., *Stigmata* (Paderborn, Germany, 2004), 47–68; M. Gustafson, "Condemnation to the Mines in the Later Roman Empire," *Harvard Theological Review* 87 (1994), pp. 421–433, ID. "Inscripta in fronte: Penal Tattooing in Late Antiquity," *Classical Antiquity* 16 (1997): 79–105 and ID.; "The Tattoo in Later Roman Empire and Beyond," in *Written on the Body*, 16–31; C. P. Jones, "Stigma: Tattooing and Branding in Greco-Roman Antiquity, *Journal of Roman Studies* 72 (1987): 139–155 and ID.; "Stigma and Tattoo," in *Written on the Body*, 1–15; P. Pedrizet, "La miraculeuse histoire de Pandare et d'Echédore, sui vie de recherches sur la marque dans l'Antiquité," *Archiv für Religionwissenschaft* 14 (1911): 54–129; W. Schönfeld, *Körperbemalen, Brandmarken, Tätowieren: Nach griechischen, römischen Schriftstellern, Dichtern, neuzeitlichen Veröffentlichungen und eigenen Erfahrungen, vorzüglich in Europa* (Heidelberg, Germany, 1960); and K. Zimmerman, "Tätowierte Thrakerinnen auf griechischen Vasenbildern," *Jahrbuch des Deutschen archäologischen Instituts* 95 (1980): 163–196.

2. C. Lombroso, *L'uomo delinquente* (Turin, Italy: Bocca, 1896), 323.

single glance the faults of *uncivilized* beings, of *being uncivilized,*
since "tattoos are the true writing of savages, their first civil registry.[3]

The mere idea that such a barbaric and pagan tradition,
which had been openly denounced in chapter XIX, verse 28 of
Leviticus ("Do not lacerate your bodies for the dead, and do
not tattoo yourselves"), condemned by the Council of Nicaea
in 325, and abhorred by the Holy Fathers, could have survived
for another fifteen centuries in such a civilized, educated, and
Catholic nation has left various commentators perplexed, if not
downright shocked.

The Assyrians whom Luciano described had tattoos, as
did the Dacians, as well as the Sarmatians, who according to
Pliny the Elder "*corpora sua inscribunt*" (marked their bodies).
The Thracians whom Herodotus observed were so covered in
ink that a new expression, *Thracianotae* (the marked Thracians),
was born. Yet, Christians did not engage in the practice, and the
devoted servants of the Holy Roman Church certainly did not
either. In reality, be it the Aryans, the Agathyrsi, the Britons, the
Canaanites, the Gelonians, the Libu, the Nubians, the Picts, or
the Scythians, tattoos immediately (and without saying a word)
denounced the barbaric nature of their bearers, even though in
Latin, terms were confused to the point that the word *nota* (mark,
letter) identified the very emblem of the civilization of letters—
writing, as might be inferred by the substitution of the Greek
word *stizein (*to wound, to pinch, from whose root the word *stigma*
was derived) with the verbs *inscribo* (to inscribe) or *imprimo* (to
imprint). The substitution was entirely fitting, since tattoos are
above all writing, an expression of a finished thought, a narration,
a vow, a piece of discourse, an epic—*history.*

Nevertheless, it was hard to accept that tattooing had such
a widespread, prolonged, and persistent presence in Italy and
throughout Europe. It is thus no coincidence that in 1880, Buckland,
in one of the first academic papers on the topic, affirmed that
"tattooing died out rapidly after contact with civilised races; but it
is somewhat singular, that no trace of tattooing as far as I'm aware
is to be found among the Egyptian, Assyrian, Greek, and Roman

paintings and sculpture, although these *civilized nations* must have come in contact with *tattooed people.*"[4]

After all, in the collective imagination of the nineteenth and twentieth centuries, the colorful marks that adorned the bodies and faces of the "essentially good" savages marked a fundamental otherness from the Eurocentric value system that was way more important that any intrinsic meaning they may have had—a moral even more than an aesthetic inferiority. Tattoos, which the popular historiography recounts as supposedly introduced to Europeans by Cook in 1769, and Bougainville in 1771, thus marked the clear yet perilously crossable line between bourgeois righteousness and criminal deviance (eccentric aristocrats and restless travelers notwithstanding).[5]

This gave rise to a partisan mythography, which in claiming the exotic origins of tattoos managed to impose (something of a rarity in the lexicon of the time) the use of a word with a Polynesian root: "The English word tattoo is derived from the Polynesian word *tatau* ... which first appeared in English in *Captain Cook's Voyages,* 1770. . . . The word *tabu,* or *taboo,* came with it. During the operation (the tattooing), a man was under *tabu.* These two are said to be the only Polynesian words in the English language. Since, the word *tattoo* has been adopted in many other European tongues."[6]

Nevertheless, the global success of the *tattoo-taboo* pairing significantly contributed to causing words that had previously referred to the same depictions in European cultures and history to fall into disuse and later be forgotten. Sinclair, an inexhaustible scholar, had himself noted that "the Italian words are *retratto* (picture), *marco* (mark), *signo* (sign), *devozione* (devotion),

---

3. Ibid., 324.

4. A. W. Buckland, "On Tattooing," *Journal of the Anthropological Institute of Great Britain and Ireland* 17 (1888): 318–328; quote appears on p. 326 (author's own italics).

5. As an example of devotional tattooing, in 1862 the Prince of Wales got a tattoo in Jerusalem; his two sons followed suit twenty years later. They were certainly not the only ones: In an 1862 publication, Godard commented that a great Russian duke had also engaged in the practice, while a few years later, Joest mentioned two kings, various emperors, and several other princes who had also decided to get tattoos.

6. A. T. Sinclair, "Tattooing: Oriental and Gypsy," *American Anthropologist* 10 (1908): 361–386.

7. Ibid., 367.

tatuaggio [tattoos]. I have usually heard *retratto, marco,* and *devozione*,"[7] to which should be added the forms *marconzito* and *'nzito* mentioned in the Enciclopedia Treccani.[8]

Thus tattooing, which had been tolerated in non-European subcivilizations as an atavistic inheritance, now supposedly eliminated by the progress toward more-evolved forms of coexistence, no longer had a safe space in Western practices, being undoubtedly considered the clearest mark of criminal tendencies. Hence the long-standing belief that in European countries, and especially Italy, these primitive forms of bodily decoration had disappeared as of antiquity, concomitantly with the elimination of ancient Greco-Roman practices. This incomplete viewpoint, at times softened by ethno-anthropological curiosity, and in other instances hardened by the firmness of positivist prejudices, could naturally do nothing *but* leave enduring traces (Lombroso notwithstanding), and according to the respected interpretation of Alfred Gell, the author of an excellent monograph, "provide a point of view on tattooing which is explicitly (rather than implicitly) European, middle-class and disapproving."[9]

This book finally does justice to decades, if not centuries, of unjustified ignorance.

---

8. *Enciclopedia Italiana di scienza, lettere ed arti, XXXIII,* 334.
9. A. Gell, *Wrapping in Images: Tattooing in Polynesia* (Oxford: Oxford University Press, 1993), 11–12.

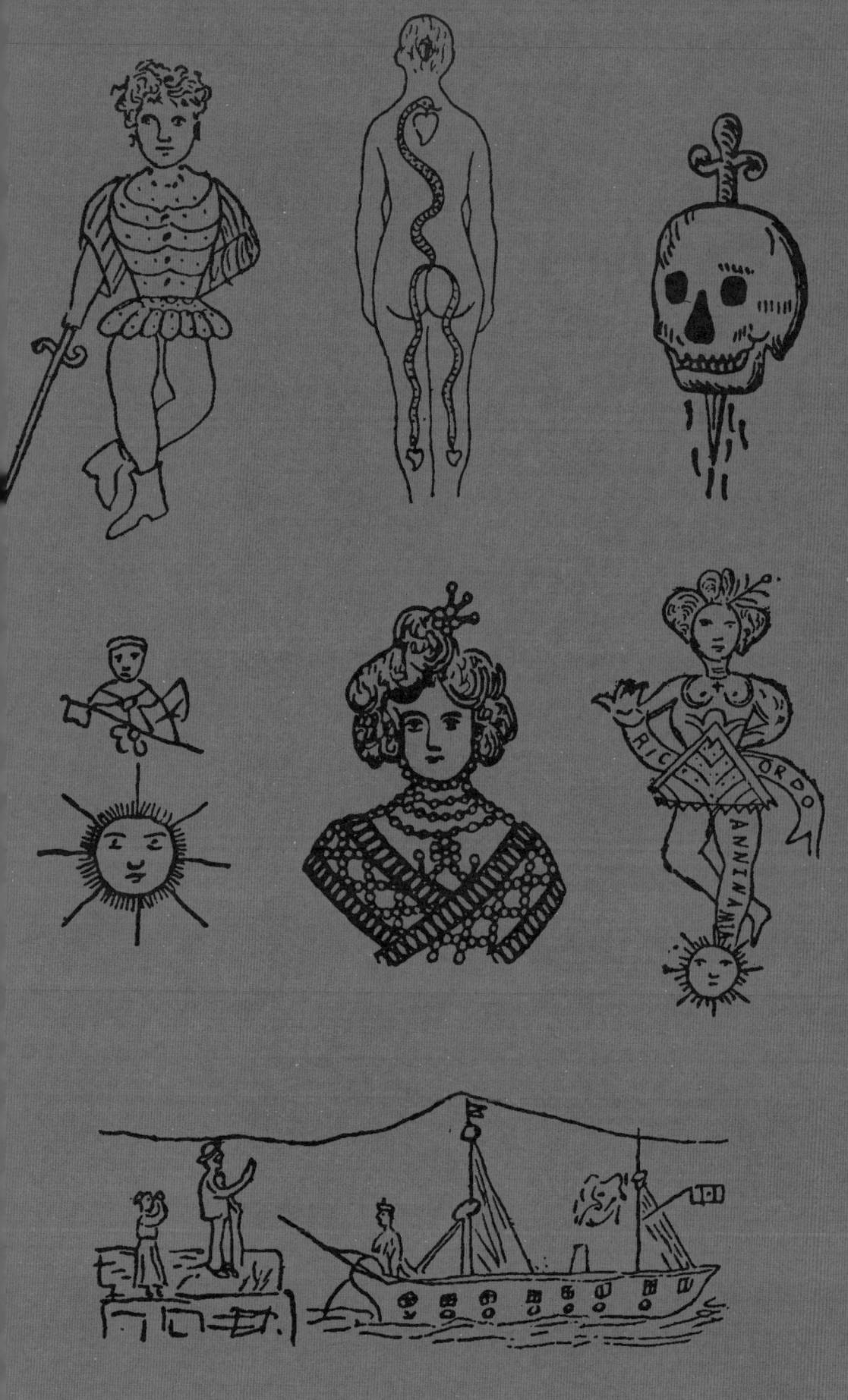

Why a Book on Tattoos of the Mediterranean Basin

— Luisa Gnecchi

It is now commonly accepted that tattoos are among man's oldest forms of artistic expression, and ongoing discoveries of anthropological evidence have confirmed the practice was widespread and culturally significant.

We don't know the precise reasons why people have always been fascinated with tattoos, nor do we know the origins and roots of the impulse that drove people toward the practice. Yet, it is indisputable that the act of engraving a sign on one's own skin is inextricably linked to the primary act of making art, with any instrument, and the mystery in which it continues to be shrouded even today is probably an integral part of its fascination.

Anyone who decides to get a tattoo is completing an act of permanent, irrational, and intimate self-expression, and whatever they choose to engrave on their skin is nearly always aimed at transforming their body in a way that reinforces their positive self-image.

Tattooing is thus a serious and profound gesture, but also simultaneously a game, as are all other forms of bodily decoration. Having fun, being playful with oneself and one's own body, is an important element of tattooing.

Therefore, tattooing had always been a positive social act in primitive civilizations, and it was only when authoritarian and repressive systems directly appropriated the practice as an instrument of punishment and humiliation that it was met with rejection and repulsion. This perhaps explains why even today, tattoos draw fascination but also concern (albeit increasingly less than in the past).

This is because the official culture continues to give tattooing the cold shoulder, relegating it as a counterculture phenomenon, even as increasing numbers of people from all social strata are embracing the practice (including publicly), without any issue.

In today's Western world, there are so many men and women who have some kind of tattoo, irrespective of age, social, ethnic, or religious origins. In Italy too, over the last few decades, the number of people with tattoos has increased tremendously, and there are now thousands of people who get tattoos. Nevertheless, there is much disinformation about what this phenomenon has represented in the past and in the world. People are particularly unaware of the history of tattooing in the areas closest to us—Italy and the Mediterranean basin. Yet, tattooing in Italy dates back to the late Neolithic period, and Italy is the proud holder of the oldest tattooed archeological discovery in the world. The body of Ötzi, a man who lived 5,300 years ago, was discovered in the Alps near Bolzano and contains some sixty-one tattoos. The history of tattoos in the Mediterranean includes incredibly interesting examples that span centuries, from the tattoos of the slaves and convicts in ancient Greece and Rome, to those of the Crusaders and pilgrims to Jerusalem and Loreto, and to those of artisans in the Middle Ages, not to mention the ones studied by Lombroso and other criminologists between the mid-nineteenth century and the turn of the twentieth. Last, the arrival of tattooed Indigenous people from the new lands that major explorers after Columbus discovered in the West and East drew fascination in Europe and the United States, giving rise to the modern tattoos that are now so globally widespread.

In recent decades there have been numerous archeological findings, along with new technological tools with which we can study them. This has allowed us to discover and analyze so many forms of tattooing from antiquity that we did not know about from various parts of the world, and to be able to affirm with certainty that the symbols found on clay human figures or reproduced on vases or frescoes are in fact tattoos.

Hence this book on the tradition of tattoos in the Mediterranean basin—now timelier than ever.

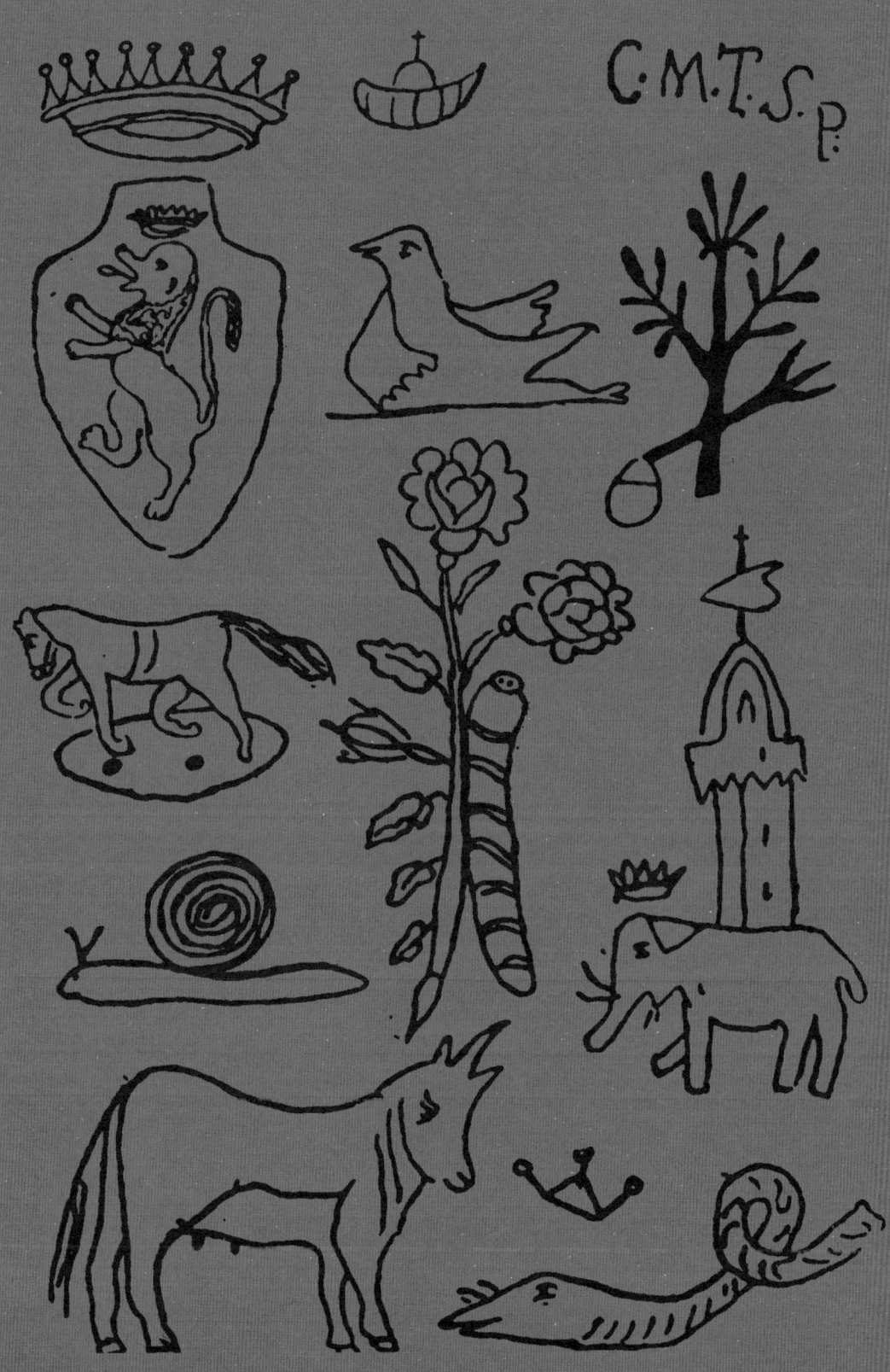

C.M.T.S.P.

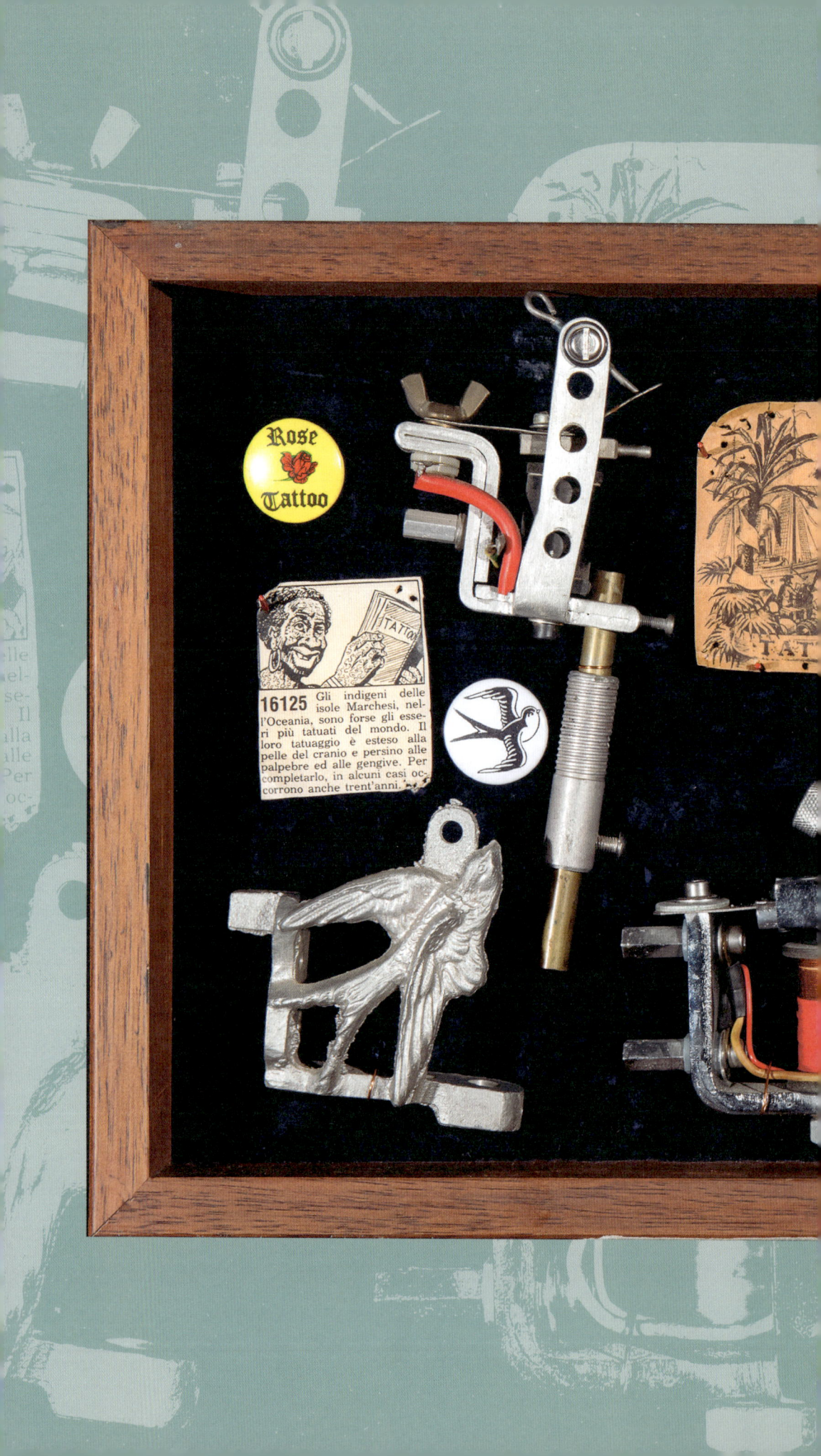

Rose Tattoo

16125 Gli indigeni delle isole Marchesi, nel-l'Oceania, sono forse gli esseri più tatuati del mondo. Il loro tatuaggio è esteso alla pelle del cranio e persino alle palpebre ed alle gengive. Per completarlo, in alcuni casi occorrono anche trent'anni.

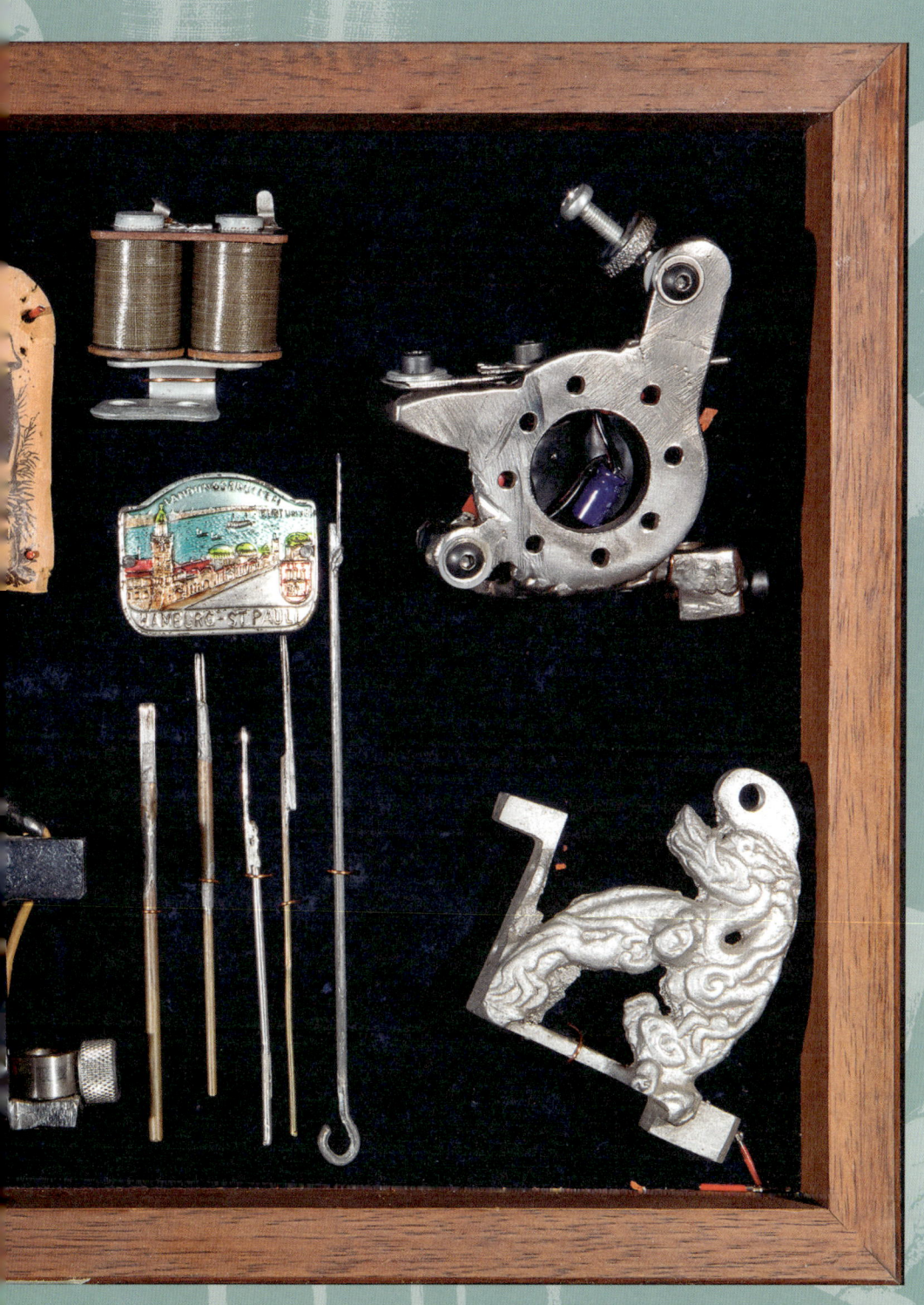

Small electrical machine for drawing tattoos and their components, twentieth century, Milan, Tattoo Museo Gianmaurizio Fercioni (Gianmaurizio Fercioni Tattoo Museum)

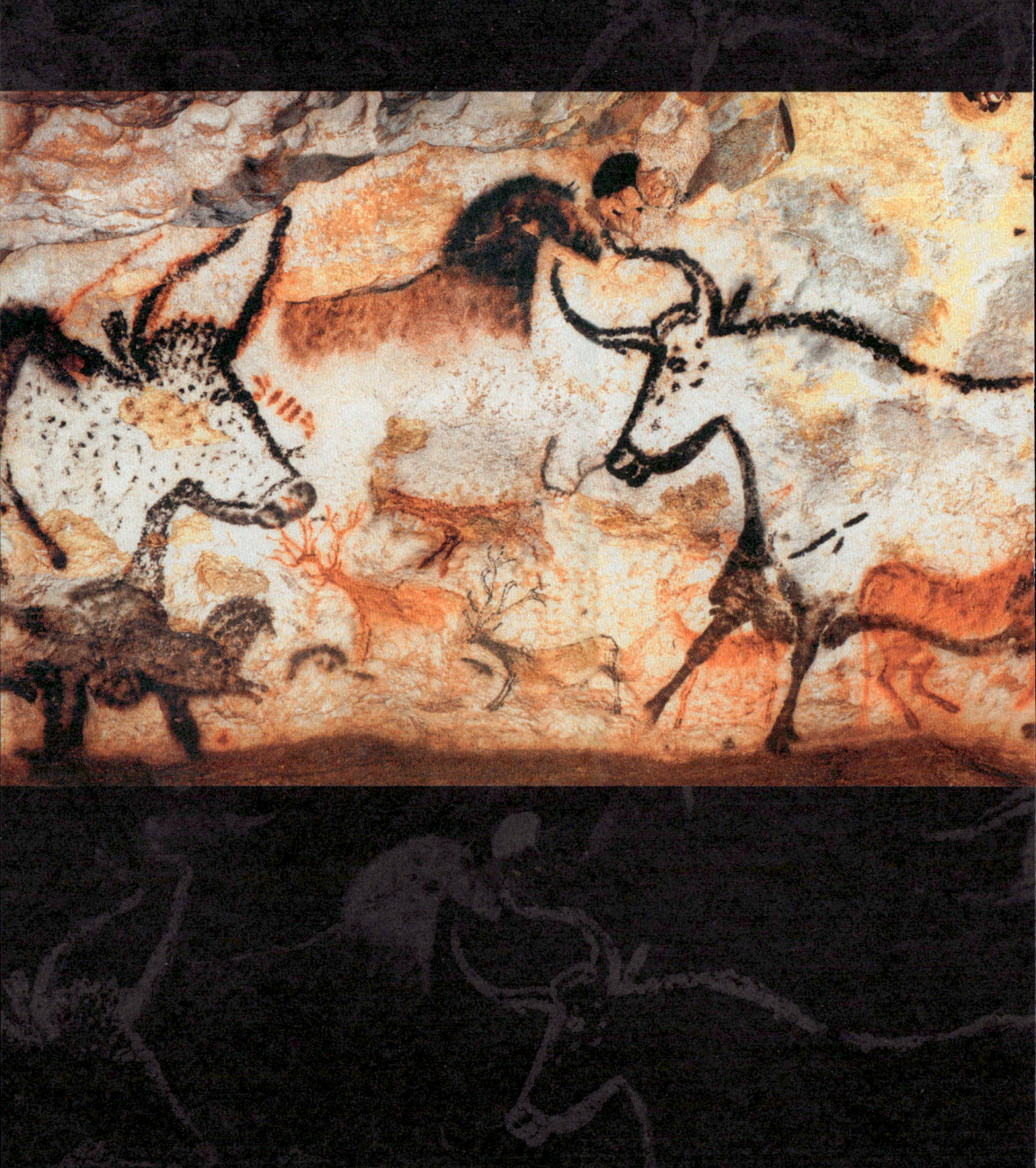

From the Lascaux Caves to the Grotte du Mas d'Azil

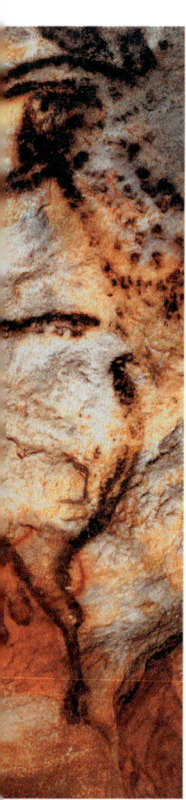

Even though they were discovered relatively recently, the Lascaux Caves have entered the popular imagination as the most famous prehistoric monument in Europe. Four boys entered the cave on September 12, 1940, completely by chance, thanks to Robot, a white puppy with a brown spot on his snout.

France was occupied by German troops at the time, having been divided since its June 25, 1940, surrender between the military zone controlled by the nationalist army (consisting of the North and the Atlantic coast) and the South (with the exception of the zone of Menton), run by the collaborationist government of Vichy France. On a warm day in mid-September, eighteen-year-old Marcel Ravidat was out walking with his dog Robot on the La Rochefoucauld-Montbel family's property in the town of Montignac in the Dordogne, when the furry creature suddenly disappeared into a cave.

Marcel recruited three of his friends to go find him: fourteen-year-old Jacques Marsal, sixteen-year-old Georges Agnel, and thirteen-year-old Simon Coencas. The group descended deep beneath ground, at least 66 feet (20 meters) from the surface. The four boys not only found their four-legged friend but looked up and discovered Lascaux's cave paintings, more than 6,000 figures painted around 17,500 years ago. It is the last known work from the European Upper Paleolithic period and the chef d'oeuvre of Magdalenian culture (15,500–9,000 BCE), so named for the La Madeleine rock shelter, which was also discovered in the Dordogne in 1863.

Four years later, in 1867, Félix Garrigou (a doctor from Tarascon) published the first scientific paper on the caves of Mas-d'Azil, another essential site for studying Magdalenian civilization, located more than 300 kilometers from Lascaux.

The publication of Garrigou's paper drew the attention of many scholars, including Saint-Just Péquart and his wife, Marthe, a well-to-do couple passionate about archeology, who during the 1930s moved to the Pyrenean department of Ariège, bordering Andorra.

Sant-Just Péquart, who was born in Saint-Laurent on March 15, 1881, and died in Montpelier on September 11, 1944, was a man of many talents. During the course of his intense life, he was a successful industrialist, a leading archeologist and paleontologist, a famous art collector and generous patron, and a close friend of Jules Cayette and Jean Prouvé. He and Marthe were fervent supporters of prehistoric archeology and were well respected by the transalpine scientific community. In 1935, Saint-Just was appointed president of the French Prehistoric Society, and the following year he took office in Mas-d'Azil, the little town in the Pyrenees home to the cave of the same name. There the couple made important discoveries about Magdalenian culture, most notably finding a set of tattooing tools, which proved the degree of technical sophistication that prehistoric tattooing had attained.

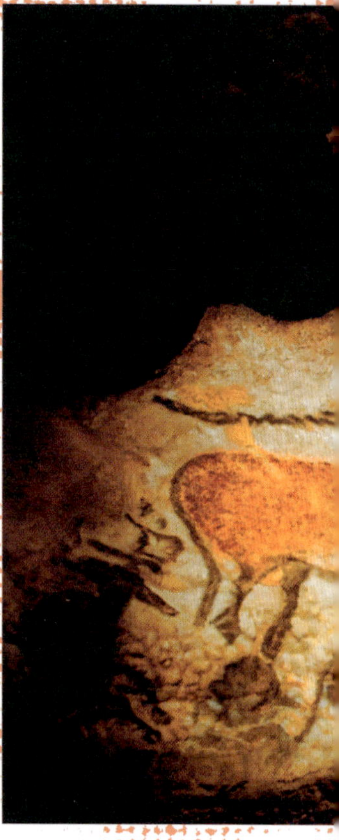

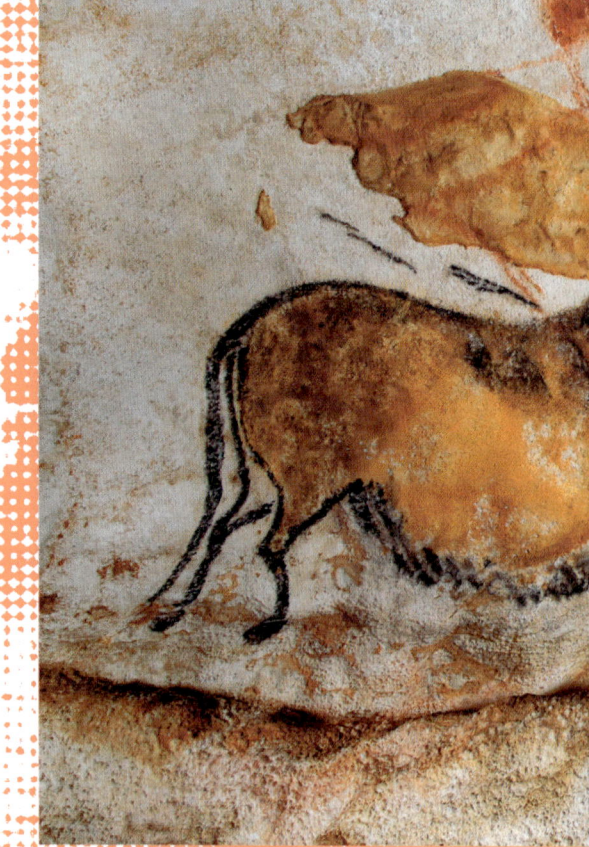

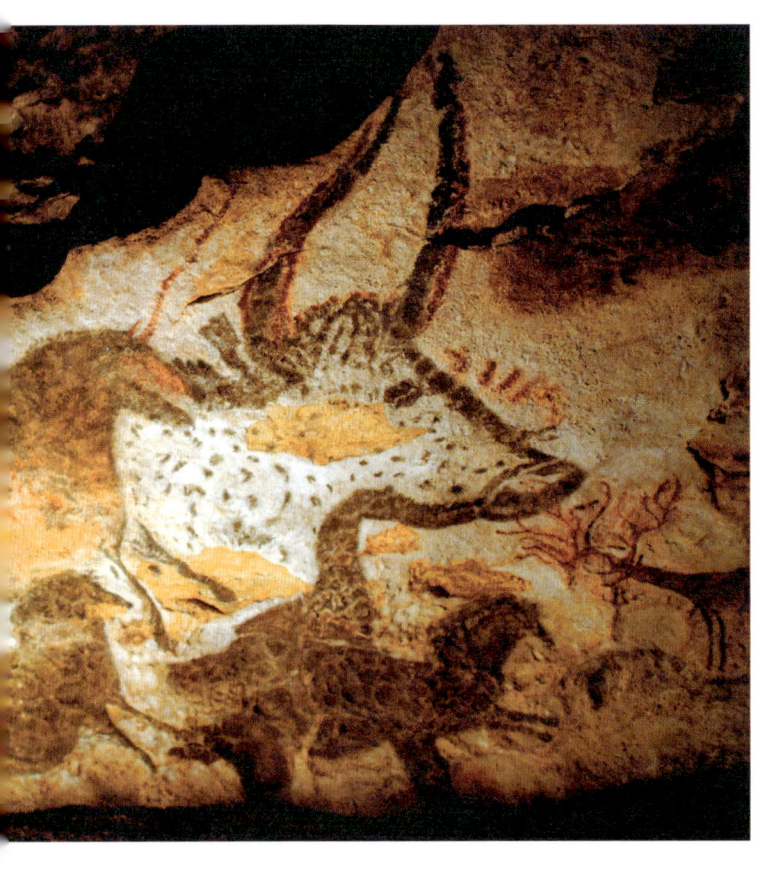

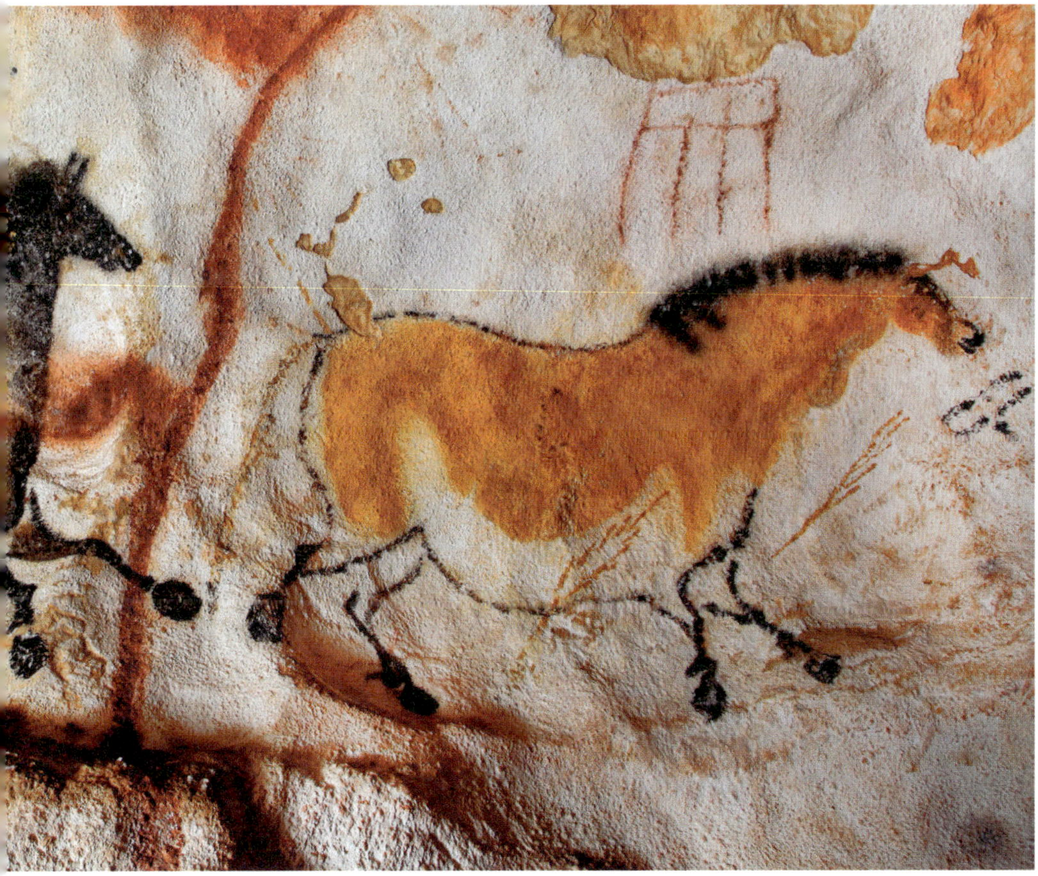

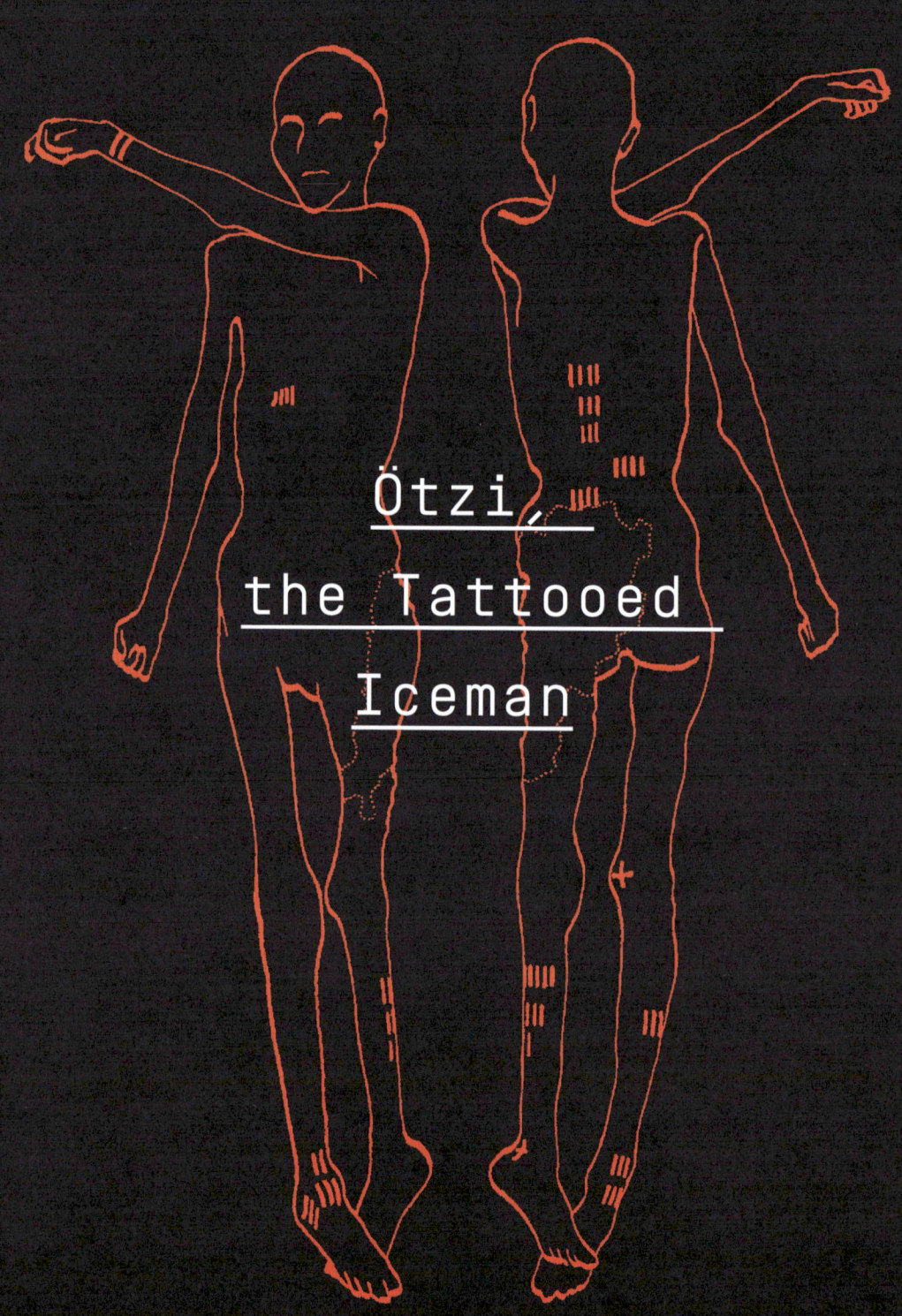

Ötzi,
the Tattooed
Iceman

—— Katharina Hersel

Discovery

On September 19, 1991, during a hike through the snow-covered Giogo di Tisa mountain in Val Senales in the Ötztal Alps, two tourists made an amazing discovery: Sticking out of a block of ice were the head and torso of a frozen, mummified human body.

Just five days later, despite poor weather conditions and the fact that they could use only makeshift tools, the corpse was recovered, along with a series of objects of unknown origin, including a copper axe and a flint dagger. The finds were sent to the Institute of Forensic Medicine at the University of Innsbruck. The next day, after having analyzed the discovered artifacts, prehistory expert Konrad Spindler declared them to be a truly extraordinary find: archeological artifacts that were "at least 4,000 years old."

The subsequent radiocarbon dating confirmed that the mummy was from the period between 3350 and 3120 BCE.[1] The iceman was thus 5,300 years old and lived during the transitional Copper Age, which followed the Neolithic period!

The Similaun Man

The mummy was officially named "the Iceman." In Italian, he is also sometimes called the "Similaun man," from the name of the glacier near where the body was found. Yet, he became famous around the world as "Ötzi," the nickname given to him by the Austrian journalist Karl Wendle, in reference to the German name for the Ötztal Alps, Ötztaler Alpen.

Studies on the mummy and the objects he carried with him have provided a kind of identikit. Ötzi was male, around forty-five years old, and a hunter who was perfectly outfitted for high mountains. He wore an expertly stitched surcoat, boots lined in goat fur, a loincloth made of soft sheepskin, a bearskin cap, and leather shoes filled with an insulating layer of straw. His tools included a long bow made of yew wood, which had not yet been finished, a quiver with fourteen arrows, two of which were ready for use and contained flint tips, a string for tightening the bow, and some other small tools. Ötzi also carried a pouch on his belt with everything he needed to start a fire, a retoucher to sharpen the flint, and a kind of first-aid kit containing birch polypore, a mushroom that had healing properties. A pannier made of hazelnut tree branches, a woven grass basket, and birch bark containers filled with leftover embers completed his kit. From the cereal grains (Einkorn wheat) found in the mummy's clothing and stomach, we can deduce that Ötzi came from an agricultural village (see images on pages 33–34).

---

1. G. Bonani et al., "AMS 14C Age Determination of Tissue, Bone and Grass Samples from the Ötzal Ice Man," *Radiocarbon* 36, no. 2 (1994): 247–250.

The mummy is still today a subject of archeological, medical, and genetic studies, which provide ongoing details and further knowledge about our ancestors from the Copper Age. According to analyses, Ötzi was quite agile, even though he was not in perfect shape: he suffered from joint pain and probably also from the aftereffects of Lyme borreliosis (a serious tick-borne disease) and was affected by ailments caused by intestinal parasites and from the gastric bacteria *Helicobacter pylori*. Although he was certainly not a sedentary man, his DNA revealed a predisposition for cardiovascular illnesses, with confirmed evidence of atherosclerosis.

In 2001, clinical analyses led to a second shocking discovery: The Similaun man had not been killed by an avalanche, nor did he freeze to death. He was actually hit in the back with an arrow. A homicide had occurred on the Giogo di Tisa mountain pass! The flint arrow tip was still stuck in his left shoulder, between his heart and lung, and showed up very clearly on radiological exams. The arrow had struck his subclavian artery, causing a massive hemorrhage, and Ötzi very probably died shortly after the event (see image 2 on page 33).

Did Ötzi know he was being followed? Was he on the run from something? There is a lot of evidence to support that hypothesis. The deep knife wound between his right thumb and index fingers, which had not yet completely healed, would suggest he was involved in a violent fight a few days prior to his death. Additionally, the fact that some of his weapons were unfinished might have been the result of an unexpected departure or sudden attack. However, food residues found in his stomach would seem to contradict the theory that he had run from something. Shortly before he died, Ötzi had actually eaten a rich meal of grains, dried venison, and dried wild goat meat. His stomach also contained traces of bracken fern, a poisonous plant. Perhaps there was a period of time during his escape when he felt secure?

We do not know with certainty who the iceman was and what exactly had happened to him during those last few days of his life. Yet, we do know that his story has continually fascinated people all over the world. The South Tyrol Museum of Archaeology in Bolzano, where Ötzi is exhibited, welcomes nearly 300,000 visitors per year, who come from every corner of the world.

The Tattoos on Ötzi's Body

Even when he was first discovered, the black marks imprinted on Ötzi's body did not go unnoticed. Famous Alto Adige mountaineer Reinhold Messner, who happened to be climbing in the area and was taking a break at the Similaun lodge during the same period, was one of the first to inspect the discovery site (see image 1 on page 33). Seeing those enigmatic marks on the mummified body, which seemed to have been branded on, Messner assumed he was a fugitive.[2] Experts from the University of Innsbruck went on to identify those lines as actual tattoos, hypothesizing that they had a therapeutic or ritualistic purpose.[3]

---

2. E. Rastbichler Zissernig, *Der Mann im Eis: Die Fundgeschichte* (Innsbruck, Austria:Innsbruck University Press, 2006), 34.

In 2008, Ötzi's entire body was photographed by using a multspectral imaging technique, which captures images in different wavlengths across the light spectrum. Those images were then made available for scientific purposes to experts and researchers around the world (www.icemanphotoscan.eu) (see images on pages 36–38).

This new technique allowed a mark on the right part of Ötzi's chest to be visible for the first time, bringing the total number of Ötzi's tattoos to sixty-one, which were then subdivided into nineteen different groups.[4] Two of these groups consist of tiny crosses on his right knee and left heel, while another seventeen are structured in sets of two to four parallel lines and distributed all over his body: on the right part of his chest, his left wrist, the lower part of his spine, his legs, and his right malleolus.

While the tattoos are now fully visible, the technique used to create them is still unclear. Was a needle used or were incisions made? In some of the tattoos, the concentration of pigments at the ends of the lines would suggest they were engraved into the skin, perhaps using a sliver of flint, into which pulverized charcoal was then rubbed.[5] In other tattoos however, the stippled distribution of the pigment would instead suggest perforation with a bone needle that had been dipped in soot. There is currently an experimental archeological study underway to determine the technique used to create Ötzi's tattoos (see image on page 35).[6]

Tattooed Marks for Therapeutic Purposes

If you line up the map of his tattoos with the x-rays, the joints underneath the tattooed marks show indisputable wear, which may have caused joint pain. Anthropological examinations performed on the skeleton have confirmed that the Similaun man would frequently travel long distances on foot.[7] The wear on his joints thus without a doubt supports the hypothesis that he was a high-altitude hunter or merchant obliged to walk long distances.

The tattoos are moreover positioned along the meridians[8] of the body, which are still used today in acupuncture to treat pain;[9] we can therefor: presume that the tattoos served to alleviate pain. This hypothesis asserting their therapeutic function remains the most substantiated theory to date.

---

3. T. Sjøvold et al., "Verteilung und Größe der Tätowierungen am Eismann vom Hauslabjoch," in K. Spindler et al., eds., Der Mann im Eis: Neue Funde und Ergebnisse (The Man in the Ice 2) (Vienna: Springer, 1995), 279–286.

4. M. Samadelli et al., "Complete Mapping of the Tattoos of the 5,300-Year-Old Tyrolean Iceman," Journal of Cultural Heritage 5, no. 16 (2015).

5. M. Pabst et al., "The Tattoos of the Tyrolean Iceman: A Light Microscopical, Ultrastructural and Element Analytical Study," Journal of Archaeological Science 36 (2009): 2335–2341.

6. A. Deter-Wolf et al., "Chalcolithic Tattooing: Historical and Experimental Evaluation of the Tyrolean Iceman's Body Markings," European Journal of Archaeology 27 (2024): 267-288.

7. W. Murphy et al., "The Iceman: Discovery and Imaging," Radiology 226, no. 3 (2003): 614–629.

8. According to traditional Chinese medicine, there are channels of energy (Qi) that run along the body, known as meridians.

Another famous discovery, made in Siberia, would seem to corroborate this theory. In 1993, the burial mound of a Scythian woman, the Princess of Ukok, emerged from the permafrost, along with some lavish personal effects and the bodies of two warriors from the Pazyryk culture. The group had lived in the Iron Age between 500 and 400 BCE. The permafrost had perfectly preserved their bodies, which were found to contain tattoos inspired by the figures of mythological animals. However, in addition to the ornamental tattoos on the skin of one of the two warriors, researchers noted areas containing tiny dots along the spine, similar to those of Ötzi. This could be proof that there were different types of tattoos, each with a different purpose (see drawing on page 39).

The parallel arrangement of the lines tattooed on Ötzi's body could have been due to a precise therapeutic sequence—the pain-relieving treatments likely had limited efficacy over time and had to be repeated.[10]

The Oldest Tattoos in the World

The black lines on Ötzi's body provide some of the oldest evidence that tattoos existed. Prior to this discovery, it was believed that the oldest tattoo was the one discovered on the face of a Chinchorro warrior from 2500 BCE, found in South America in what is now Chile.[11] However, Ötzi's tattoos are now in the running for the title of oldest tattoos in the world, along with those on the Gebelein mummy preserved at the British Museum, dating back to 3351–3092 BCE (see drawing on page 39).

Indelible Records

The large number of illustrated volumes devoted to the history of tattoos, and self-experimentation in artistic projects such as artist and performer Nicole Wilson's *Ötzi*, completed in 2012 and 2016,[12] demonstrate the interest in the Similaun mummy's mysterious tattoos. The fascinating story of the Iceman has also provided inspiration to celebrities such as Brad Pitt, who in 2007 got a tattoo on his left forearm of the unmistakable outlined body of Ötzi.

9. L. Dorfer et al., "A Medical Report from the Stone Age," *The Lancet* 354 (1999). 1023–1025.

10. P. Hégy, "Réflexions sur les tatouages d'Ötzi: Une nouvelle hypothèse diagnostique," *L'Anthropologie* 108 (2004): 107–109; and A. Zink et al., "Possible Evidence for Care and Treatment in the Tyrolean Iceman," *International Journal of Paleopathology* 25 (2019):110–117.

11. A. Deter-Wolf et al., "The World's Oldest Tattoos," *Journal of Archaeological Science: Reports* 5 (2016): 19–24.

12. www.nicolewilson.com/O-tzi.

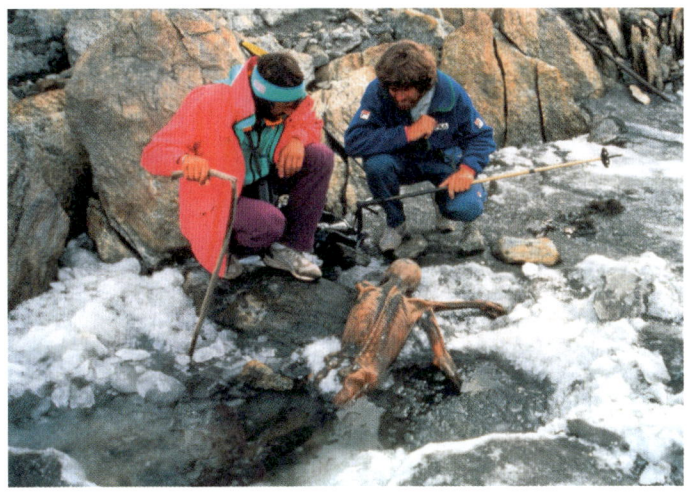

On September 21, 1991, two days after the amazing discovery,
mountaineers Reinhold Messner and Hans Kammerlander inspect
the site where the Similaun mummy was found. Bolzano, South Tyrol
Archeological Museum.

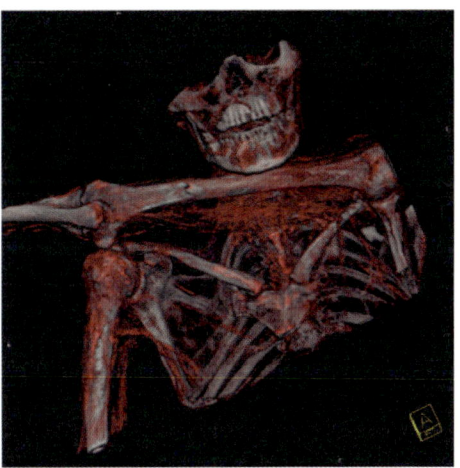

Arrow tip sticking out of Ötzi's left shoulder,
visible on CT scans. Bolzano, South Tyrol
Archeological Museum.

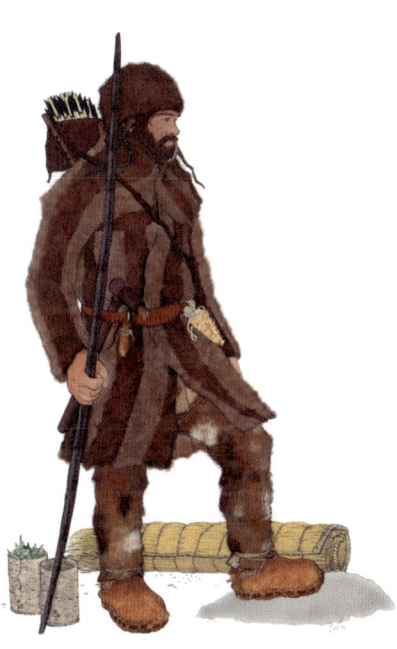

How the Similaun man would have looked.
Drawing by Sara Welponer. Bolzano, South Tyrol
Archeological Museum.

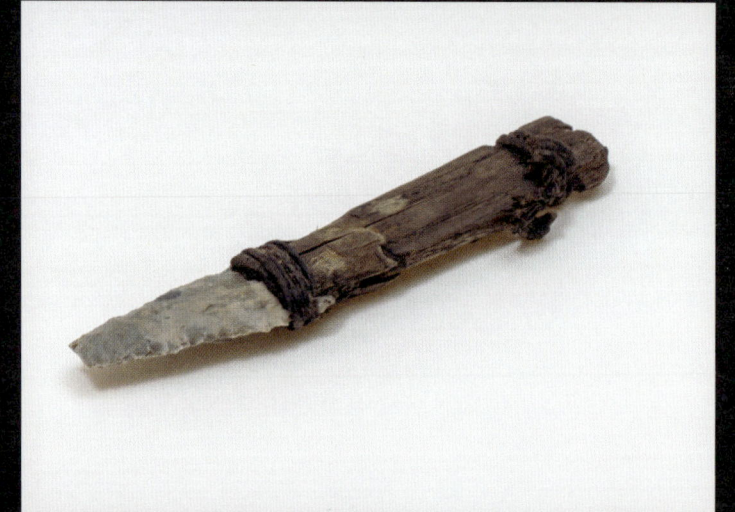

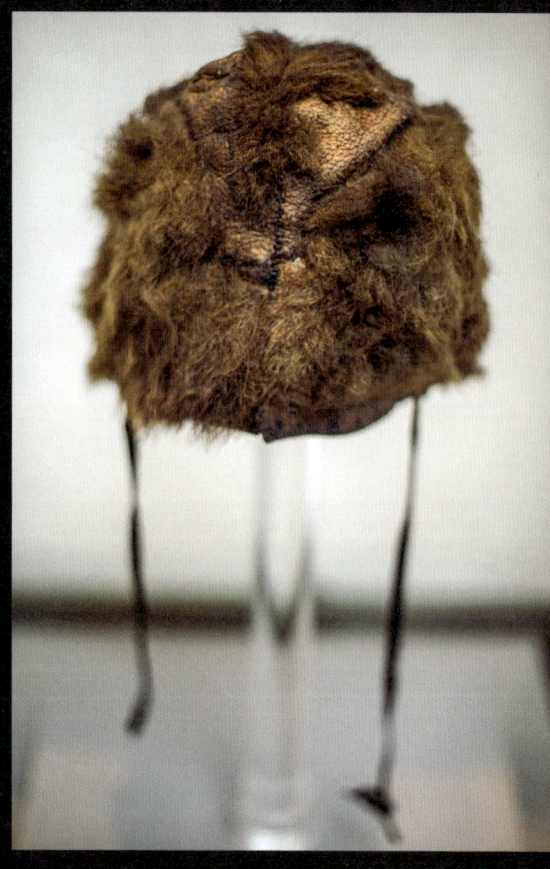

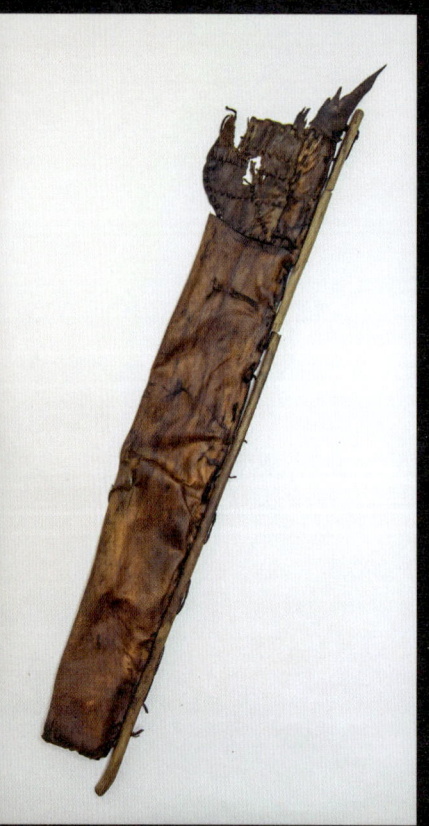

Clockwise from bottom: Arrow holder, flint dagger with case, bearskin hat, all belonging to the Similaun man. Bolzano, South Tyrol Archeological Museum.

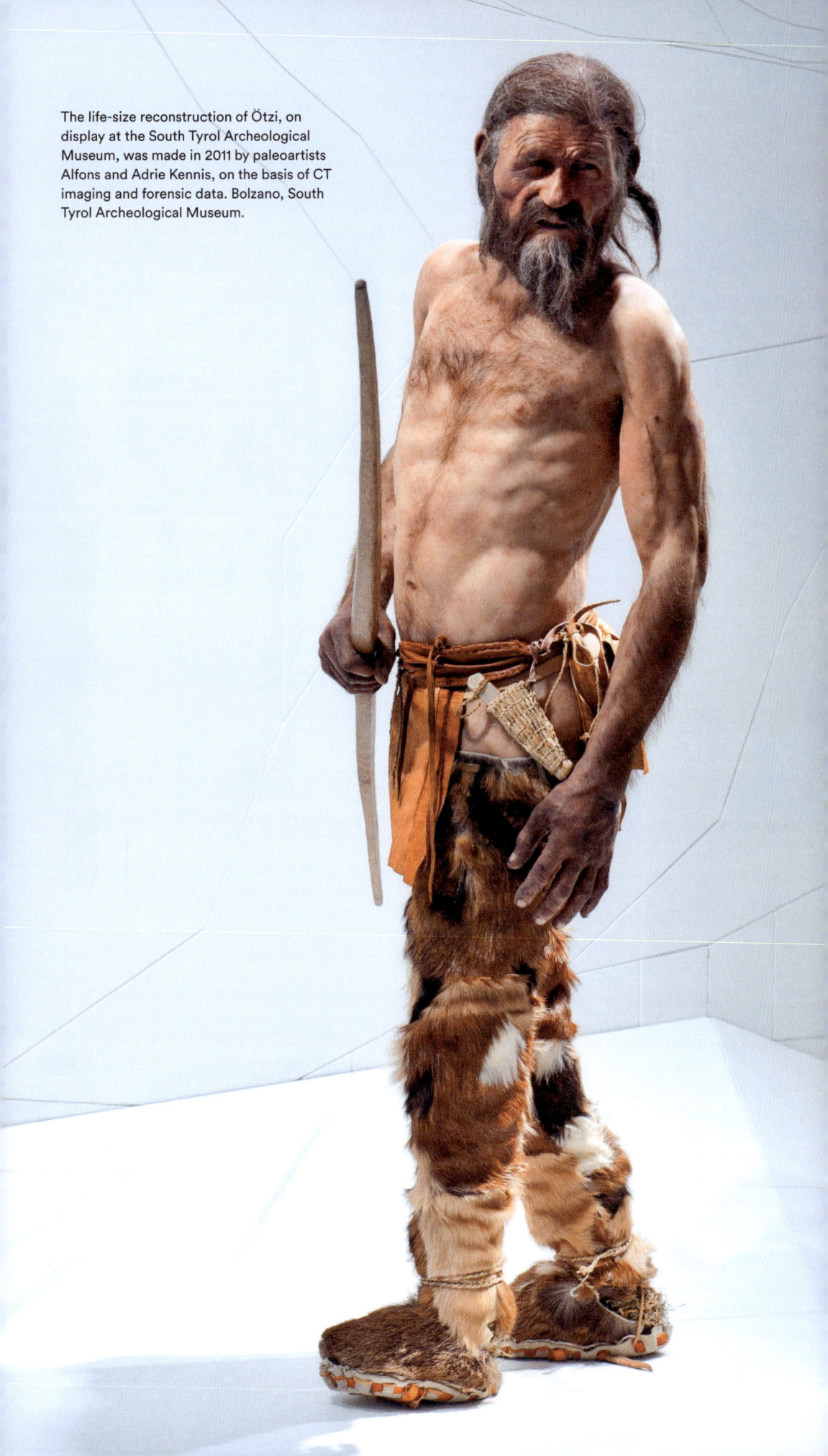

The life-size reconstruction of Ötzi, on display at the South Tyrol Archeological Museum, was made in 2011 by paleoartists Alfons and Adrie Kennis, on the basis of CT imaging and forensic data. Bolzano, South Tyrol Archeological Museum.

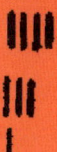
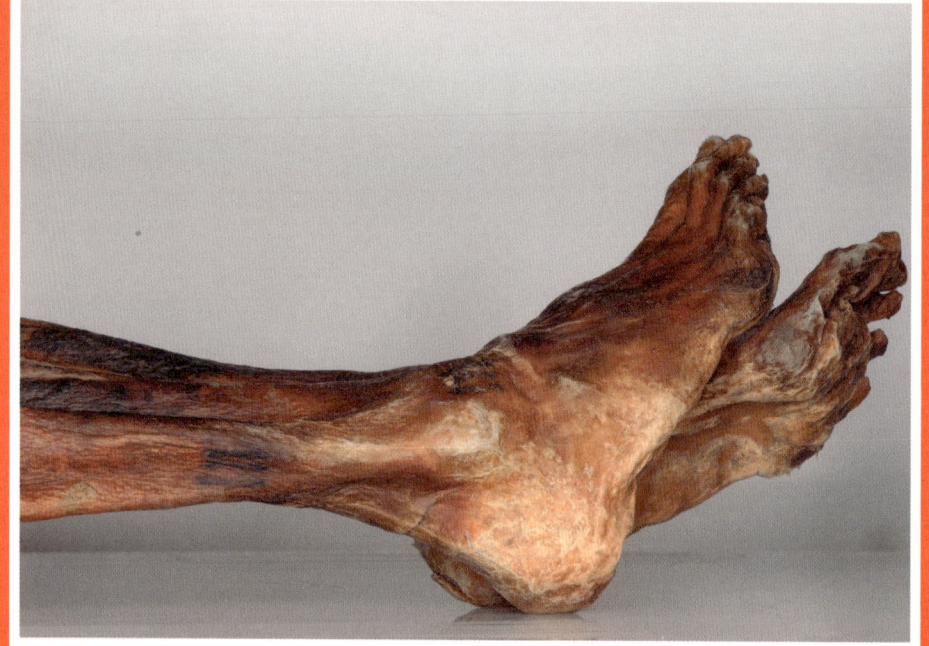
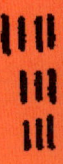
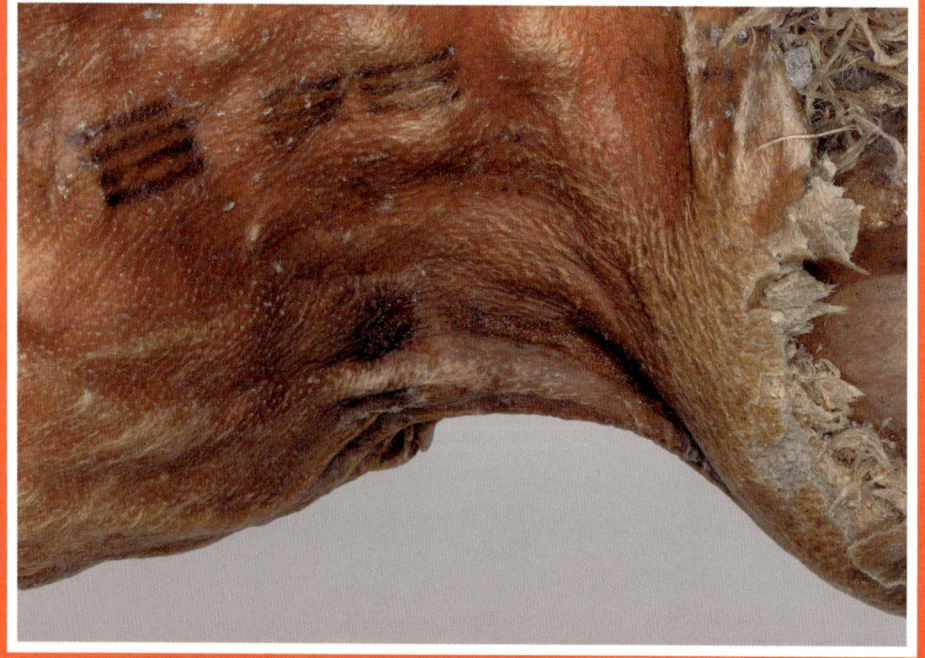

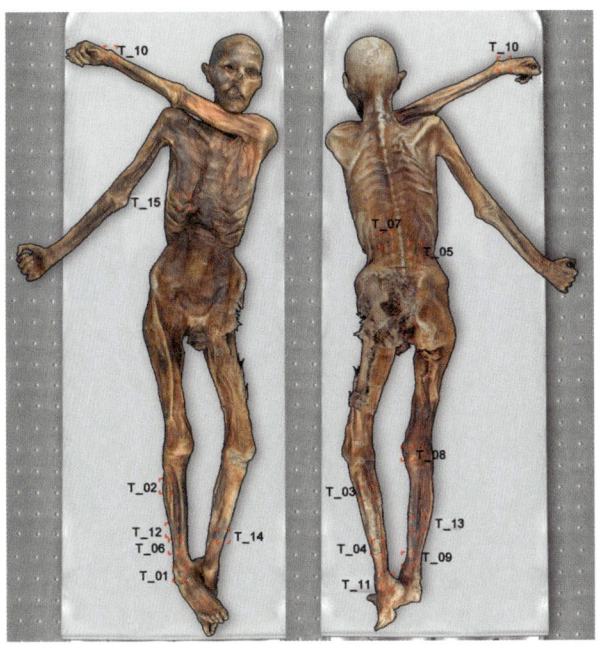

Placement of the sixty-one tattoos on the Iceman's body. Bolzano, South Tyrol Archeological Museum.

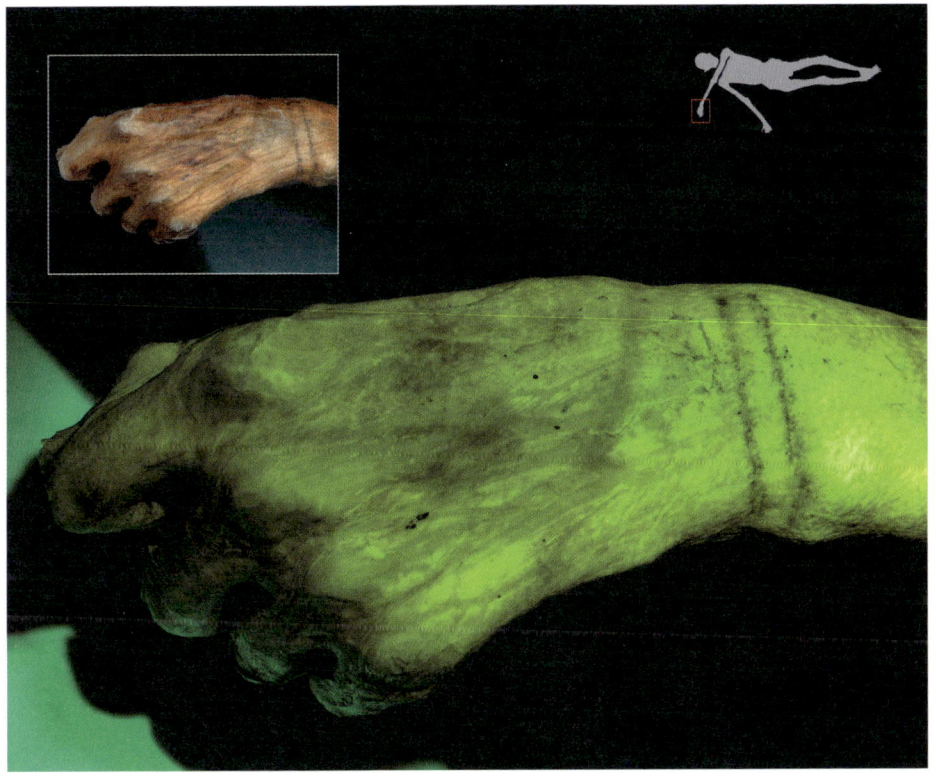

On this and next page: The majority of the tattoos on the Iceman's body are visible to the naked eye. Bolzano, South Tyrol Archeological Museum.

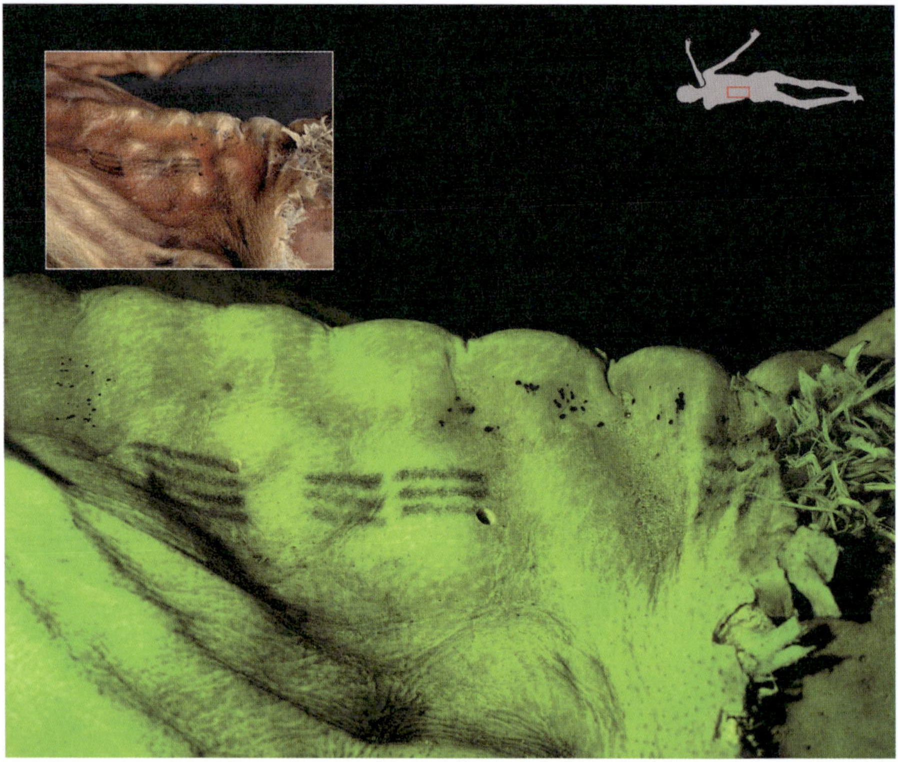

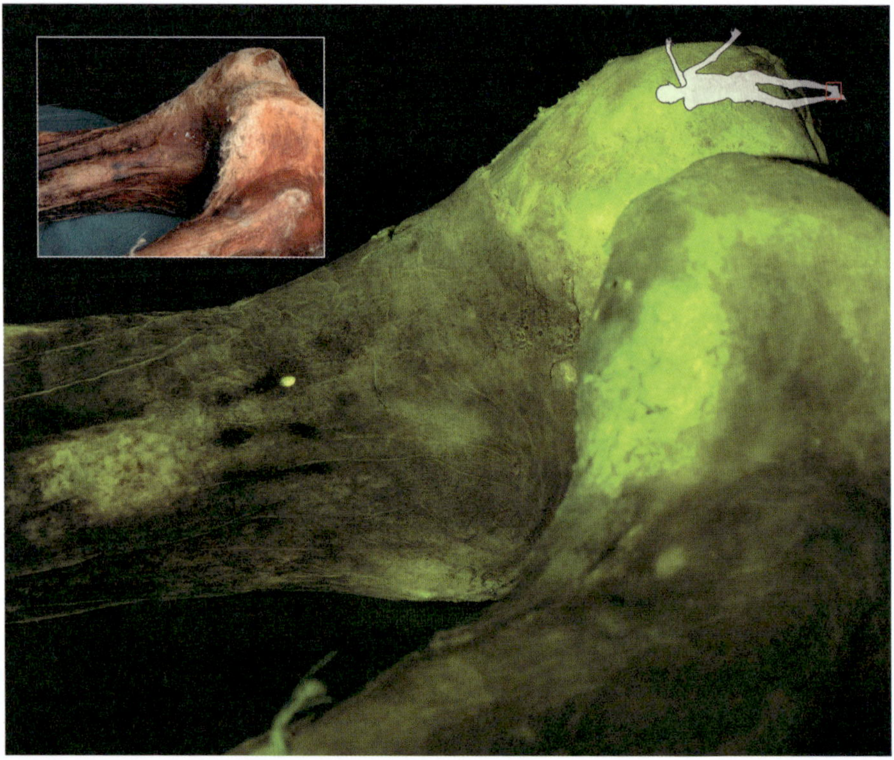

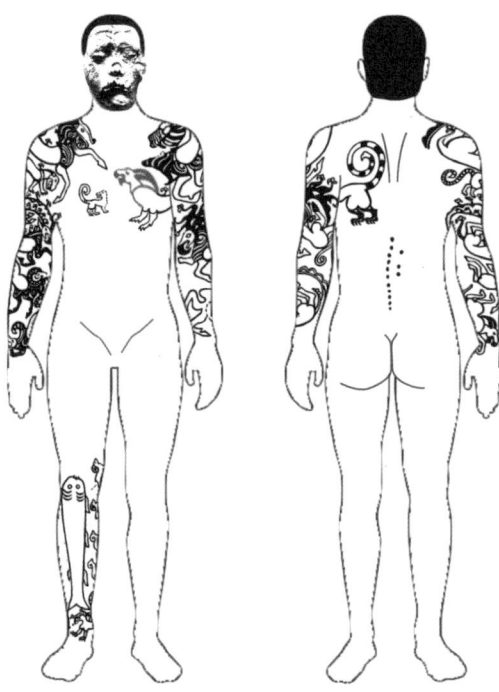

Tattoos on the body of a warrior of the Pazyryk culture, in *Scythians: Warriors of Ancient Siberia (London:* British Museum, 2021), 106–109.

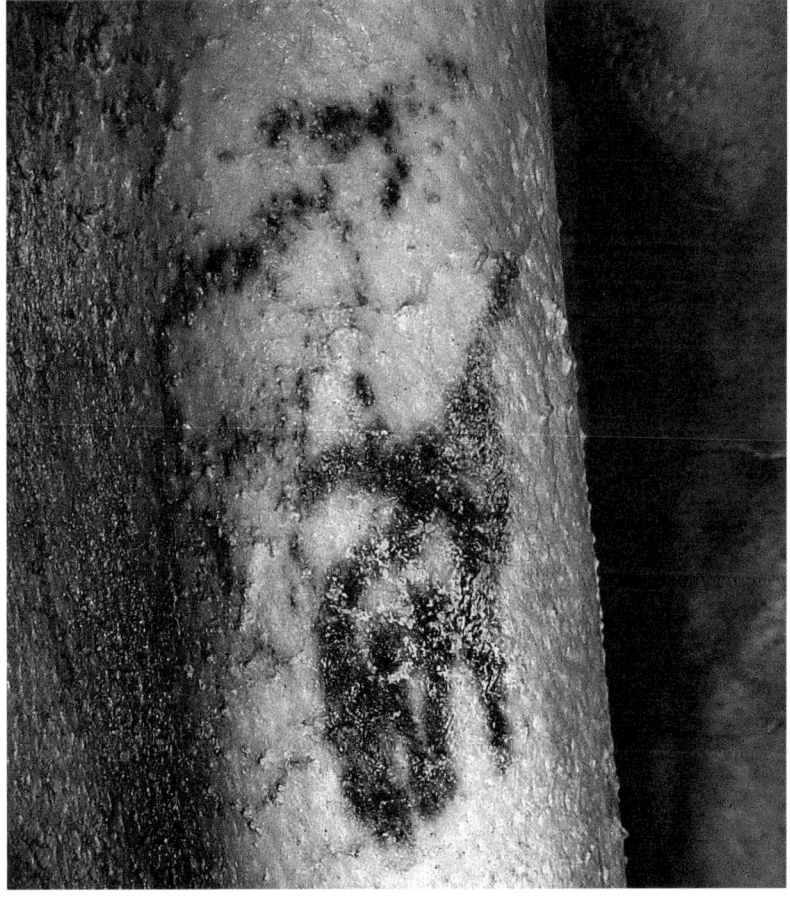

Tattoos on the mummy of the Gebelein man, preserved at the British Museum, London. Together with the Iceman, these are the oldest tattoos that have been discovered in the world to date (Ötzi: 3350–3120 BCE, Gebelein man: 3351–3017 BCE). London, the British Museum.

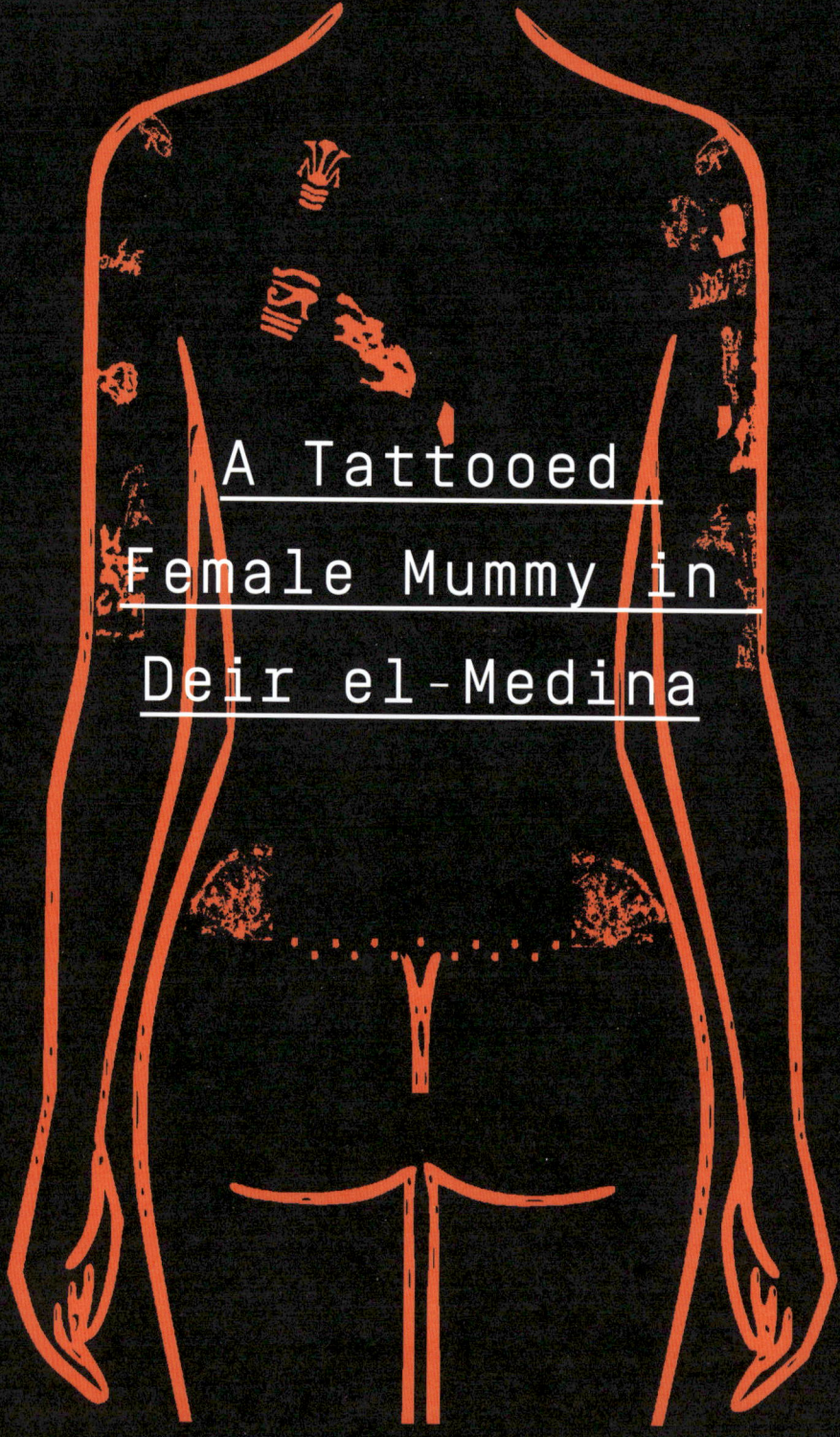

A Tattooed Female Mummy in Deir el-Medina

In 2014, the French Institute of Eastern Archeology (IFAO) conducted research on Theban tomb 291 in Deir el-Medina (belonging to royal workmen Nu and Nakhtmin) in order to inventory and study preserved human remains that had originally been found in the chamber of tomb TT 290 (belonging to royal workman Irynefer). Since this site had been heavily ransacked, it contained a broad mixture of human remains. The artifacts and mummification techniques observed onsite suggest that the material dates primarily from the Ramesside period, although certain sepultures appear to be from the beginning of the Twenty-First Dynasty. During the evaluation phase, we identified at least thirty tattoos on the neck, shoulders, back, and arms of a mummified female bust. Unlike previous examples of tattooed mummies in Egypt, which showed only geometric and abstract patterns, the tattoos found on this mummy were figurative and represented pharaonic Egyptian imagery.

The torso, measuring 25 × 11 × 6 inches (64 × 27 × 14 centimeters), was found unwrapped, with the exception of one strip of bandaging on the right forearm. The head, hands, and legs were no longer present. The mummy had been eviscerated, although there were no visible cuts; this could be an indication of transvaginal or transperineal evisceration, a practice that has recently been documented in other mummies from the New Kingdom. The osteological analysis led us to estimate that this woman was between the ages of twenty-five and thirty-four when she died. Since the torso was discovered mixed in with the rest of the TT 290 group, it was impossible to ascertain whether the individual had been buried with any funeral trousseau. Moreover, it was not possible to reattach the head, legs, or hands, to the extent they were still present. Consequently, our interpretations of the mummy were based exclusively on the tattoos.

In order to identify these tattoos, we used a combination of traditional photography, photographic enhancement techniques, and infrared photography. Thanks to special software, we were able to apply a photographic enhancement technique known as decorrelation stretch to a photo of the mummy, which allowed us to stretch the images to mimic the look of the skin prior to mummification. In 2016, we used an infrared sensor to identify tattoos that were otherwise unidentifiable in visible light. These infrared images proved particularly effective in contrasting the pigment of the tattoos with the mummified skin. By combining these techniques, we identified at least thirty tattoos on the mummy's neck, shoulders, arms, and back.

The drawings on pages 48–49 reconstruct the distribution and approximate position of the tattoos as viewed from the front, back, and side. Tattoos were present on the neck and upper arms, but not in the torso space between them, nor along the collarbone. They extended down the outer portion of both arms to the elbow. There were no tattoos below this point, although we were not able to observe the wrists or hands. There were also tattoos on the mummy's back, three of which were close to the left shoulder blade.

On the basis of the look and distribution of the tattoos, we can make various observations. They were done prior to mummification, since the designs clearly appear to have been distorted from the shrinking of the skin during the mummification process. They are generally located in areas of the body that were exposed and visible. Tattoos were found on the neck and along the arms, but not on the abdomen or inner shoulder, where the straps of a dress would usually be found. Previous research has demonstrated the erotic undertones of tattoos in these areas of the body, but in this case their placement avoids points that were traditionally associated with eroticism or fertility.

Many of the tattoos were also in areas that most likely required the intervention of another person, such as the upper back or neck. This suggests they were done by one or more members of the community, while their intentional placement in visible areas indicates that they were meant to be seen by all. In choosing the location of the tattoos, sensitive areas were not avoided, and in fact some tattoos were placed in extremely delicate areas of the body, such as the neck. Last an important guiding principle in positioning the tattoos seems to have been symmetry, given that identical tattoos were placed symmetrically on the neck, lower back, and upper arms.

The discoloration and distortion of the skin made it difficult to identify all tattoos with certainty. Some of them, on the shoulders and arms, were too faded to be recognized. The following discussion focuses on the tattoos that could be identified in a substantiated way (even if only provisionally). While the symbolism and value of each tattoo can be considered individually, the symmetrical arrangement of the designs and the recurring patterns suggest they should be interpreted as a single set.

The tattoos on the neck may be viewed as the central part of the entire decorative system, above all because the themes in this area of the body are repeated on the shoulders and back. The tattoos appear in two rows and look like a group of amulets placed on the woman's throat. The upper row shows an Eye of Horus, surrounded by two seated baboons; the lower row contains two Eyes of Horus, with two Nefer signs between them. The Eyes of Horus, the Nefer signs, and the sitting baboons have all been previously confirmed to be amulets or magical symbols. We might wonder why these tattoos were drawn specifically on the throat. Given that they were very visible, they might be a graphic representation of amulets. If this were the case, this group of tattoos would have served an important protective function. Indeed, for Egyptians, the neck was one of the most vulnerable parts of the body, which explains why amulets were often placed around it. In this instance, the act of permanently affixing the image of an amulet could therefore have been interpreted as a way of permanently imprinting magical power onto an individual. These considerations suggest that this was a person who actively cared for and protected others—in other words, a sorceress. Sorceresses also said magic spells, and this woman had most likely deemed it advantageous to cover her throat with magical symbols, so as to imbue her actions with magical powers.

It is particularly noteworthy that the theme of the Eyes of Horus reappears on the shoulders. This means that whether you saw the woman from the front, back, or side, you would always see the divine eyes.

On her shoulders, beneath each set of Eyes of Horus, is the outline of a coiled snake with its head looking forward. Snakes were often depicted on magical objects and were also considered powerful supernatural beings. Beneath the coiled snakes on both arms is a design in the form of a cross, which further emphasizes the symmetry of the tattoos. In this case, these designs are linked to the idea of perpetuating life (or reincarnation in the afterlife).

On the right arm, just below the cross, there is another tattoo that could be interpreted as a sistrum handle with the head of the goddess Hathor on it. If, like the tattoos on her neck, those on her arm were activated through dance or movement, then every time this woman moved her right arm, this would result in a ritual shake of the handle. Other Hathoric elements also appear on her left arm. Just above the elbow, there is a scene with two Hathoric cows that are fighting and wearing menat necklaces.

All the tattoos on this woman's body seem to be connected to a type of magic that was unrelated to protection. The tattoos instead appear to be more strictly associated with the idea of power and divine action. The placement of permanent tattoos on her body not only would have connected her to the divine through Hathoric symbols but would have also enabled her to assume important religious or magical roles. This suggests that tattooing served a twofold purpose: to protect, but also to help complete actions that had a significant role in the life of communities.

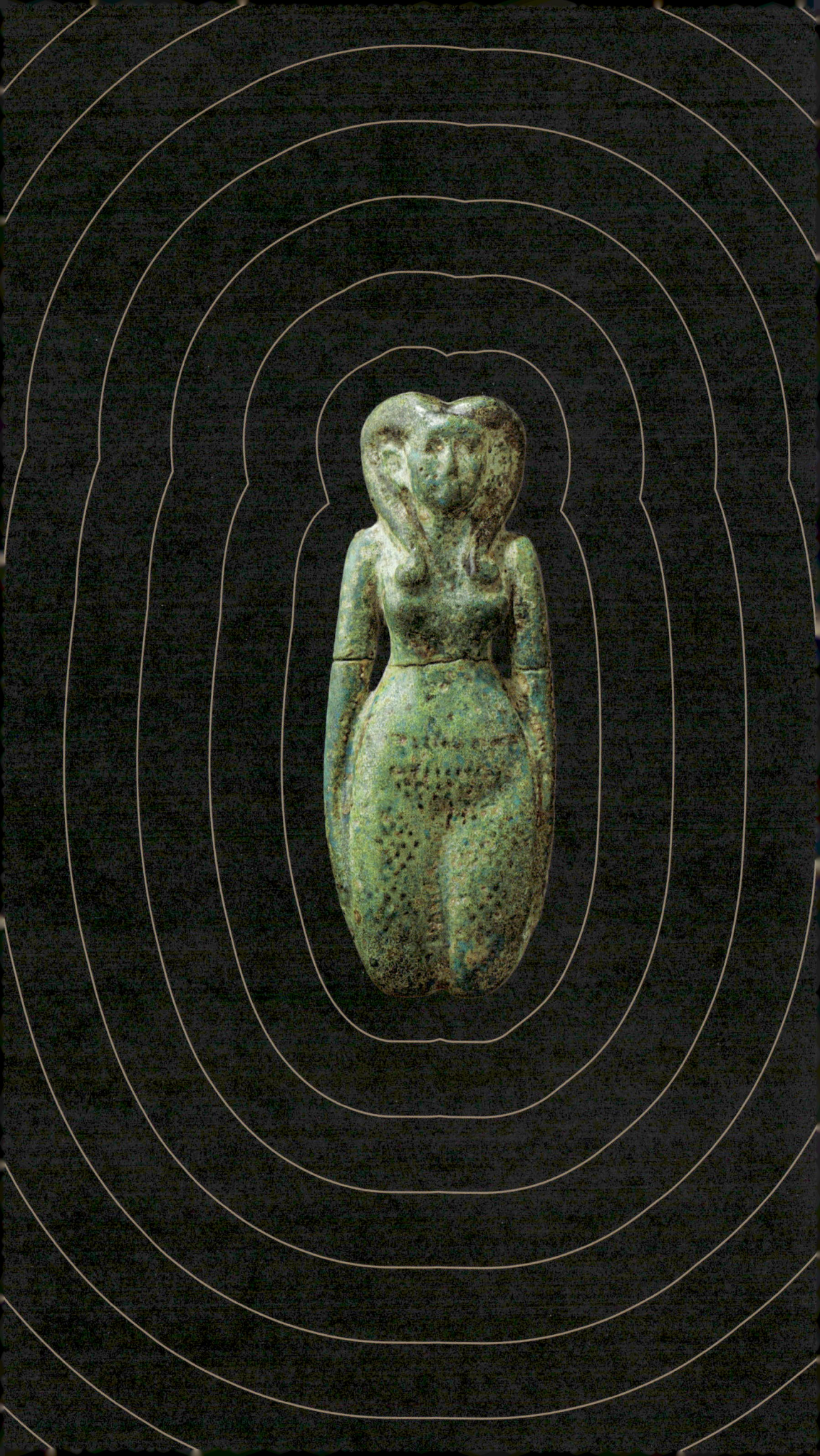

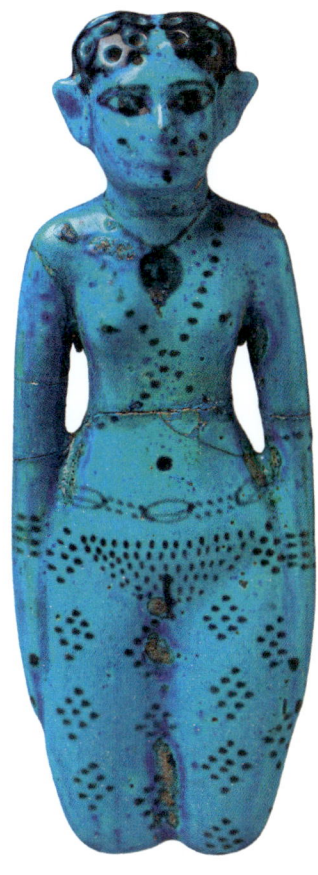

Figurine of a tattooed woman from the Middle Kingdom of Egypt. Paris, Louvre Museum.

Standard-bearing statue of Penbui. Turin, Museo Egizio (Egyptian Museum).

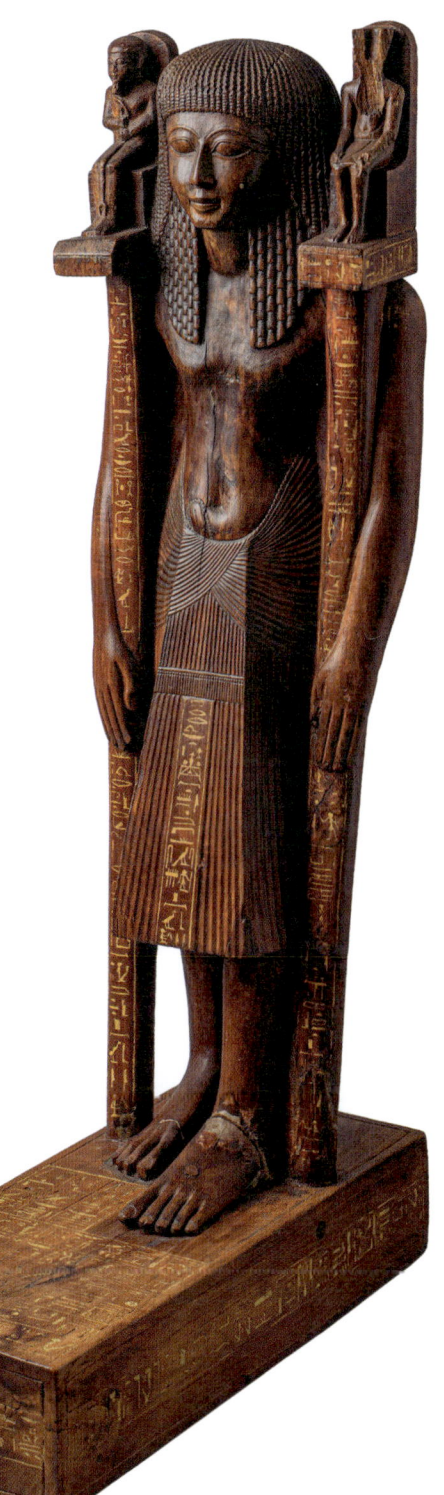

On opposite page:
Figurine of a tattooed woman from the Middle Kingdom of Egypt. New York, Brooklyn Museum.

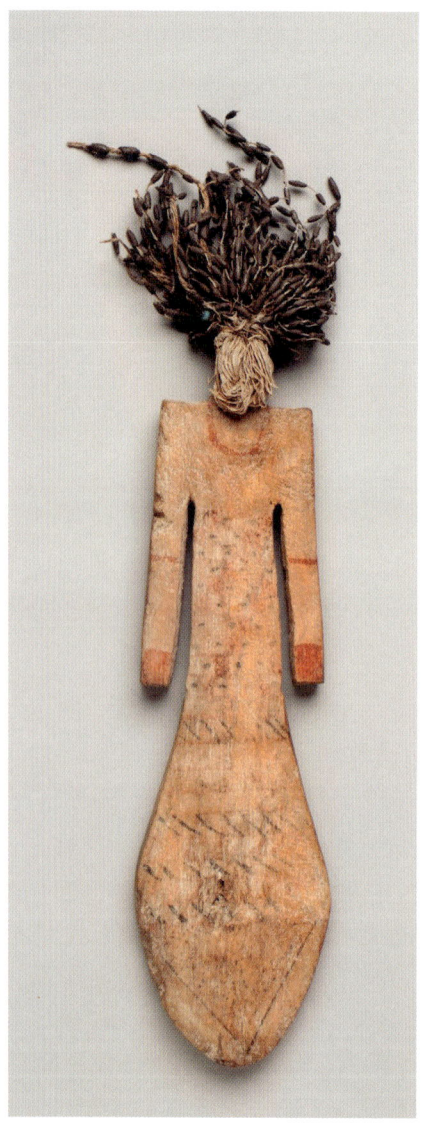

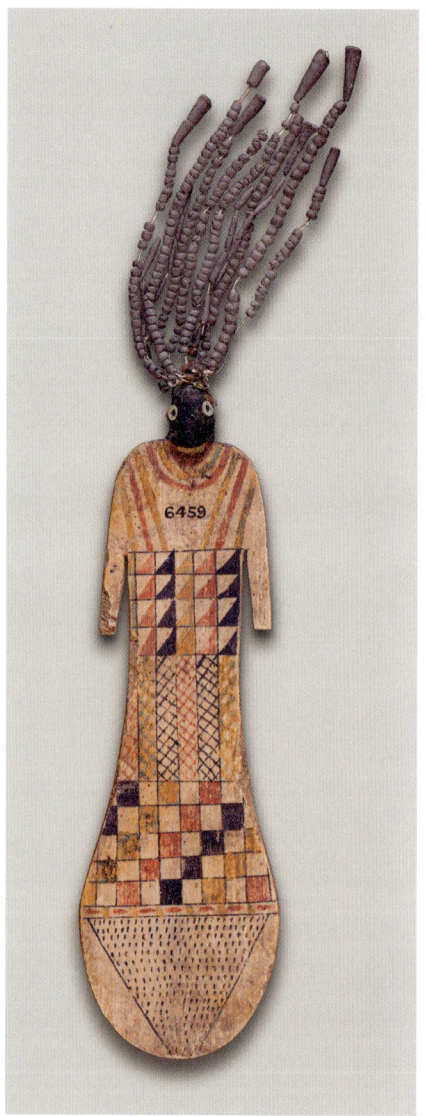

Wood paddle doll. New York, Brooklyn Museum.

Wood paddle doll. London, the British Museum.

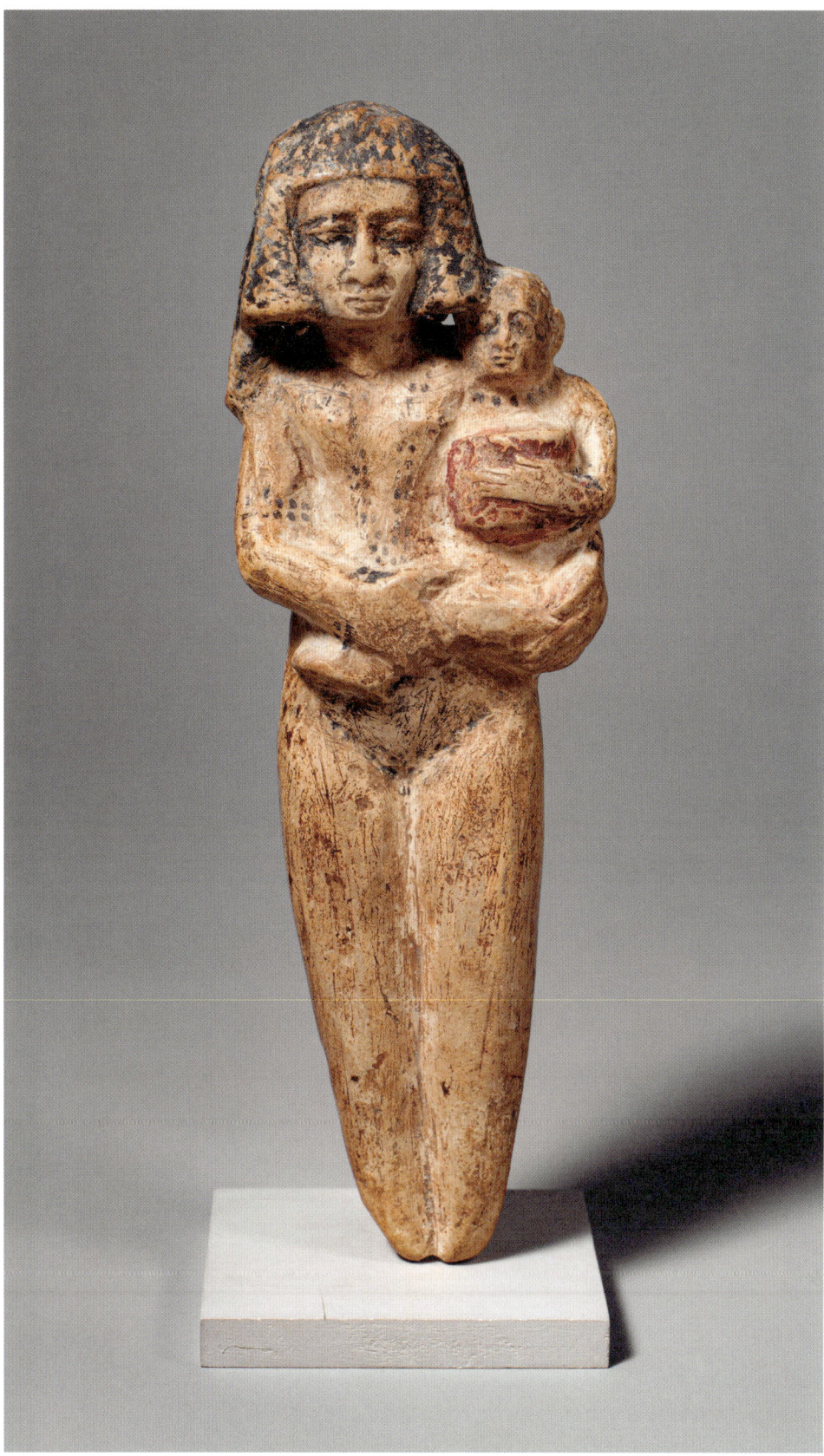

Figurine of a tattooed woman from the Middle Kingdom of Egypt. New York, the Metropolitan Museum of Art.

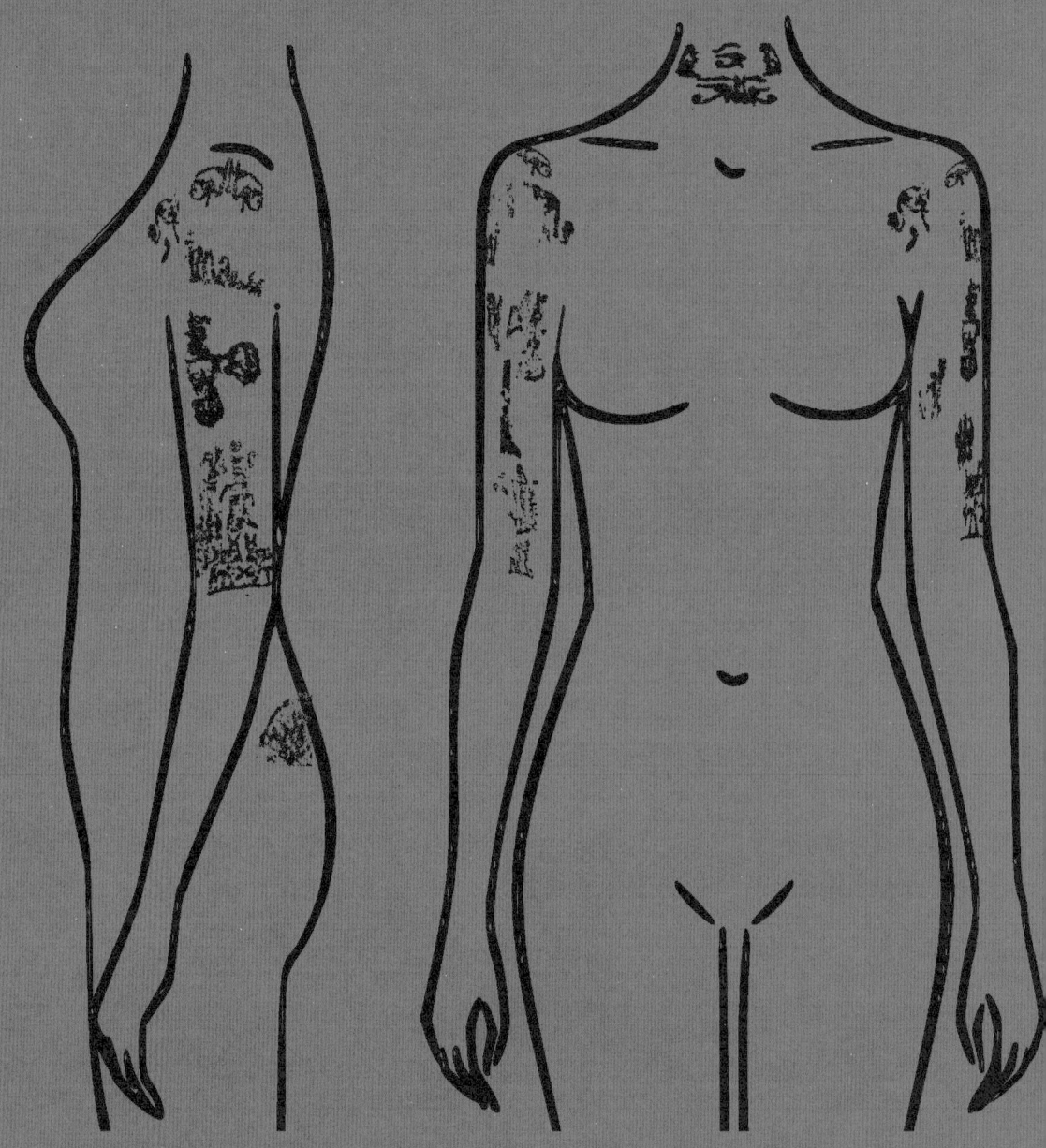

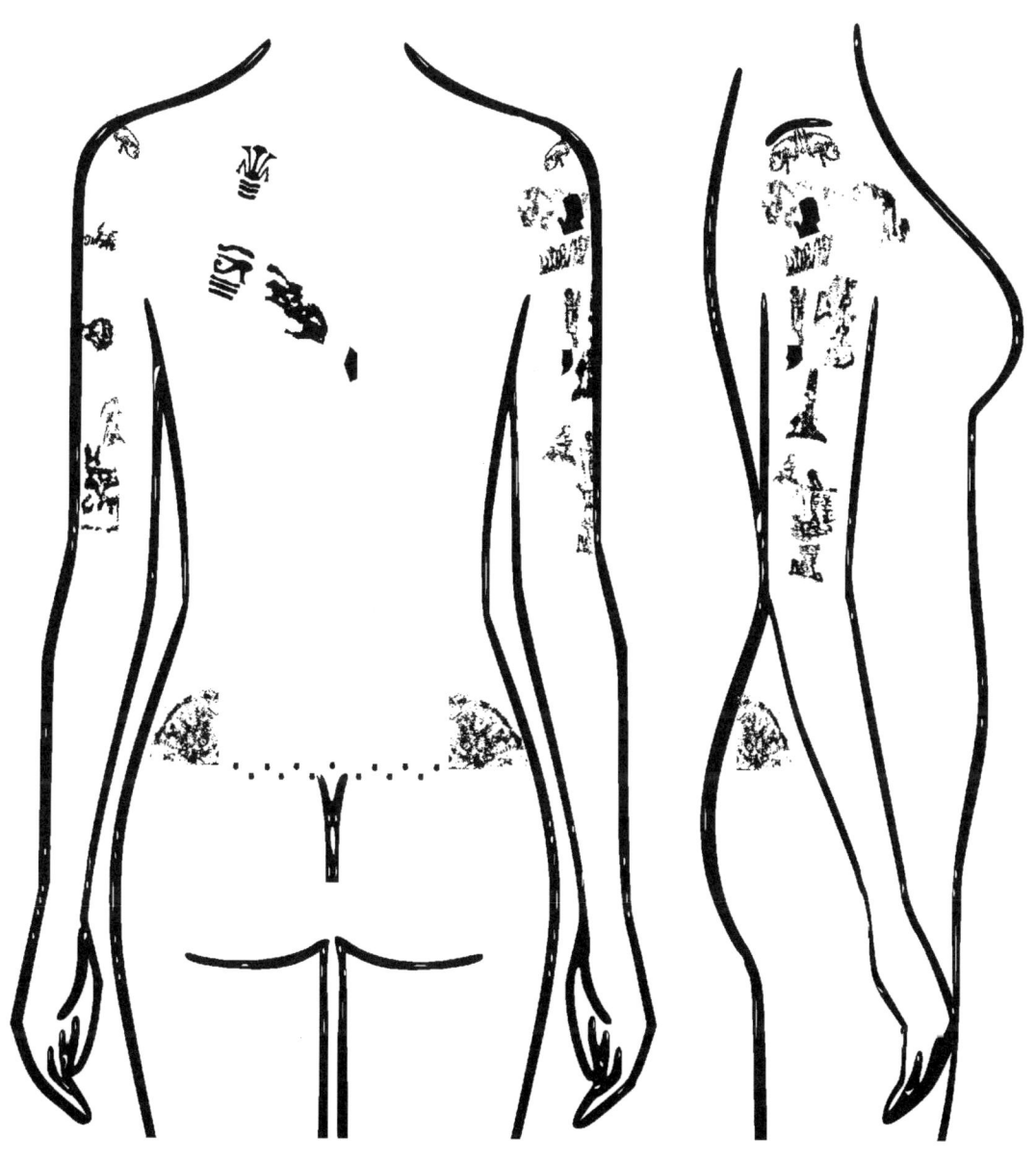

Drawings showing location of tattoos on the mummy. © Anne Austin

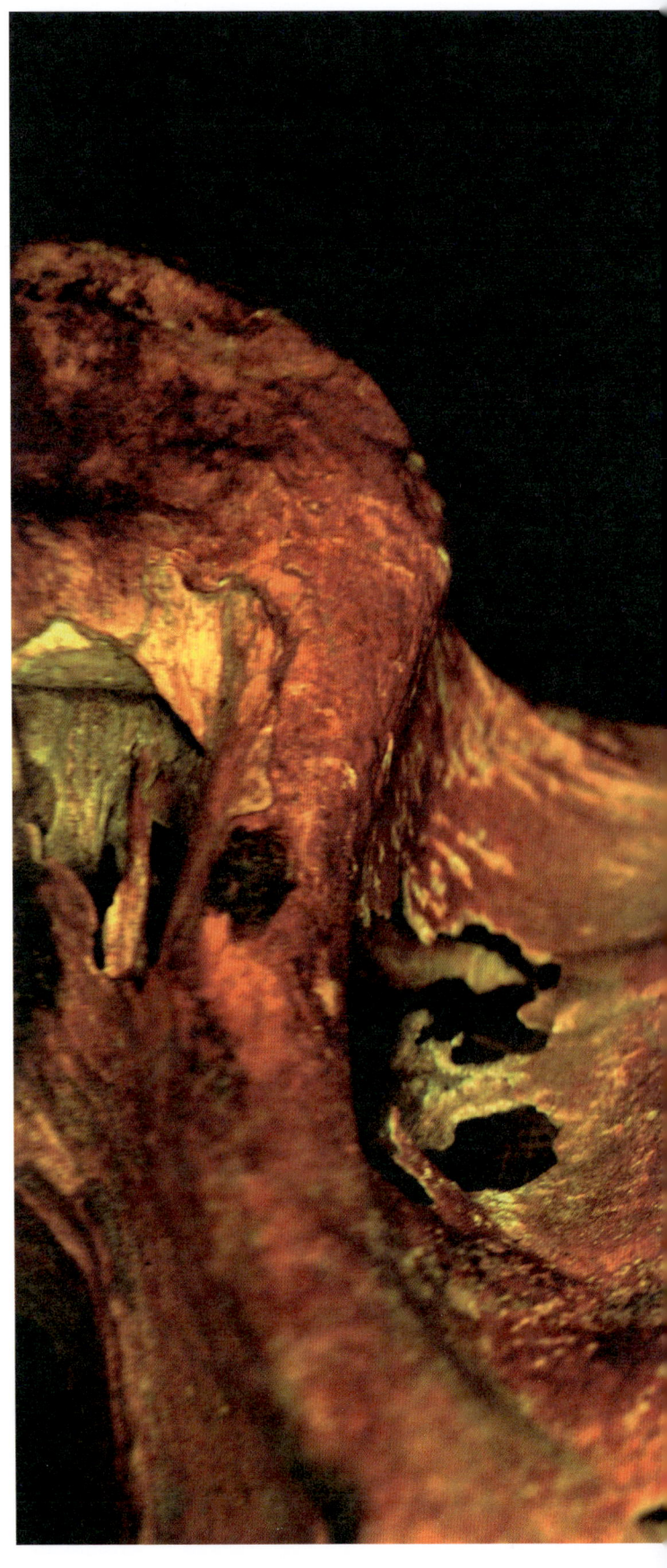

Photograph of the mummy's
tattooed neck.
© Anne Austin

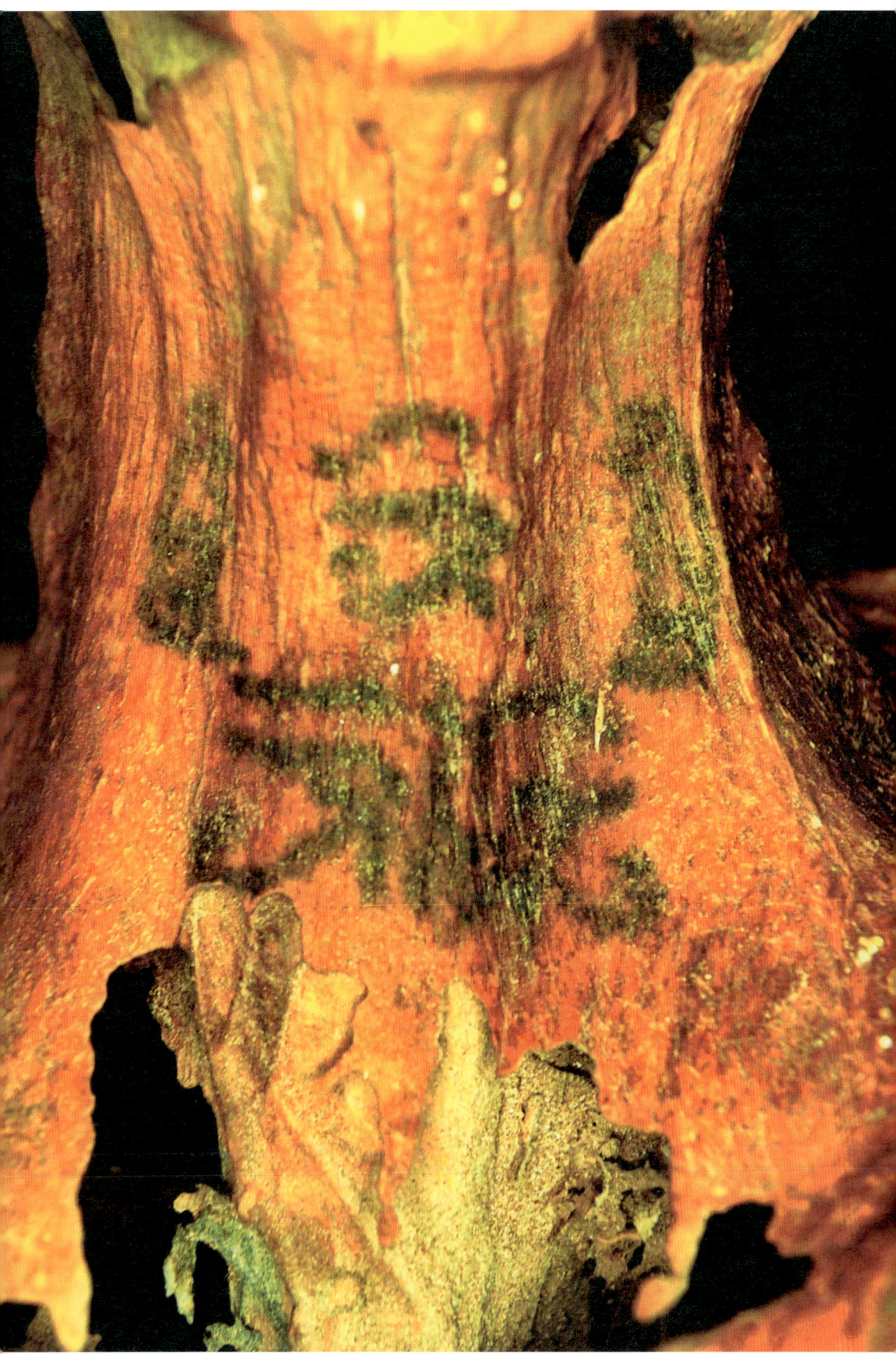

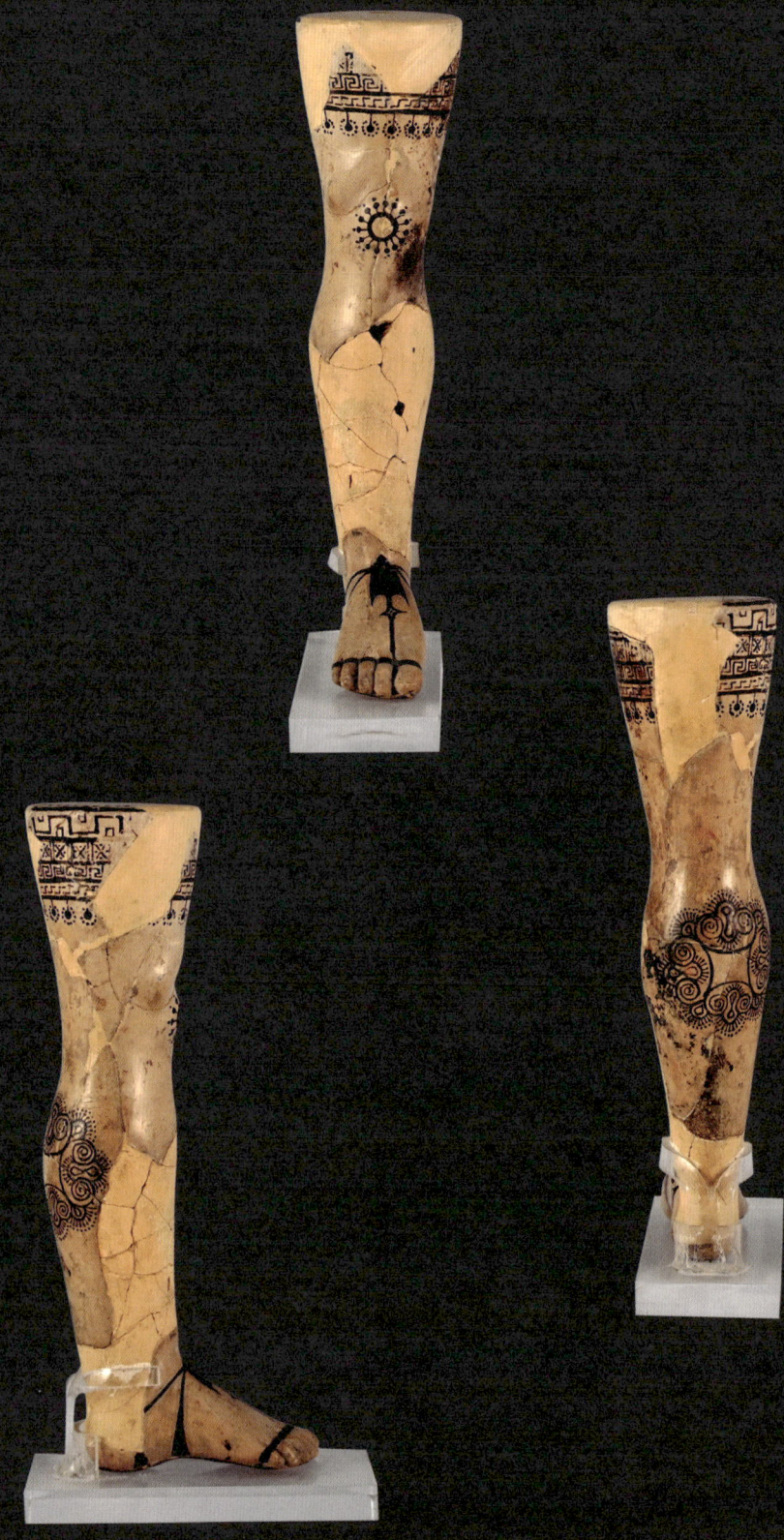

Terra-cotta unguentarium in the shape of a right leg, imported from Rhodes, circa sixth century BCE.
Cerveteri, Parco Archeologico di Cerveteri e Tarquinia–Museo Nazionale Archeologico Cerite (Archeological
Site of Cerveteri and Tarquinia–National Archeological Museum of Cerite).

Although it cannot be confirmed with absolute certainty (they might just be temporary decorations), the most-recent scientific discoveries allow us to speculate that the decorative motifs on a sixth-century BCE unguentarium from Rhodes that was found in Cerveteri in a tomb of the Banditaccia Etruscan necropolis (grave I, tomb 1) might represent tattoos.

The presence of a foreign artifact should come as no surprise. Indeed, there has been considerable modern evidence of artifacts of Greco-Oriental origin in the Banditaccia Necropolis, as in other Etruscan burial centers. Such items confirm the significance of ancient long-distance trade, as proven by discoveries of luxury items (notably numerous ceramic products) that were imported by remote production centers.

In this sense, the designs depicted on the right leg of the purified clay unguentarium are very similar (in terms of their scale, colors, spacing, and form of inscription on the skin) to the patterns tattooed on the upper and lower limbs of the Thracian women portrayed on Greek vases of that time, as may be deduced from a comparison of the respective images.

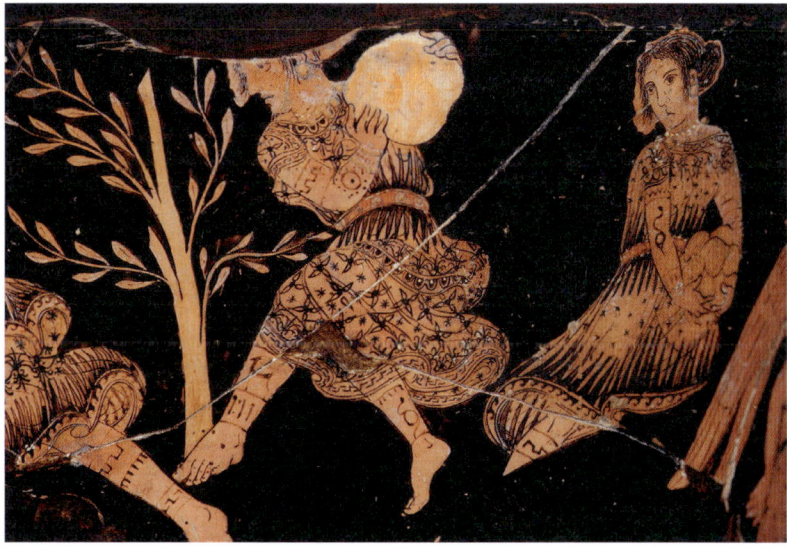

Detail of a krater depicting Thracian women attacking Orpheus, 360 BCE. Amsterdam, Allard Pierson Museum.

The Tattooing
of Artisans in
Italy and Europe
After the Fall
of the
Roman Empire

The Mark of Cain, Mark, *Nzito,* Sign, and Devotion

When the Roman Empire ended, tattooing was no longer widespread and was probably done only in certain isolated communities, in private homes, and primarily for religious purposes. Nevertheless, a considerable number of people must have still engaged in the practice for Pope Adrian (in 787 CE at the Council of Cealchythe in England) to feel it his duty to issue an edict for the precise purpose of prohibiting it (along with circumcision).

However isolated and secret, tattooing did occur in various places throughout the Middle Ages, although the many different words used to refer to the practice have made it difficult to identify. These terms differ both from one another and from the Latin terms. Words such as mark, *nzito,* sign, devotion, and, most commonly, the mark of Cain were used to refer to tattoos during this period.

In medieval culture, tattoos were prohibited (albeit tolerated in pilgrims) and had solely negative connotations. Medieval canon law divided men into three hierarchically ordered classes: At the top were those who prayed, followed by those who fought, and last those who worked the land. Excluded from "respectable society," their work activities were considered unnoble. The worst jobs were considered to be those working in contact with blood (one of the biggest taboos of the Middle Ages in the West): surgeons and butchers, not to mention executioners, who were considered to be worst of all. These people were called by the derogatory term "*scalabrini*" and were forced to live outside the city.

Soldiers were conversely excluded from the category of dishonored people because they were considered to be protectors of Christianity.

People working in trades where they got dirty (anyone from street cleaners to dyers), people in the entertainment professions (jesters, actors), and nomadic tradesmen in general were also considered disgraced.

Around the tenth and eleventh centuries, many categories of artisans joined together in highly selective guilds and associations, in order to escape prejudice and protect themselves. Each artisan guild chose a holy protector and a symbol of recognition that "nobilized" them and united them as a group. This afforded them more strength in their struggle against isolation and social disdain, enabling them to gain newfound professional dignity and different acknowledgment as a group. The connection to one's own guild and the symbol that represented it became very strong when the guilds of artisans, business owners, and certain categories of salaried workers had to fight to gain space and political power in the strict, closed hierarchy of feudal society. A tattoo with the symbol of one's trade became the distinctive mark in artisans' fight for social emancipation, and the practice grew rapidly throughout Europe, where it survived for a few decades.

Tattoos in and of themselves summed up the most-important values in the struggle of the newly emerging middle class. A tattoo of the symbol of one's guild expressed a strong link of belonging. The demand for professional dignity through a provocatory act—tattooing— represented an official declaration refusing the taboo against blood. Ultimately, Cain was chosen as the protector of all artisans. The Lord tattooed Cain (branding was considered to be a tattoo) after he killed Abel. He sent him "to roam the earth as a fugitive among men" but affixed a mark on his forehead as a sign that no one should kill him.

The artisans of that period referred to their tattoos as "the mark of Cain." Their mark demanded their right to dignity. The executioners (the lowest of the low) were probably the first tattooers. They were the ones with the instruments and technical knowledge to do so, since they were responsible for tattooing those condemned to death.

Cain is commonly considered to have committed the first homicide. He was the first criminal, the first subverter of order, and the first one responsible for creating violence and barbarity. Yet, however surprisingly, the Bible states that Cain was the founder of the city (i.e., of civilization)—the establisher of law and order (Genesis 4:17). After the assassination of his brother, the Lord showed him how horrendous his act was, and, in response to Cain's terror ("Whoever finds me will kill me"), proclaimed, "Anyone who kills Cain will suffer vengeance seven times over." He then "imposed on Cain a sign, lest any who found him should attack him." Various elements can be noted from this profound and mysterious episode. God prohibits anyone from killing Cain, and then the assassin himself becomes the founder of civilization (i.e., of a city) Enoch, named after his son) that rises from the desert. It becomes a thriving center for law and worship, but also technology (through Tubal-Cain) and art (through Jubal).

Perhaps some other forms of tattooing were practiced during the Middle Ages, of which we are not aware. Surely, tattoos were used as a sign of belonging to groups of various kinds, whether criminal, political, or religious. Certainly, some people got a tattoo with the name of their loved one, and there were definitely tattoos recognizing illegitimate children or heirs to power or property. In Portugal, there were tattoos containing magic potions that were believed to be able to cure fevers and infections. In Siena, where the contrade (urban wards) continued to be a way of recognizing the inhabitants of various neighborhoods, there was an ancient tradition of getting a tattoo with the symbol of one's contrada.

Therefore, while tattooing in the Middle Ages was clearly viewed upon poorly and was primarily practiced as punishment or as a mark of infamy, it also survived in its most-positive forms of expression, in an isolated and hidden manner.

Blacksmith emblem

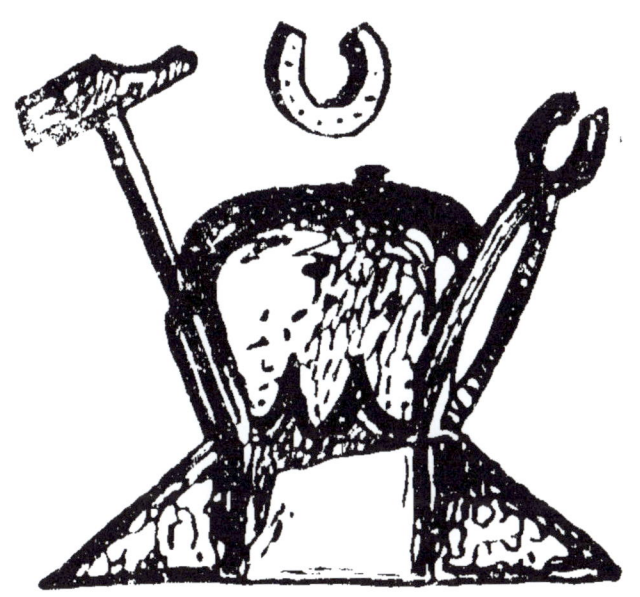

Tailor emblem

Stonecutter emblem

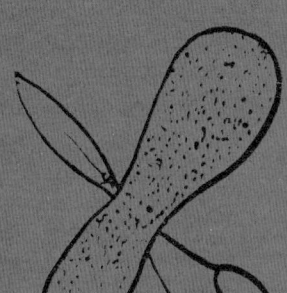

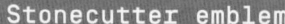

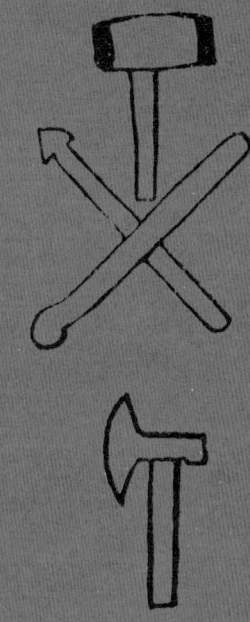

Baker emblem

Cobbler emblem

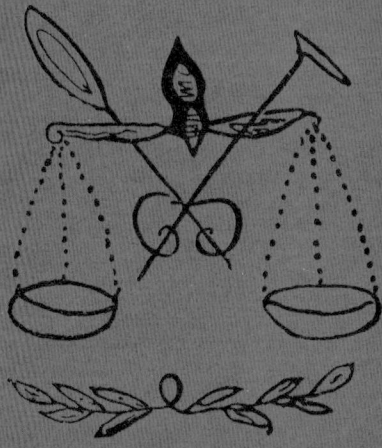

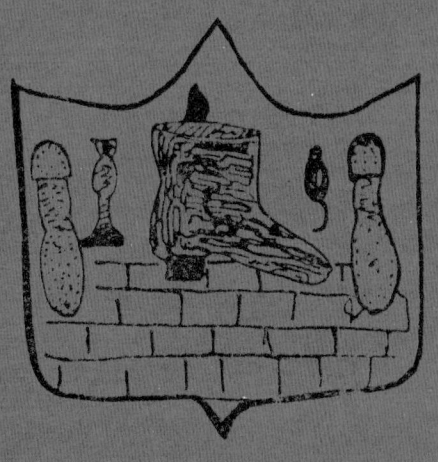

Love tattoo

Bootmaker emblem

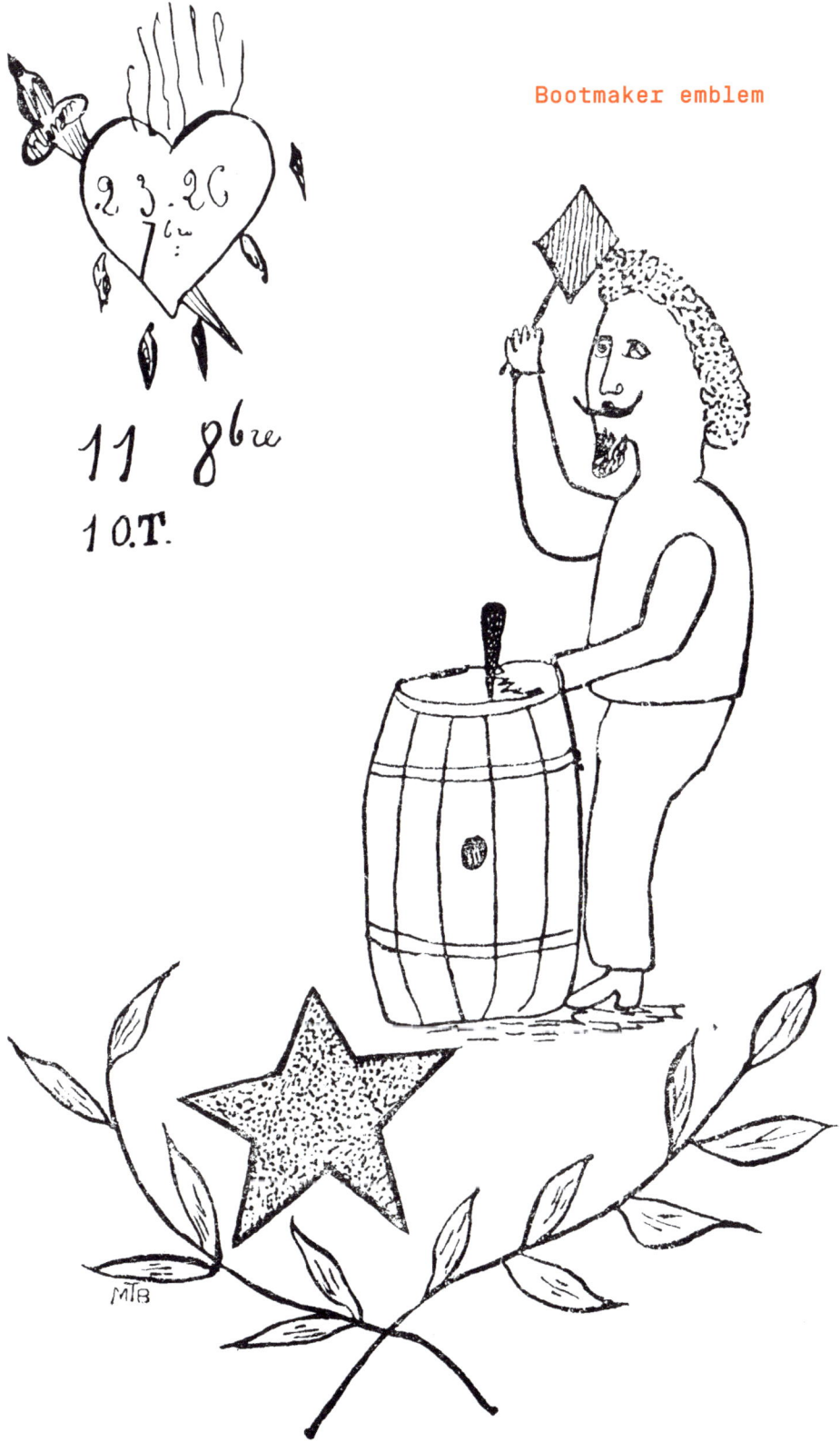

Bricklayer emblem

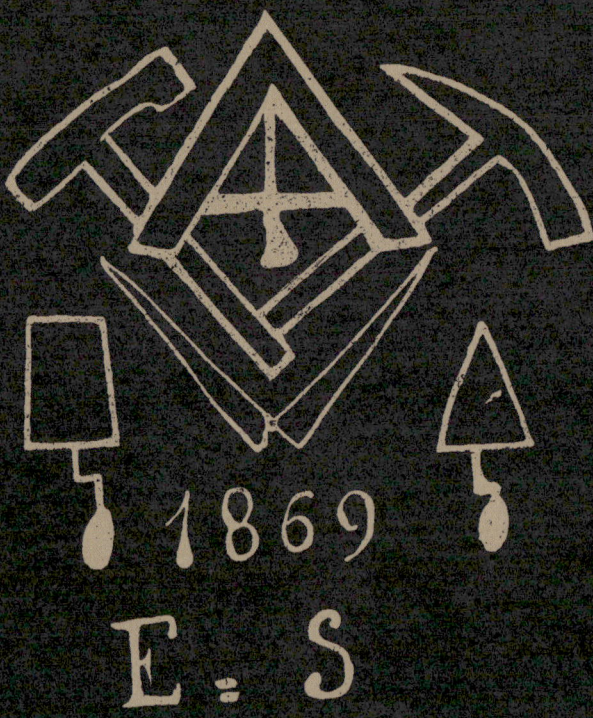

Cart driver emblem

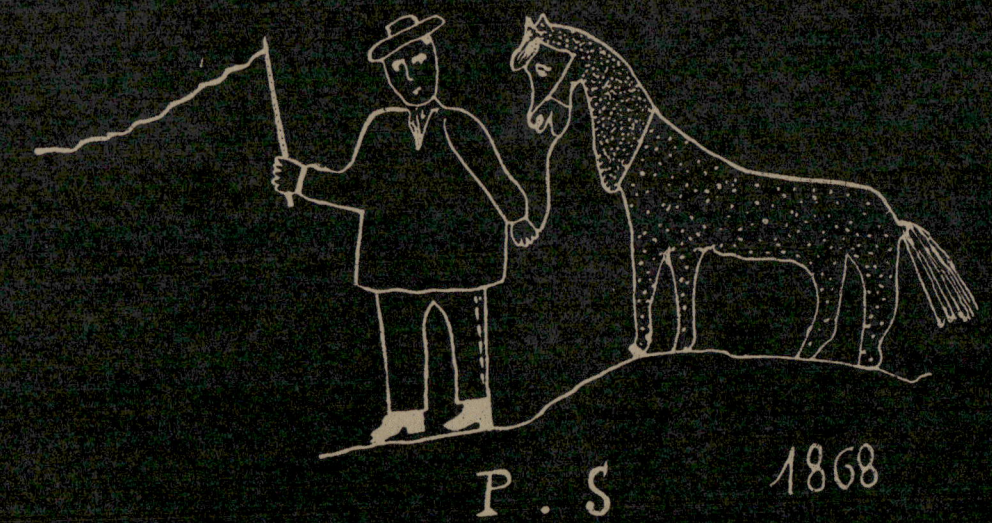

Tattoos from certain contrade in Siena

Snail

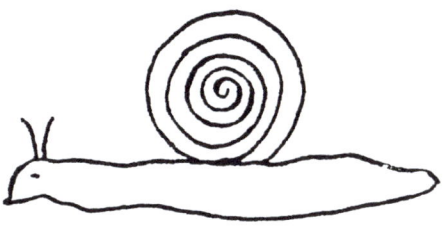

Tower

Seashell

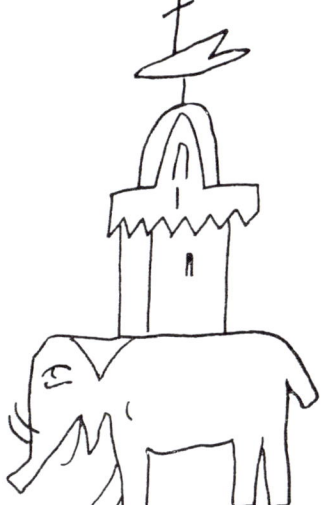

Wave

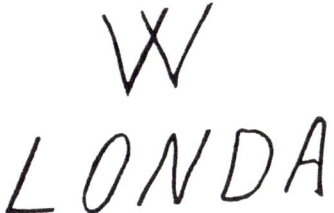

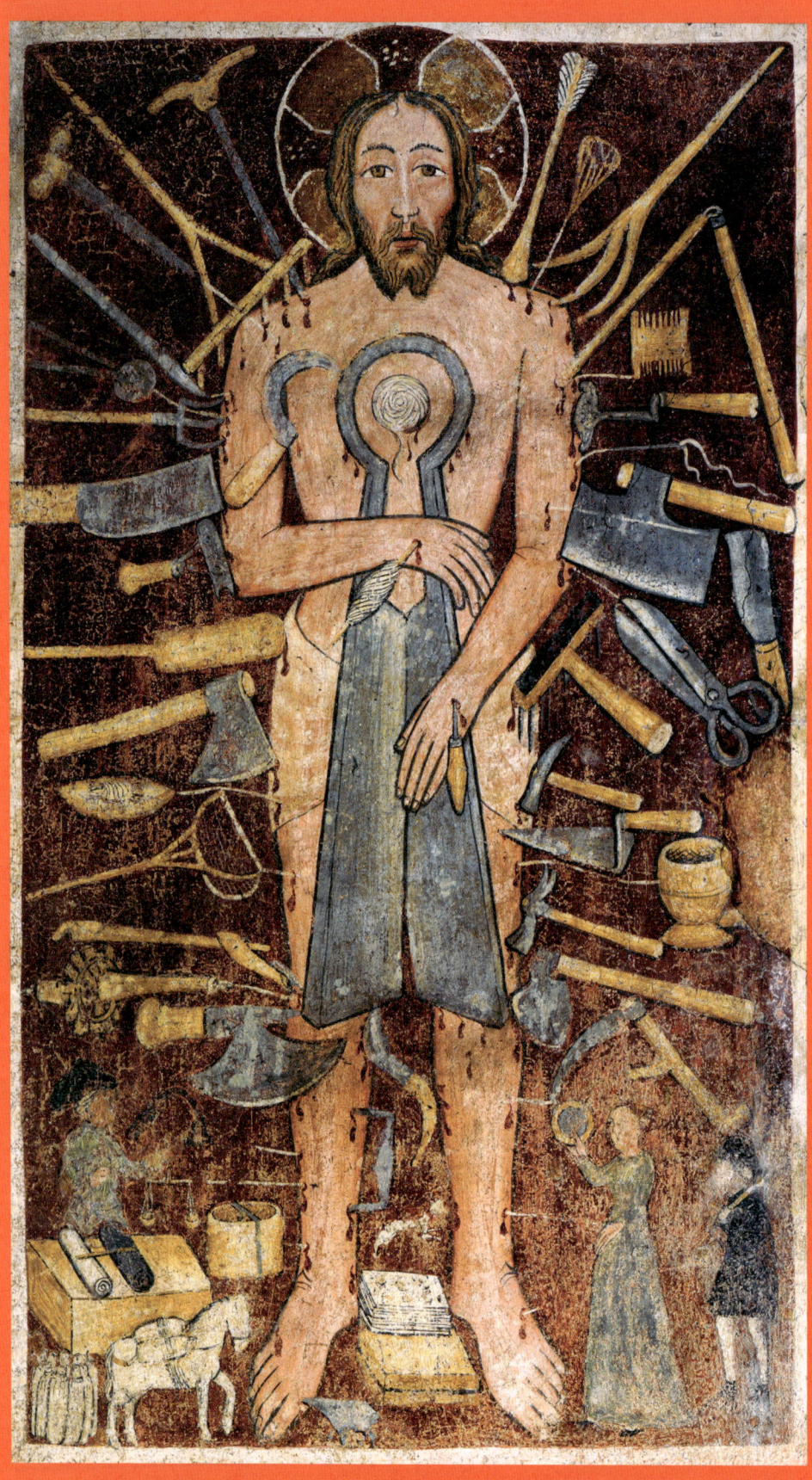

Anonymous, *Cristo della Domenica,* late fifteenth century. Biella, Duomo di Santo Stefano
(Santo Stefano Cathedral).

The Sunday Christ

From the early fourteenth century to throughout the sixteenth century, the practice of decorating the interior and exterior walls of churches with frescos and paintings depicting the so-called Sunday Christ spread throughout Italy and Europe. These images served as an admonishment to artisans and peasants, reminding them of the precept of "sanctifying holy days."

The image is always that of a suffering Christ. The basic message is the condemnation of sin through the depiction of men acting in ways that conflict with the church's teachings, men once again destroying God. Per ancient popular pictorial tradition, this Christ thus served the didactive purposes of better conveying the wrongdoings of whoever worked on Sunday.

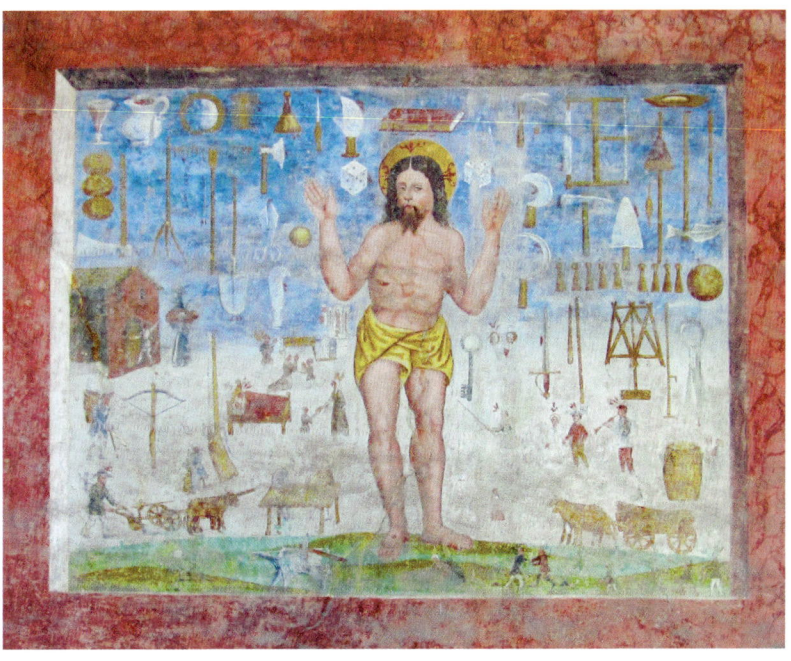

Anonymous, *Cristo della Domenica*, circa 1557. Tesero (Trento), Chiesa di San Rocco (Church of Saint Roch).

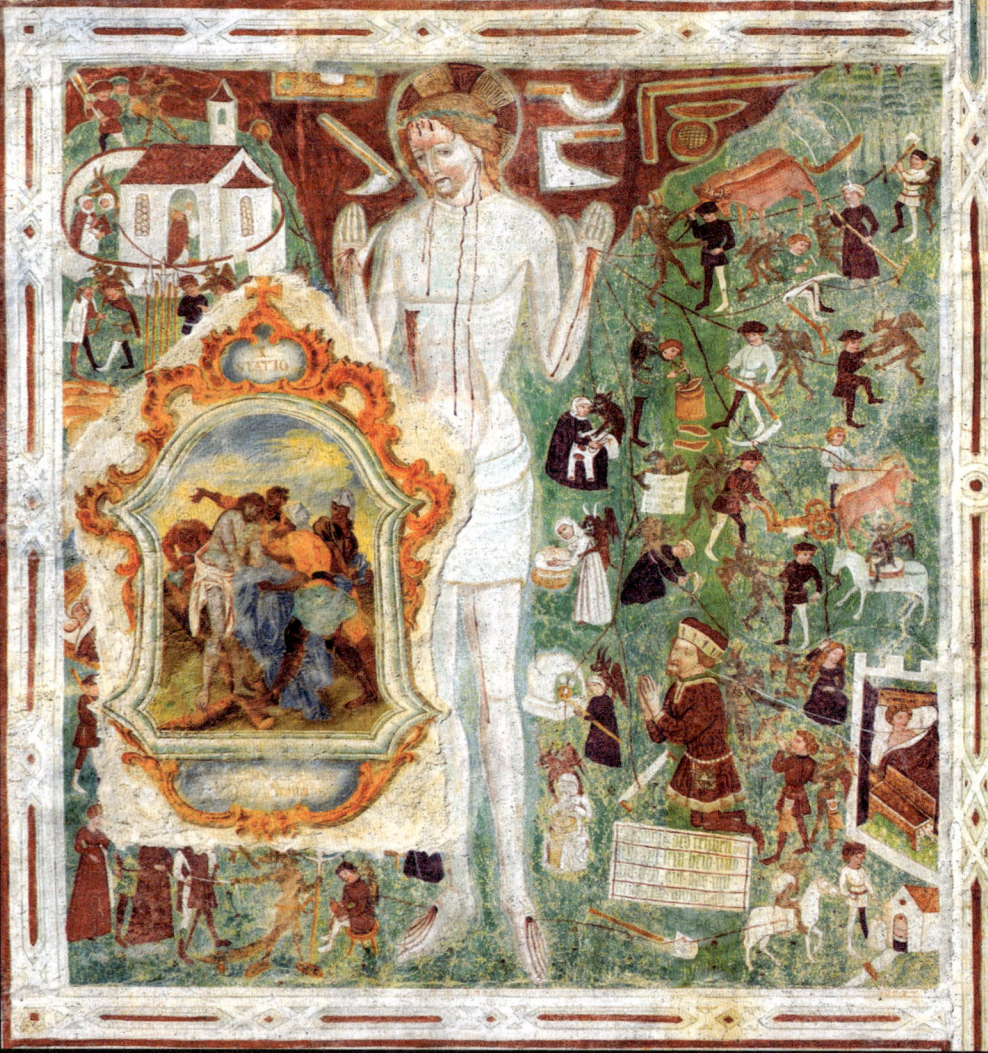

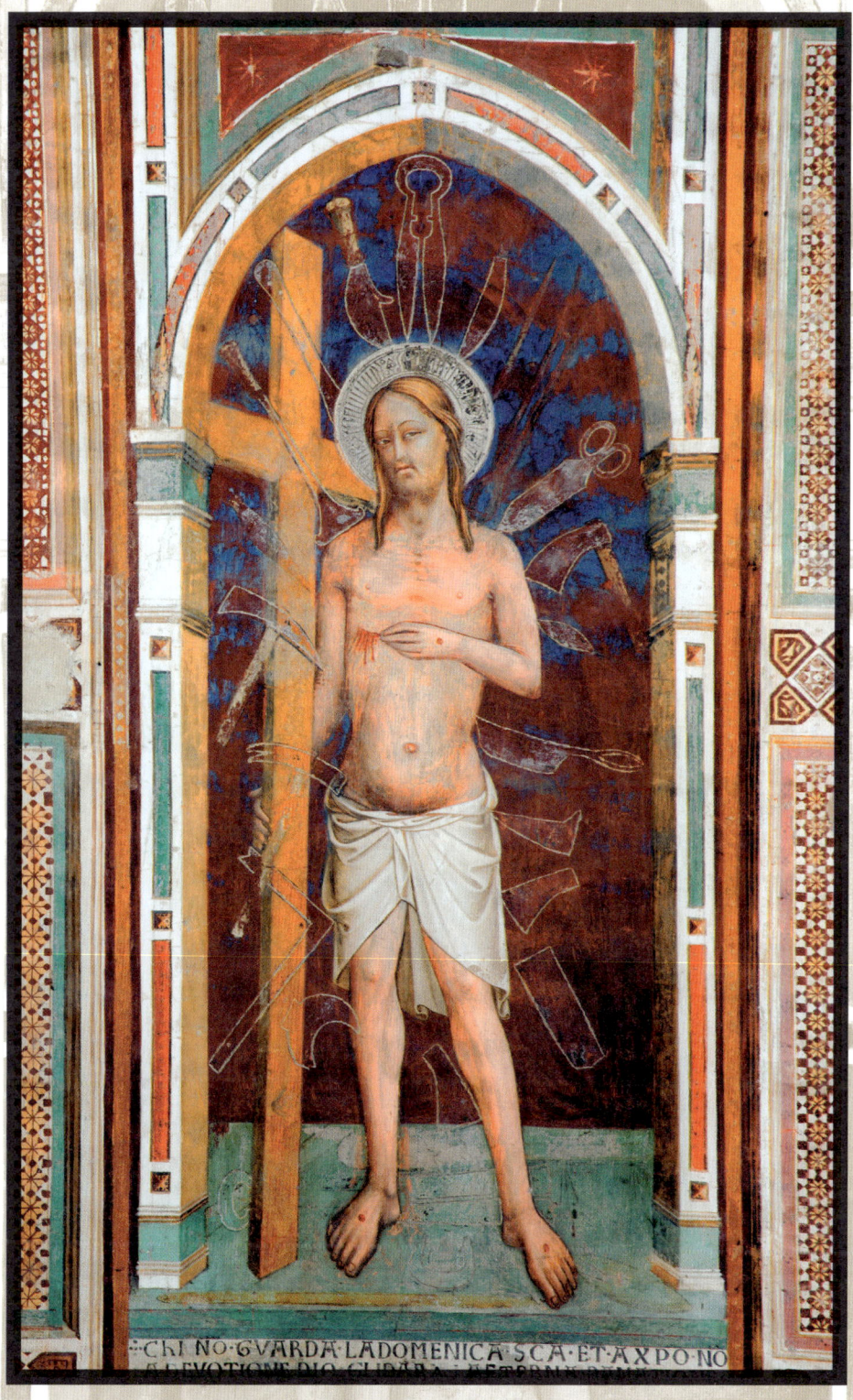

CHI NO GUARDA LADOMENICA SCA ET AXPO NO
A EVOTIONE DIO GUDARA A ETERNE DENATO

Mariotto di Cristofano, *Cristo della Domenica*, 1420–1425. Florence, Abbazia di San Miniato al Monte
(San Miniato al Monte Monastery).

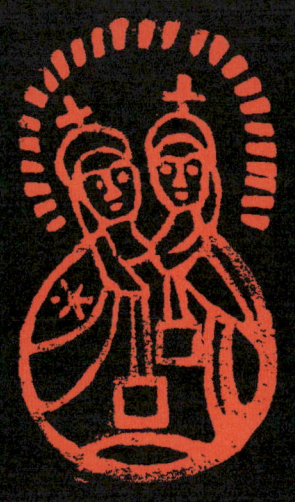

Devotional Tattoos in Italy: The Case of Loreto and the Connection to Jerusalem

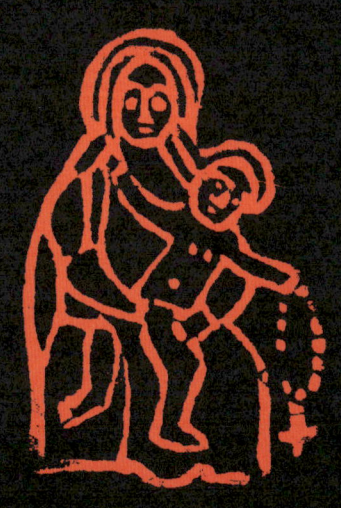

—— Guido Guerzoni

Devotional Marks

When ethnologist Caterina Pigorini Beri released her book *Costumi e superstizioni dell'Appennino Marchigiano* (Customs and Superstitions of the Apennine Mountains of the Marche), published in Città di Castello in 1889 by printmaker-publisher S. Lapi, she included an essay titled "I tatuaggi sacri e profani della Santa Casa di Loreto" (Sacred and Secular Tattoos of the Holy House of Loreto), in which she revealed the results of a lengthy research project on tattoos done in Loreto in the late nineteenth century.

Mapping out "the superstitions, fables, legends, and beliefs of the Apennine Mountains of the Marche," the author was struck "by a unique custom found among nearly all inhabitants of the Picenum region of ancient Italy, bordered by the Tronto River, Umbria, and Abruzzo. This very simple, civilized, and intelligent people, which seems to have assimilated and practically adopted Umbrian and Etruscan cultures, engages in tattooing, which is particularly popular among men. This was easily determined, since tattoos are generally applied on the arm, close to the wrist. I was surprised to see the deep-blue symbolic marks on laborers working in the fields with their sleeves rolled up. They had tattoos of figures, maxims, crosses, or symbols of passion involving the sun and moon. There were tattoos depicting the Holy Spirit, with one or two pierced hearts, sometimes beneath a cross placed on top of a globe, other times atop a star, and a thousand instances of the song lyric '*Eterno, incancellabile non ti scordar di me*' [*eternal, indelible don't forget me*]. The practice appears to be so natural and so common that no one talks about it. In fact, as far as I know, no one from the area has ever mentioned this strange custom, which is unique to the region and has and must necessarily have considerable ethnographic and historical importance."[1]

In reality, Pigorini Beri's statement was not entirely true, since her discovery was not completely new. Cesare Lombroso had actually observed, prior to 1878, that in the vicinity of the Loreto Sanctuary, people practiced "a devoted illicit trade . . . since there are specific *marcatori* ["markers"] in its proximity, who receive sixty to eighty cents per tattoo."[2] This practice, according to the Verona physician,

1. C. Pigorini Beri, *Costumi e superstizioni dell'Appennino Marchigiano*, Città di Castello 1889, 291. In the previous year, the same author had published a preview titled *I tatuaggi sacri ed erotici della Santa Casa di Loreto* in *L'illustrazione italiana XV*, 51 (1888), 415–419.

2. C. Lombroso, *L'uomo delinquente studiato in rapporto alla antropologia, alla medicina legale ed alle discipline carcerarie*, vol. I, *Delinquente nato e pazzo morale* (Turin, 1843), 300–301. The first edition of this serendipitous text was published in the same city by the same publisher in 1878.

was also widespread elsewhere. Various Lombard pastors favored a "cross, overlapping a sphere and a heart, and encircled by candles," and the image of the Blessed Sacrament was loved "especially among Neapolitans," along with crucifixes, figures of patron saints, and the heads of the dead. People from Romagna and Abruzzo frequently adorned their limbs with Christograms featuring a capital H,[3] which were similar to those Giuseppe Pitrè had identified in Sicily.[4]

Additionally, while visiting Loreto in the late 1870s, the abbot Antonio Stoppani observed that despite the prohibition, which had been in effect since 1860, strange-looking people were waiting along the road leading to the shrine, parading in front of cobbler's benches, where they "blasted and banged wooden beams like castanets" inviting "people towards something I did not understand."[5] Stoppani, the author of *Il bel paese,* stayed for a few minutes waiting before watching "in the heart of Italy, the most indecorous scene of tattooing."[6] The Lombard monk's disgust was not mitigated by the fact that "each of the roughly cut plates" depicted "a saint, a Virgin Mary, and a cross, such that customers could choose whichever figures of those religious symbols they wished to have imprinted onto their skin."[7] He instead grew angrier when he saw "right in front, a fresh-faced and seemingly naïve and smiling young girl" who chose "I don't know what symbol or saint," giving over "her arm . . . to that ugly mug manning the bench. That depraved man began to dye the cuts of the incision with black varnish, then applied the plate onto her poor arm, pressing it so that the cuts of the incision were permanently imprinted in black; he then began the ignominious carnage. Grasping a steel dagger, his hand moving almost mechanically in a convulsive shudder, he began to prick her, drawing blood from the poor little girl, going over and over across the cuts of the incision, until all of that filth had been absorbed."[8]

The practice of tattooing religious symbols was not new and was in fact definitely widespread as of the sixteenth century. Indeed, it continued to find fans among men and women alike until the 1950s, to the significant outrage of conformists. It was no coincidence that when setting up the Marches stand at the Italian Ethnography Exhibition held in Rome for the 1911[9] International Exhibition, Lamberto Loria presented a pair of young newlyweds about to get tattoos of matrimonial emblems, per *the custom in Loreto prior to 1860.*[10] Likewise,

3. C. Pigorini Beri, *Costumi e superstizioni,* 303.

4. G. Pitrè, *Usi e costumi, credenze e pregiudizi del popolo siciliano raccolti e descritti da Giuseppe Pitrè* (Palermo, Italy, 1870–1913), vol. I, 465. In addition to the year of grace, monograms for Mary and the triad G.M.G.—Jesus, Mary, and Joseph—were fairly common.

5. A. Stoppani, *Il bel paese* (Milan, 1881), 164.

6. Ibid.

7. Ibid., 166.

8. Ibid. This description coincides with the one Pigorini Beri provided on p. 302: "The worker, using a pen consisting of three points of steel (picchetta) attached to a handle with a thick piece of tarred thread, traces the borders with tiny thick points; as soon as it's done, the patient's skin is slightly stretched on each side so that the blood can escape: therefore a deep blue (indigo) ink is rubbed onto the skin, which seeps down and sets in there permanently, leaving the precise design. The operation is painful but after twenty-four hours the pain is gone."

9. *Catalogo della Mostra di Etnografia Italiana in Piazza d'Armi* (Bergamo, Italy, 1911).

10. Ibid., 148

sixty years later, the last tattooers living in the region of the Marches sanctuary told Daniela Gambuti, who cataloged the 337 boxwood stamps and a related set of 340 stamps that prior to 1973 were at the Museo Nazionale delle Arti et delle Tradizionali Popolari (National Museum of Art and Popular Traditions) in Rome[11] that even children between the ages of ten and fifteen[12] were getting tattoos as late as the postwar period.

An Issue of Skin: Historiography Before History

Even though there were only eight years between the books by Stoppani (1881) and Pigorini-Beri (1889), we can immediately see how much the two authors differ. Stoppani demonstrates no interest in this practice, let alone a *positive* interpretation. He makes his disgust more than apparent in the pages devoted to the tattoos studied by Lombroso and his disciples. Pigorini, conversely, is aware of the fact that the Loreto tattoos, and religious tattoos in general,[13] when "judged excluding their *historical environment*, could produce unique errors and mislead anthropology scholars, who would be straying from the truth by applying the principles of positive science to them."[14] She therefore tried to go back to the origins of the phenomenon, demonstrating unique independence and depth of judgment, at a time when tattoos evoked only criminality in Italy.

In this specific case, however, we found ourselves faced with a unique phenomenon. According to the author of *Costumi e superstizioni,* who managed to get hold of nearly "a hundred ancient fruitwood printing blocks (possibly engraved with a nail), and two awls or *pens,* with which the color of the strange hieroglyphs was injected into live flesh," which had been seized from a sexton,[15] the molds could be grouped into six main categories: (1) tattoos pertaining to the Order of St. Francis,[16] (2) tattoos pertaining to the Society of Jesus,[17] (3) tattoos pertaining to the Order of Franciscans and the Society of Jesus;[18] (4) various religious tattoos;[19] (5)

---

11. D. Gambuti, *Schedatura dei tatuaggi del Santuario di Loreto giacenti al Museo Nazionale delle Arti e delle Tradizioni Popolari* (La Sapienza University of Rome, School of Literature, years 1973–74).

12. D. Gambuti, *Schedatura,* 109.

13. Pigorini Beri on p. 302 affirmed that "tattoos in Loreto have an exclusively mystical origin; we cannot conflate them with the tattoos that come from primitive civilizations: these tattoos are what could be called an institution."

14. C. Pigorini Beri, *Costumi e superstizioni,* 300.

15. Ibid., 292.

16. Ibid., I–II of the appendix: "monstrances, a symbol of the Franciscan order, St. Francis rosary, symbols of the Passion of Christ according to the order of St. Francis, St. Francis with the stigmata and rosary, Saint Clare with the palm and pyx, the Madonna of Angels with part of the coat of arms of Pope Sixtus V, the Immaculate Conception, the 'eternal dream of tho Franciscans.'"

17. Ibid., III–VI: "monstrances, the Christogram IHS, the sacred heart of Jesus with the symbols of the Passion of Christ, the sacred heart of Mary, stylized forms of crucifixes, Our Lady of the Seven Sorrows, the Sorrowful Mother."

18. Ibid., VII–VIII: "image of the Madonna of Loreto with child, Madonna of Loreto with the symbol of the sacrament, Madonna of Loreto and the Crucifix of Sirolo."

19. Ibid., IX–XX: "the Passion of Jesus Christ, Our Lady of Good Counsel, Our Lady of Genazzano, Madonna del Carmine, Queen of Heaven, emblems of the Passion of Jesus, Saint Michael the Archangel who kills the dragon, Saint Emygdius, a bishop who protected Ascoli Piceno from earthquakes (particularly important to the people of Abruzzo), angels with elements of the Passion of Jesus, Saint Philomena."

tattoos pertaining to love;[20] and (6) other themes, which included tattoos of young brides (doves, per the proverb "The Word became flesh and made his dwelling among us"), sailors (anchors and flowers), and widows, with a skull and crossbones and the motto *memento mei* or *memento mori* inscribed underneath.[21]

These items were enough to cause some degree of embarrassment to Italy's scientific community, which had by and large attested to secularly positive positions. This embarrassment explains the silence that for so long marked knowledge about this practice. Indeed, the rediscovery of tattooing coincided with the resurgence of studies in popular traditions and folklore. It is no coincidence that almost ninety years after Pigorini Beri's work, the next three publications on devotional tattoos were in 1977.[22]

Nevertheless, in order to understand how Italy came to be so hesitant—since Pigorini's work conversely had a broad international impact—we need to return to the devotional function of the ancient custom. This aspect was criticized under the dogmas of the anthropological school of positivism,[23] which for at least twenty years, and not just in Italy, insisted on the atavistic, deviant, "modern, and non-European characteristics of tattooing. These theories (which were devoid of any historical basis) identified tattooing as the connecting point between the savages described by contemporary anthropologists, explorers, and geographers, and the "urban cavemen" who were responsible (or potentially responsible) for the most-heinous crimes against civil society.

The Taboos of Tattoos

We can therefore imagine how the various experts, authors of unintentionally comedic masterpieces such as *Tatuaggi artistici in disertori francesi* (Artistic Tattoos in French Defectors) or *Tatuaggi anarchici in delinquenti monarchici* (Anarchic Tattoos in Monarchic Criminals), who proudly opened their own treatises with the following canonical quote by Théophile Gautier: "The most brutal man, feels, in an instinctive way that the decoration traces a line of impassable demarcation between himself and the animal. And when he can't put the emblem on his clothes—he will embroider his own skin,[24] worriedly received the work of Pigorini, a female ethnographer and researcher of fables challenging a legion of male scientists.

---

20. Ibid., XI: "hearts with arrows, hearts linked to a chain as a testament of love, a dove with an olive branch as a sign of peace, two linked hearts topped with a star, which may have expressed a sailor's love."

21. Ibid., XII.

22. Father Floriano Grimaldi in the book *Loreto* published on pp. 126–131 photographic reproductions of some seventy molds from the sixteenth century conserved at the Holy House; Italo Tanoni published "Il tatuaggio sacro a Loreto," in *Ricerche di storia sociale e religiosa* 12 (1977): 105–119; Cleto Corrain, Mariantonia Capitanio, and Floriano Grimaldi published "Il tatuaggio religioso in Loreto" in *Ravennatensia* 6 (1977): 381–396.

23. See P. Leschiutta, "Le pergamene viventi: Interpretazioni del tatuaggio nell'antropologia positiva italiana," *La ricerca folclorica: Contributi allo studio della cultura delle classi popolari* 27 (1993): 129–138; and J. Caplan, "Speaking Scars: The Tattoo in Popular Practice and Medico-Legal Debate in Nineteenth-Century Europe," *History Workshop Journal* 44 (1997): 104–142.

24. This quote introduces a book by Abele De Blasio (his first name might explain the Neapolitan scholar's aversion to the mark of Cain), *Il tatuaggio*, 7.

The first obstacle was epithelial taboo—the embarrassment for that harrowed use of the integument, which forced them to overcome the Manichean conception of "social skin" that Terrence Turner described so well: "The surface of the body becomes, in any human society, a boundary of a particularly complex kind, which simultaneously separates domains lying on either side of it and conflates different levels of social, individual, and intra-psychic meaning. The skin (and hair) is the concrete boundary between the self and the other, the individual and society."[25]

The devout pilgrims of Loreto (both men and women) were blamed not only for having permanently deformed their limbs with tattoos, but for having made the act (and its aftereffect) public. This public exposure was then continually repeated, revealing their affinity with a social group. Tattooing was thus more a statement of private identity than it was a religious act, which was intolerable given the middle-class clichés about showing the body, social weakness, and the unsightliness of nudity.

Devotional tattoos, insofar as they expressed noble and commendable sentiments, a nonmetaphorical incarnation of a constant and unwavering faith, shattered several taboos with a single blow: "Believers" tattooed parts of their body that were exposed to the light of the sun, and did so in front of their peers.

As Italo Tanoni observed, pilgrims would indeed often "get tattoos on their forearms, close to the hand, and even on the hand itself; it was almost like they were trying to imitate the stigmata of St. Francis, who under the legends of the Friars Minor was given a prophecy in the form of an acrostic of the word PICENUM (P-ortatur J-uxta C-onerum E-dicula N-azarene V-irginis M-ariae), which supposedly announced, nearly a half century prior, the transfer of the Holy House."[26]

Without going into the merits of the debate on the misappropriation of stigmata (the Greek word *stigma* did actually refer to tattoos), and not just the stigmata of St. Francis, I'll stress the symbolic nature of the placement, as Giovanni Crocioni also recalls: "The peasants often had tattoos and did not hesitate to display the deep blue lines on their arms, right above the wrist, which were practically a point of pride and privilege.[27]

Similarly, if we look at the shapes and sizes of the wooden molds Father Grimaldi put in his book[28] (60–70 boxwood stamps exhibited at the Apostolic Palace of Loreto, attributed to a sixteenth-century artisan), although they vary from a minimum of 0.79 × 1.6 inches (2 × 4 centimeters) (artifact 887, *Cuore di Gesù trafitto da una spada* [Heart of Jesus Speared by a Sword])[29] to a maximum of 2 × 3 inches (5 × 8 centimeters) (artifact 848, *Crocifisso* [Crucifix]),[30] nearly all have a

---

25. T. Turner, "The Social Skin: Bodily Adornment, Social Meaning and Personal Identity," in T. Cherfas and R. Lewin, eds., *Not Work Alone: A Cross Cultural View of Activities Superfluous to Survival* (London, 1980), 112–140, in particular 139.

26. I. Tanoni, *Il tatuaggio sacro a Loreto*, 107.

27. G. Crocioni, *La gente marchigiana nelle sue tradizioni* (Milan, 1951), 124.

28. F. Grimaldi, *Loreto*, p. 126.

29. Ibid., 128.

30. Ibid., 126.

length that proves they were used to tattoo the crook of the arm or back of the forearm.[31]

This was an incredibly visible place to get a tattoo, given the rural habit of having one's arms uncovered, which confirms how a wide range of tattoos were used as a monstrance—a true insignia of Christ. We can understand the nineteenth- and early-twentieth-century criminal anthropologists' distress when confronted with such audacity. It was as if the skin were reduced to a letter patent of eternal devotion, a living and pulsating holy scripture traced onto the arms and hands of its bearer, which remained forever inscribed on their flesh as evidence of their own faith until their earthly death.

Therefore, under Lombroso and De Blasio's standard classification system (tattoos pertaining to love, a nickname, a vendetta, graduation, contempt, a profession, beauty, time period, ethnicity, obscenities, or hereditary, symbolic, psychological, or religious themes), the reasons for getting a tattoo were supposedly imitation, idleness, intention, religious fervor, noble passions, erotic passions, nudity[sic], atavism, and, last, religion.

Hence the difficulties encountered in justifying such a phenomenon: In the case of Loreto, in fact, the incredibly vast range of motives is surprising (more than 400 in all were identified) as is their paradoxical modernity (for example, the popularity of the images of Saint Philomena and of the Immaculate Conception). As Pigorini Beri indeed observed, "No other sacred place has as many tattoos as Loreto,"[32] although it's not easy to determine the precise moment when devotional tattoos (which had been done in Jerusalem as of the fifteenth century) also arrived in Loreto.

Scholars know that "it is an old custom for Christian pilgrims to Jerusalem to be tattooed there with some religious symbol, their name, or initials, and the date of their pilgrimage. The Armenian word for a pilgrim is *māhdĕsī* (*māh* death, *dĕsī* I saw")[33]—a term that was identical to the one that referred to a tattoo gotten in Jerusalem. This was a common tradition for other denominations and pilgrims as well. Muslims often got tattoos in Mecca with the date of the pilgrimage, their name or initials, and other sacred symbols: "An Arab pilgrim to Mecca is styled *Hā'jji* or *Hājj*, and so are his tattoo devices imprinted there."[34]

There is extensive evidence showing that these practices were fairly widespread among Christians. Pilgrims who reached the Holy Land in the fourteenth century unequivocally reported the St. Thomas Christians performing christenings with a flame. Niccolò da Poggibonsi believed the practice to be specific to "the Indians and Ethiopians . . . they are christened by making the sign of the cross with a hot iron,"[35] while Leonardo Frescobaldi, who left Florence on August 10,

---

31. See, in Grimaldi's book *Loreto*, the photographs reproducing artifacts no. 851, Madonna del Carmine e crocifisso (Madonna del Carmine with Crucifix, 1.3 × 3.4 in, [3.2 × 8.6 cm], p. 126; artifact no. 860, San Michele Arcangelo (Saint Michael the Archangel, 1.2 × 3.9 in. [3 × 9.8 cm], p. 127); artifact no. 862, Cuore di Gesú col monogramma di S. Bernardino (Heart of Jesus with Monogram of Saint Bernardino, 1.8 × 3.1 in. [4.5 × 8 cm], p. 127); and artifact no. 867, Madonna di Loreto (Madonna of Loreto, 1.6 × 3.1 in. [4 × 8 cm], p. 128).

32. C. Pigorini Beri, *Costumi e superstizioni*, 296.

33. A. T. Sinclair, *Tattooing: Oriental and Gypsy*, 362.

34. Ibid., 363. The practice was even widespread in Medina.

35. N. da Poggibonsi, *Libro d'Oltremare di Fra Niccolò da Poggibons* (Bologna, Italy, 1881), 210.

1384, maintained that "in Cairo there are many generations of Christians . . . who perform baptisms with fire, burning points on the head and temples, or just in the head and on one temple, or just on the head, depending on the generation."[36]

One century later, the Swiss Dominican friar Felix Fabri, who left Venice for the Levant in 1483, noted in the diary of his second pilgrimage that "one of them uncovered his right shoulder in my presence and showed us a round red scar thereon . . . and told us that the abbot of St. Catharine's monastery on Mount Sinai has a golden wheel, which he puts upon burning coals and, when it is hot, lifts it off with tongs and brands the pilgrim, who is bared to receive it, thus on his right shoulder."[37]

Loreto-Jerusalem: One-Way or Return Trip?

We have yet to establish how the phenomenon was passed down from the Jerusalem or Marche origins. To that end, it is useful to compare Pigorini and Stoppani's descriptions with those of the French traveler Jean de Thévenot, who visited the holy sites of Palestine in the spring of 1658. On Monday, April 29, he spent the entire day with his travel companions

"Getting Marks put upon our Arms, as commonly all Pilgrims do; the Christians of Bethlehem (who are of the Latin Church) do that."[38] The transalpine report is rich in details, and the similarities with the practices in Loreto are astonishing. Indeed, even in Jerusalem, tattooers displayed various wooden molds, from which pilgrims could select their desired image. The mold was filled with coal dust and then pressed to the skin, in order to create a perfect print. At that point, tattooers took the pilgrim's arm with their left hand and stretched out the skin, while their right hand gripped "a little Cane with two needles fastened in it, which from time to time they dip into Ink, mingled with Oxes Gall, and prick your Arm all along the lines that are marked by the Wooden Mould."[39] After having poked the needles along the lines left from the stamp, the tattooers would wash the patient's arm, check for any mistakes, and then start over, repeating the procedure, in some cases up to three times. Once they had finished, they'd wrap up the arm. After they were tattooed, pilgrims would usually get a low-grade fever, and their limbs would be swollen for two or three days. After that, the scab that had formed beneath the bandage would fall off, revealing the outline of the tattoos, which stayed "Blue, and never wear out, because the Blood mingling with that Tincture of Ink and Oxes Gall, retains the mark under the Skin."[40]

Thévenot's description is thus nearly identical to the ones given by Fynes Moryson during the 1580s,[41] Georges Sandys in 1615 ("the pil-

---

36. L. Frescobaldi, *Viaggio in Terrasanta*, Novara 1961, 24.

37. F. Fabri, *The Book of the Wandering of Felix Fabri* (London, 1896), chapter IV, part I, 102a.

38. J. de Thévenot, *The Travels of Monsieur de Thevenot into the Levant. In Three Parts viz. into I. Turkey. II. Persia. III The East Indies/Newly Done out of French* (London: Lovell, 1687), 201–202.

39. Ibid., 202.

40. Ibid.

41. F. Moryson, *An Itinerary Written by Fynes Moryson Gent. First in the Latine Tongue, and Then Translated by Him into English: Containing His Ten Yeeres Travell Through the Twelve Dominions of Germany, Bohmerland, Sweitzerland, Netherland, Denmarke, Poland, Italy, Turky, France, England, Scotland, and Ireland. Divided in III Parts* (London: John Beale, 1617).

grims are usually marked with the names of Jesus, Mary, Jerusalem, Bethlehem, or the Jerusalem cross"[42]), the Scottish William Lithgow in 1640,[43] the Prussian Otto Friedrich von der Gröben in 1675, or the Lutheran pastor Johann Lund in 1711.[44]

We pose that fraught question yet again: Was it the pilgrims and crusaders coming back from the Levant who imported this practice to Italian soil, waving their deep-blue arms like devotional trophies? Or was tattooing invented on the shores of the Adriatic and exported abroad by some sexton from Loreto? Or did the two practices have independent origins and their own histories, as might be deduced from the passage in which Lombroso notes that "a Venetian had the symbol of the Madonna of Vicenza, and two Lombards that of Caravaggio, often having the date of pilgrimage tattooed onto them."[45]

All these hypotheses are still viable, although to date the prevailing theory is that tattoos were imported from the Levant as of the 1580s, simultaneously with the development of the form of worship promoted by Pope Sixtus V, who was originally from the Marche, a member of the Order of St. Francis, and the son of Marianna da Camerino. It was here that the first Capuchin convent was established, thanks to the work of Caterina Cybo. The Capuchins had the highest honor of sweeping the floor of the Loreto shrine. Pope Sixtus V expanded the Porziuncola church in Assisi and made it much more ornate. He also encircled the city of Loreto with walls, reinvigorated the roles of Loreto knights, and expanded the Illyrian College, demonstrating all of his devotion for the holy house and for Loreto.[46]

Nevertheless, Pigorini herself noted that tattooing was present even before Sixtus V, potentially through the intermediary of the Franciscans. Indeed, it was supposedly the friars who, protecting the holy places of Jerusalem, introduced the pleasures and pains of the Levantine needles to the naive central Italians. This may also demonstrate why, in addition to the widespread presence of Marian symbols, the tattoo stamps included a plethora of Franciscan motifs. These included "St. Francis, who lived nearly a century prior to the transfer, symbols of the Passion of Christ, and the crucifix of Sirolo, which has an even more miraculous history (if that's possible) than the Holy House, and whose tradition dates back a century and a half earlier to the convent of Sirolo St. Francis founded."[47]

---

42. G. Sandys, *A Relation of a Journey Begun An. Dom. 1610* (London: W. Barrett, 1615), 200.

43. W. Lithgow, *The Totall Discourse of the Rare Adventures and Painefull Peregrinations of Long Nineteene Yeares Travayles, from Scotland to the Most Famous Kingdomes in Europe, Asia, and Affrica: Perfited by Three Deare Bought Voyages, in Surveighing of Forty Eight Kingdomes Ancient and Moderne* (Nicholas Okes, 1640), 285.

44. J. Lund, *Die alten jüdischen Heiligthümer, Gottesdienste und Gewohnheiten, Amburgo* (Heinrich Muhlius, 1711), 732.

45. C. Lombroso, *L'uomo delinquente*, 314.

46. For these reasons, according to Pigorini, "Sixtus V, by instituting all the privileges for the city of Loreto, with the obligation to battle the Turks, established that the emblem of the city of Loreto was the Virgin seated atop the Holy House, placed above three mountains, between two pear tree branches with the motto Felix Lauretana Civitas, thus symbolizing part of his coat of arms as well as his name Felix Peretti cardinal of Montalto. Indeed, the engravings precisely show a Madonna encircled by angels and supported by an entire pear tree with two gigantic pears at the top." C. Pigorini Beri, *Costumi e superstizioni*, 298.

47. Ibid., 296.

In contrast to this hypothesis are others that imagine the long arm of the Society of Jesus, considering the attention the Jesuits gave to disseminating printed material, medals, and scapulars, and the strong push exerted on devotions that were still developing, such as the devotion to the Heart of Jesus and the devotion to the Heart of Mary. In this latter case, the insertion of Franciscan themes would be explained by the desire to feed into the mythology of the flying house, through a mass cutaneous mythography, which would have supposedly affirmed its temporal primacy. However, the underlying problem is the absence of official sources to formally prove it: As Italo Tanoni observed, "The main orders that cared for the Loreto sanctuary were the Franciscans and the Society of Jesus, but it's hard to believe they could have started this practice: The archives of the Holy House do not contain any written document to this effect."[48]

It remains a mystery, although I hope that research will resume with renewed vigor, perhaps finding an answer to the Loreto mystery.

---

48. I. Tanoni. *Il tatuaggio*, 110. Furthermore, Tanoni himself comments on p. 114: "To that end, we must note that the religious historical sources from the Loreto sanctuary are completely silent on this."

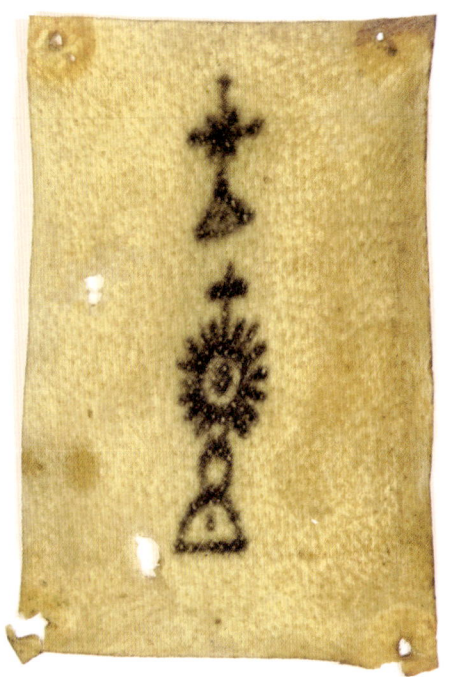

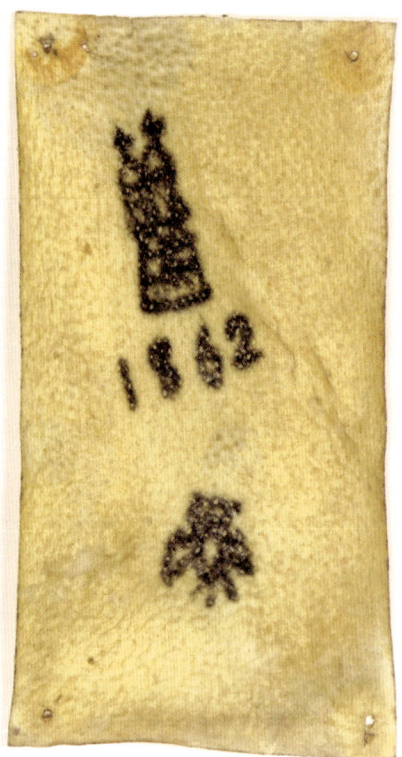

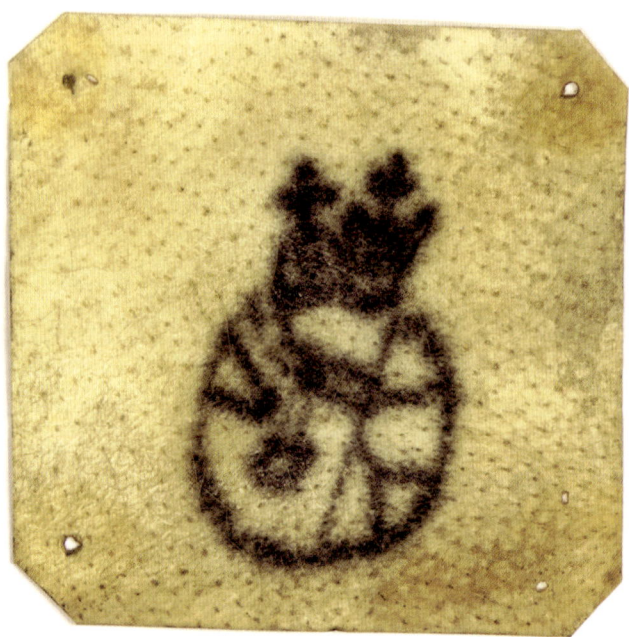

Strips of tattooed skin with religious themes connected to the cult of Madonna of Loreto, late nineteenth century (?). "Luigi Cattaneo" Collection of Wax Anatomical Models–Sistema Museale di Ateneo (University Museum System), University of Bologna.

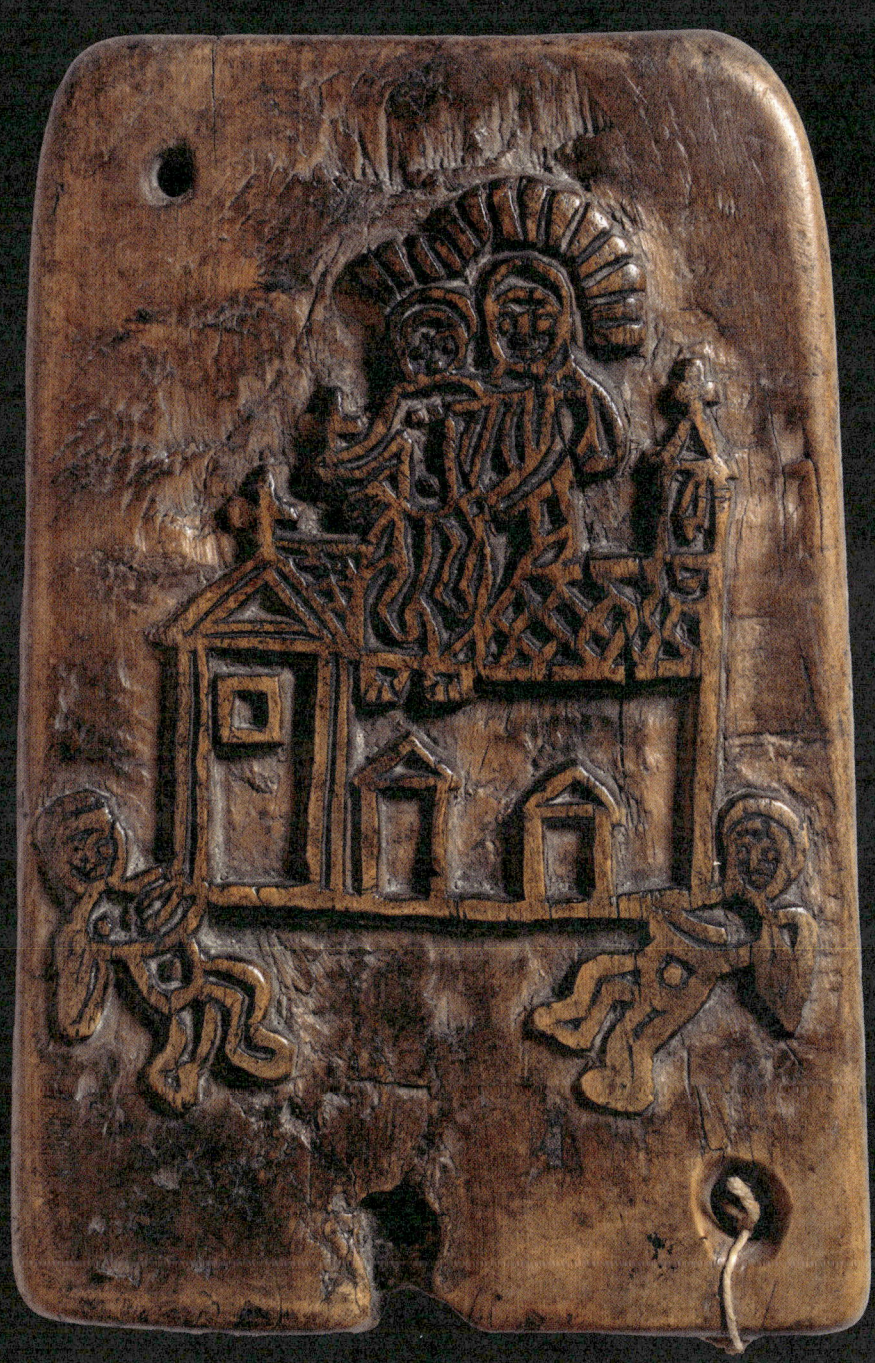

This and following page: Boxwood stamps for transferring the tattoo's design onto the skin, before piercing with needles, nineteenth century. Rome, *Museo delle Civiltà* (Museum of Civilization), Popular Traditions and Arts Collection.

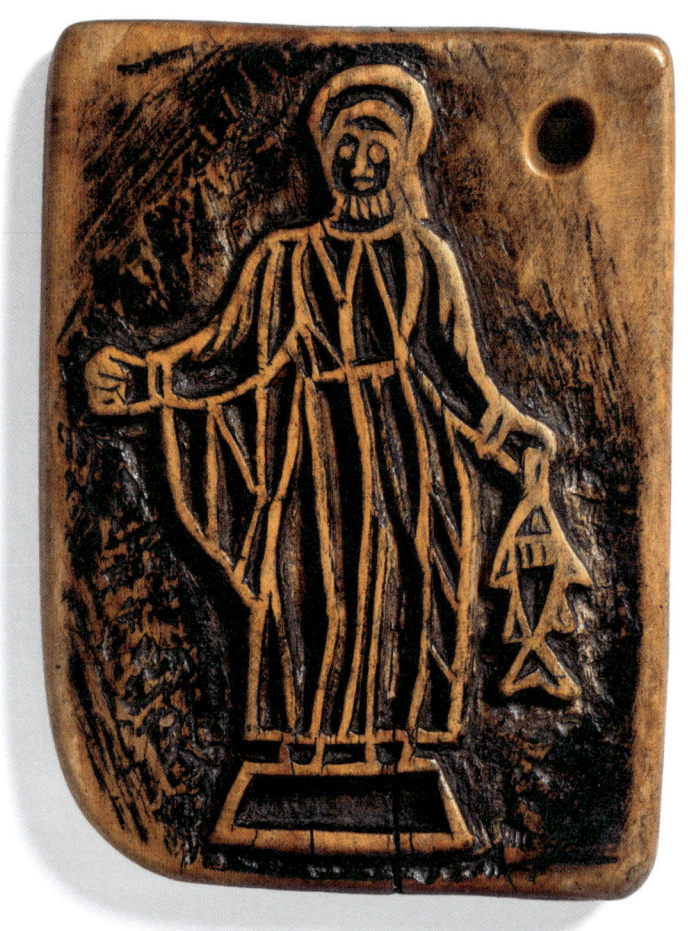

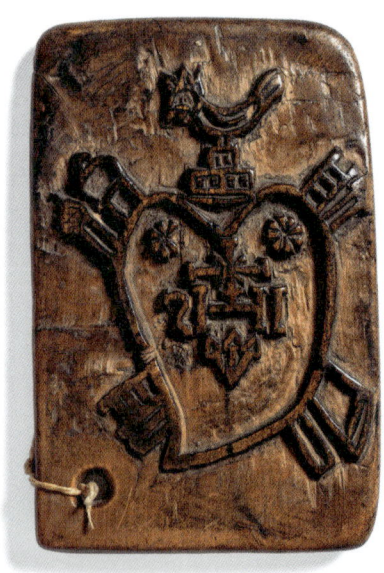

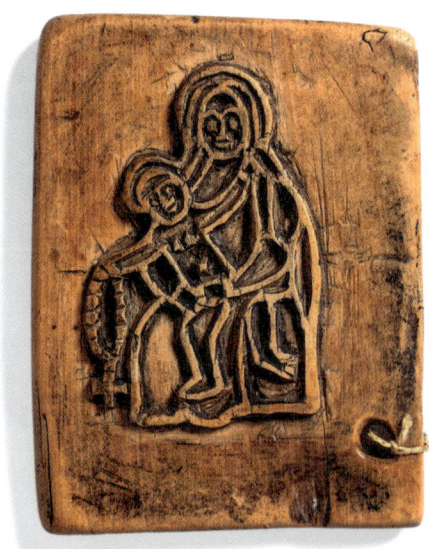

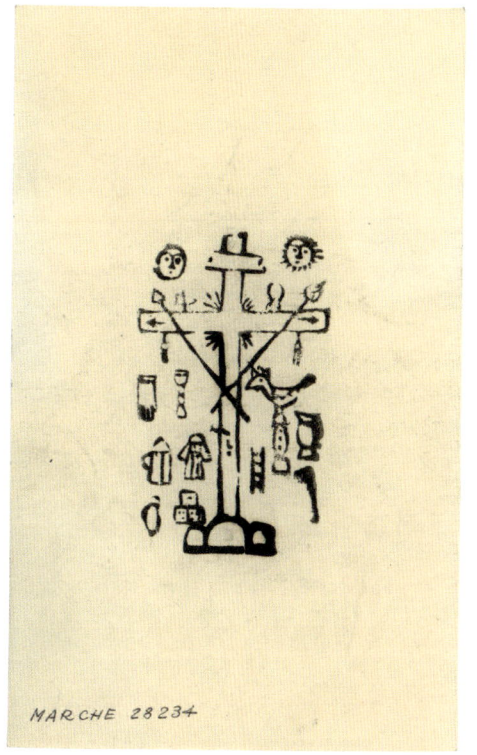

MARCHE 28234

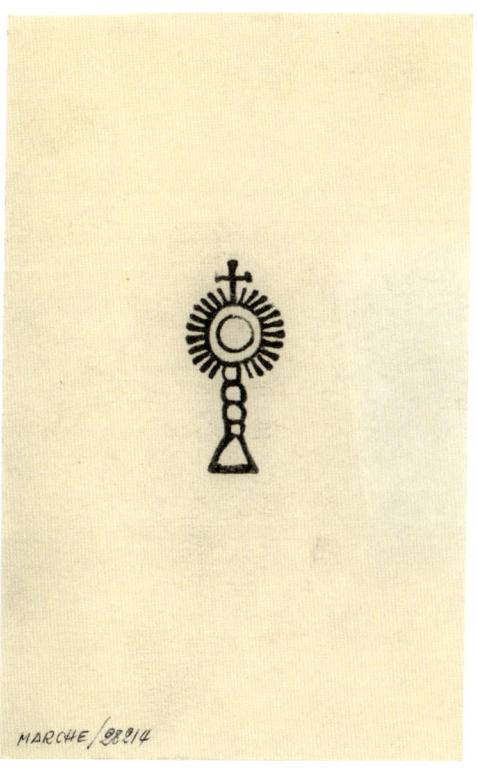

MARCHE/28214

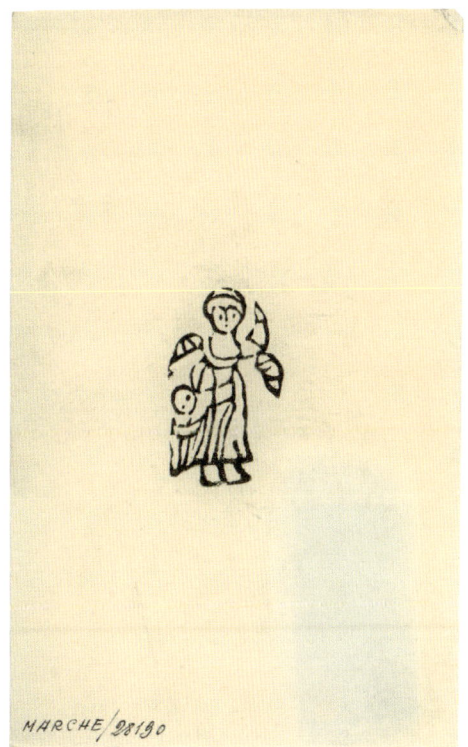

MARCHE/28130

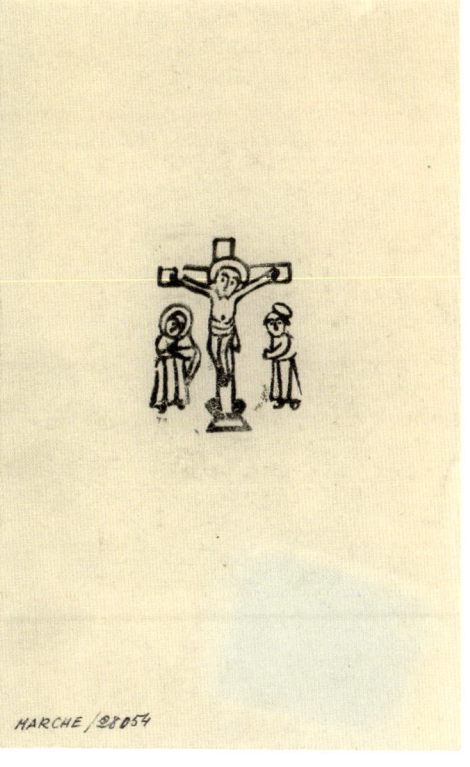

MARCHE/28054

This and following pages: Sheets stamped with the tattoos of Loreto, twentieth century. Rome, Museo delle Civiltà, Popular Traditions and Arts Collection.

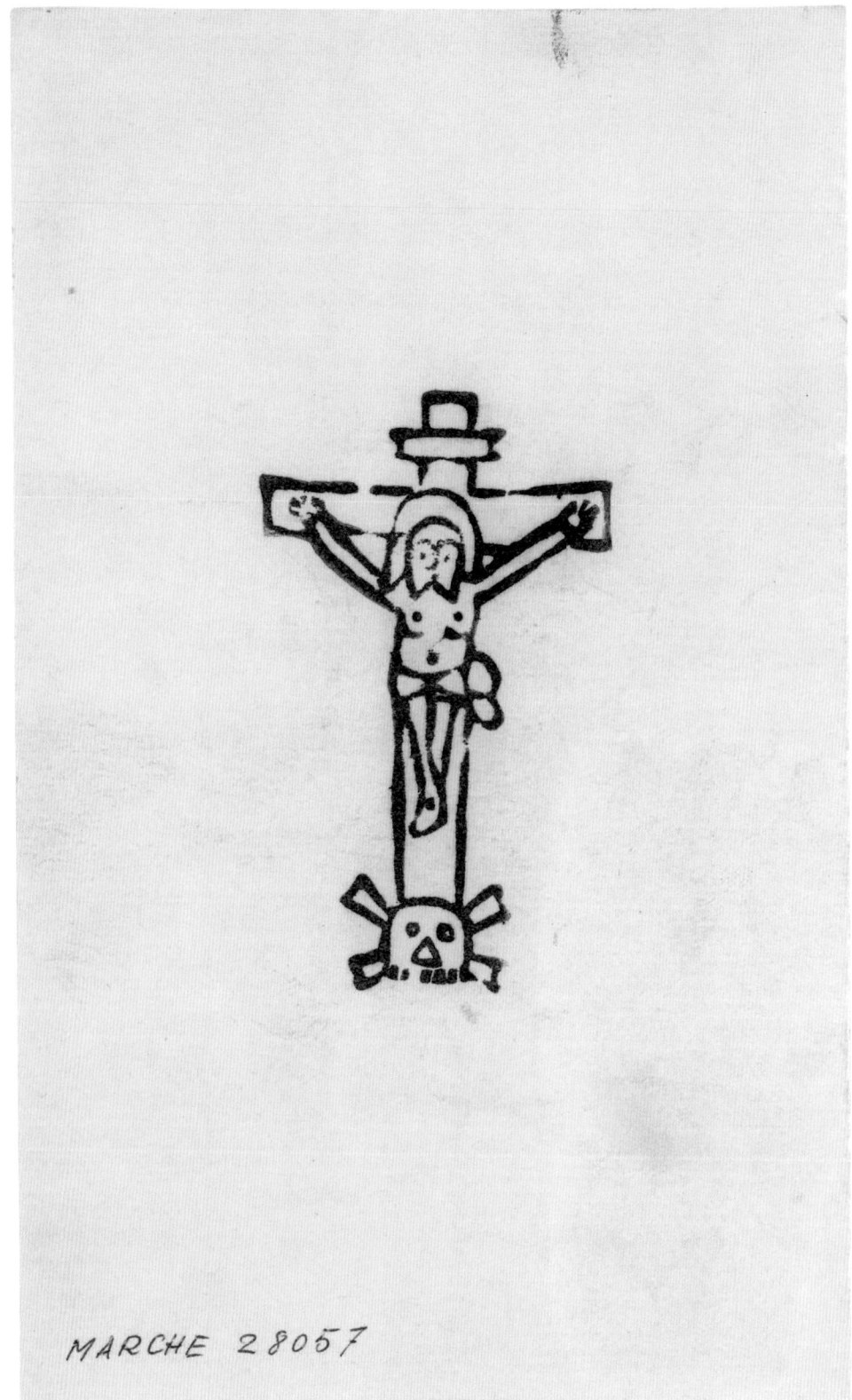

MARCHE 28057

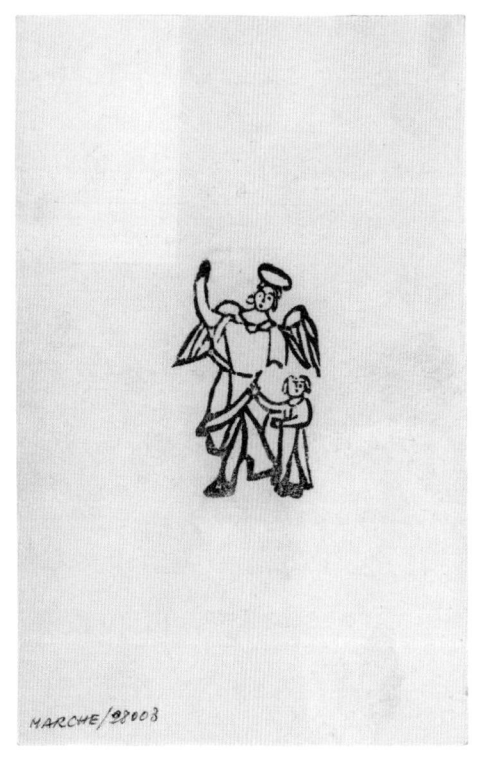

MARCHE/28008

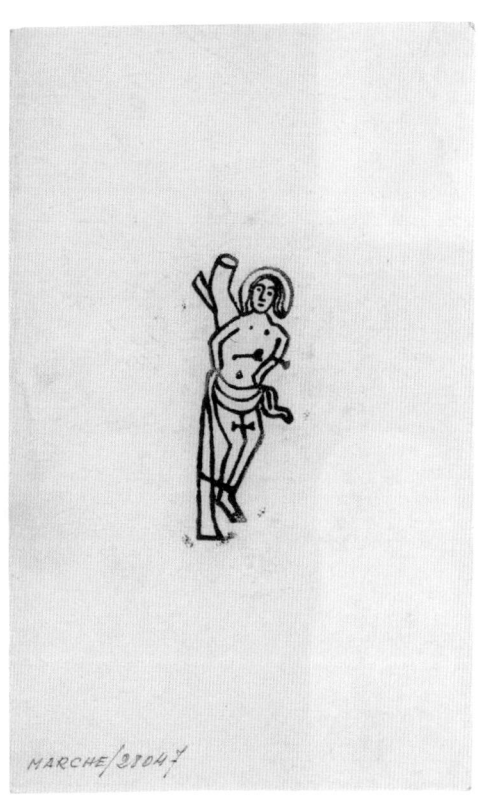

MARCHE/28047

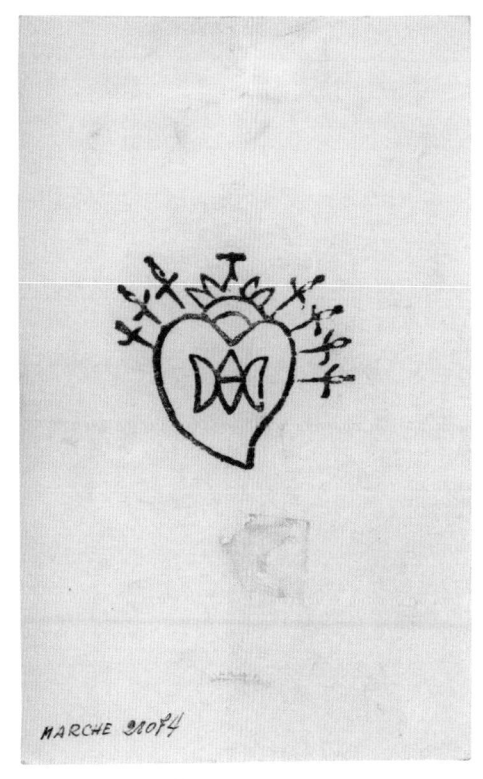

MARCHE 28074

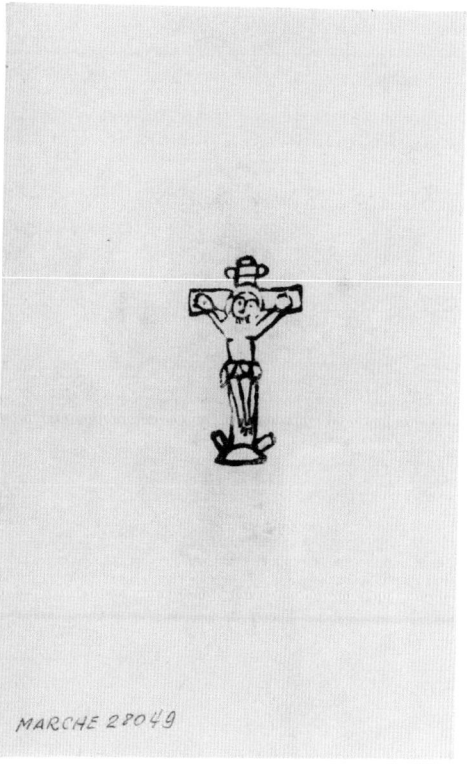

MARCHE 28049

— Guido Guerzoni

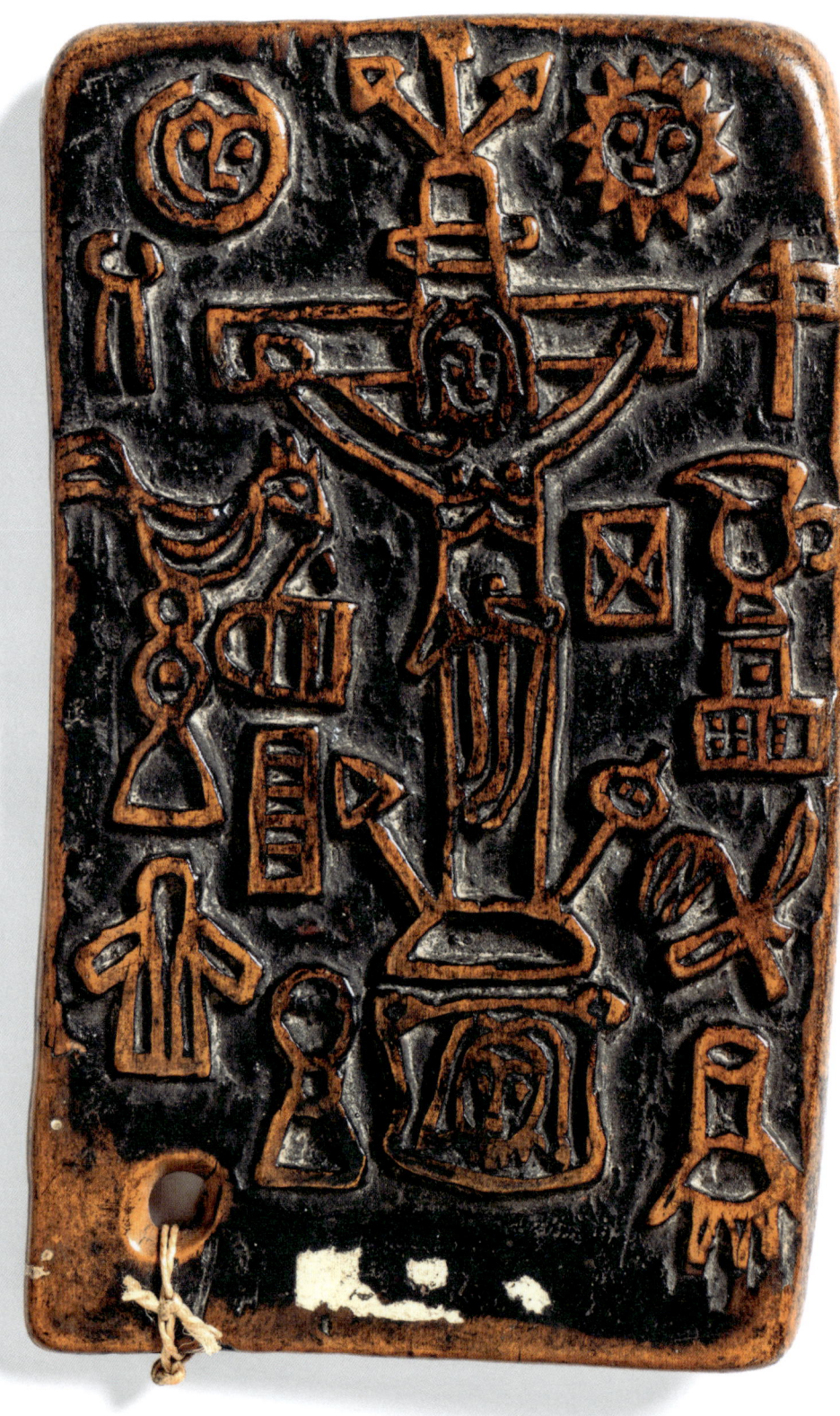

Boxwood stamp for transferring the tattoo's design onto the skin before piercing with needles, nineteenth century. Rome, Museo delle Civiltà, Popular Traditions and Arts Collection.

Print from Loreto tattoo stamps, twentieth century. Rome, Museo delle Civiltà, Popular Traditions and Arts Collection.

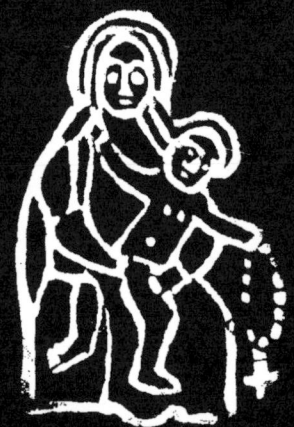

IDDIO
MIHADA
GIUDICARE

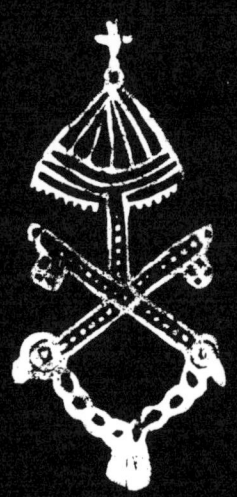

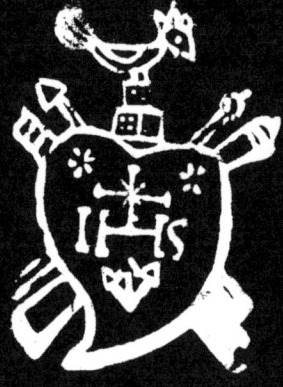

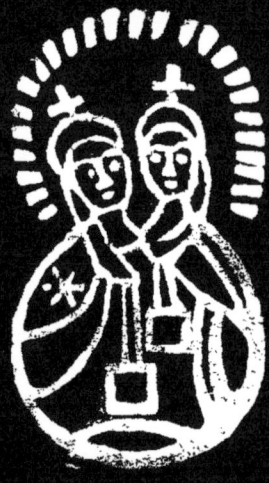

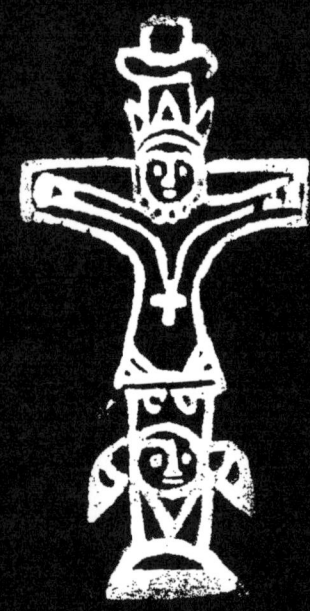

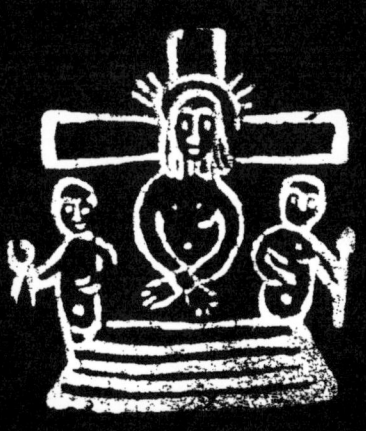

Prints from Loreto tattoo stamps, twentieth century. Rome, Museo delle Civiltà, Popular Traditions and Arts Collection.

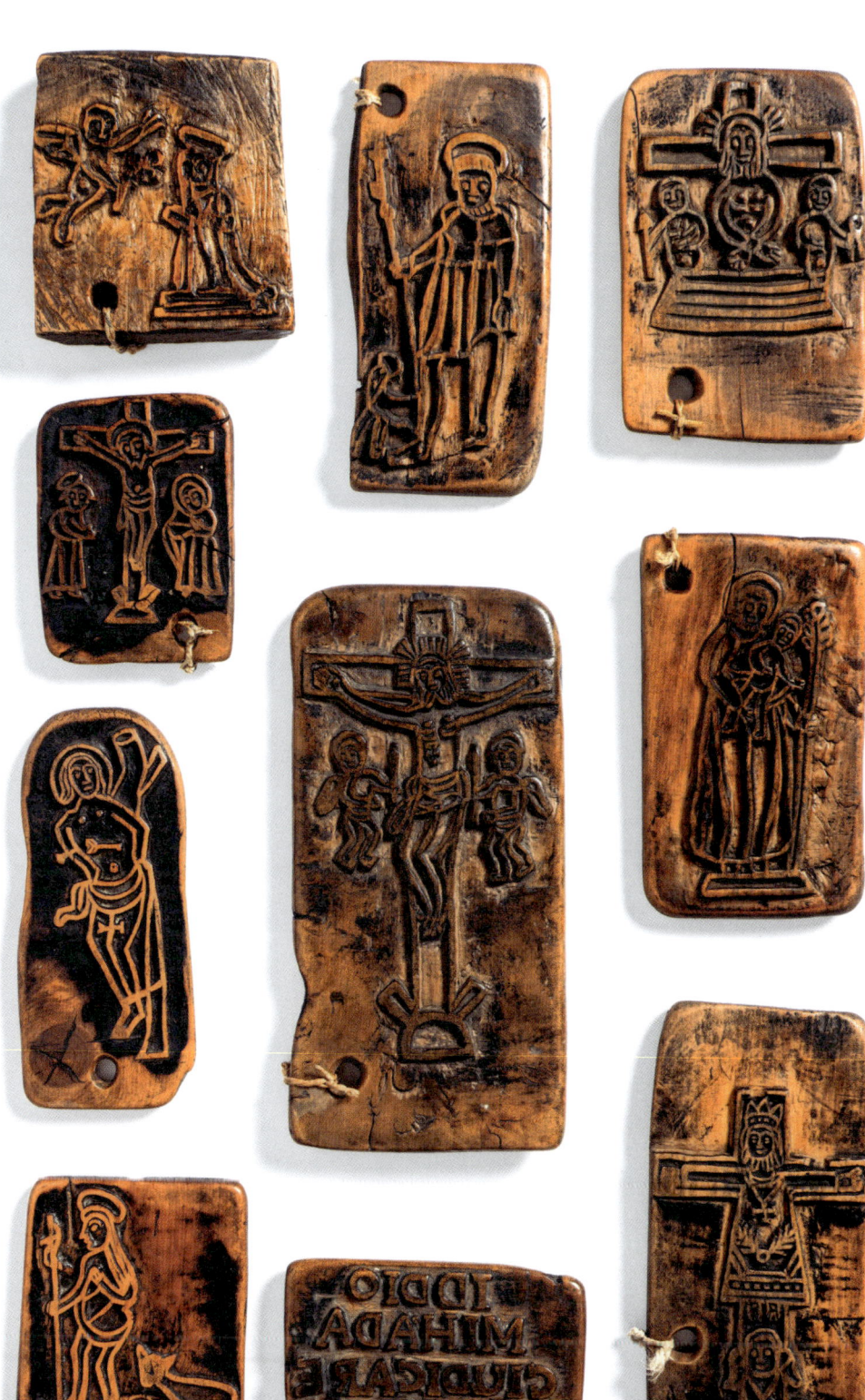

Boxwood stamps for transferring the tattoo design onto the skin, prior to piercing with needles, nineteenth century. Rome, Museo delle Civiltà, Popular Traditions and Arts Collection.

— Guido Guerzoni

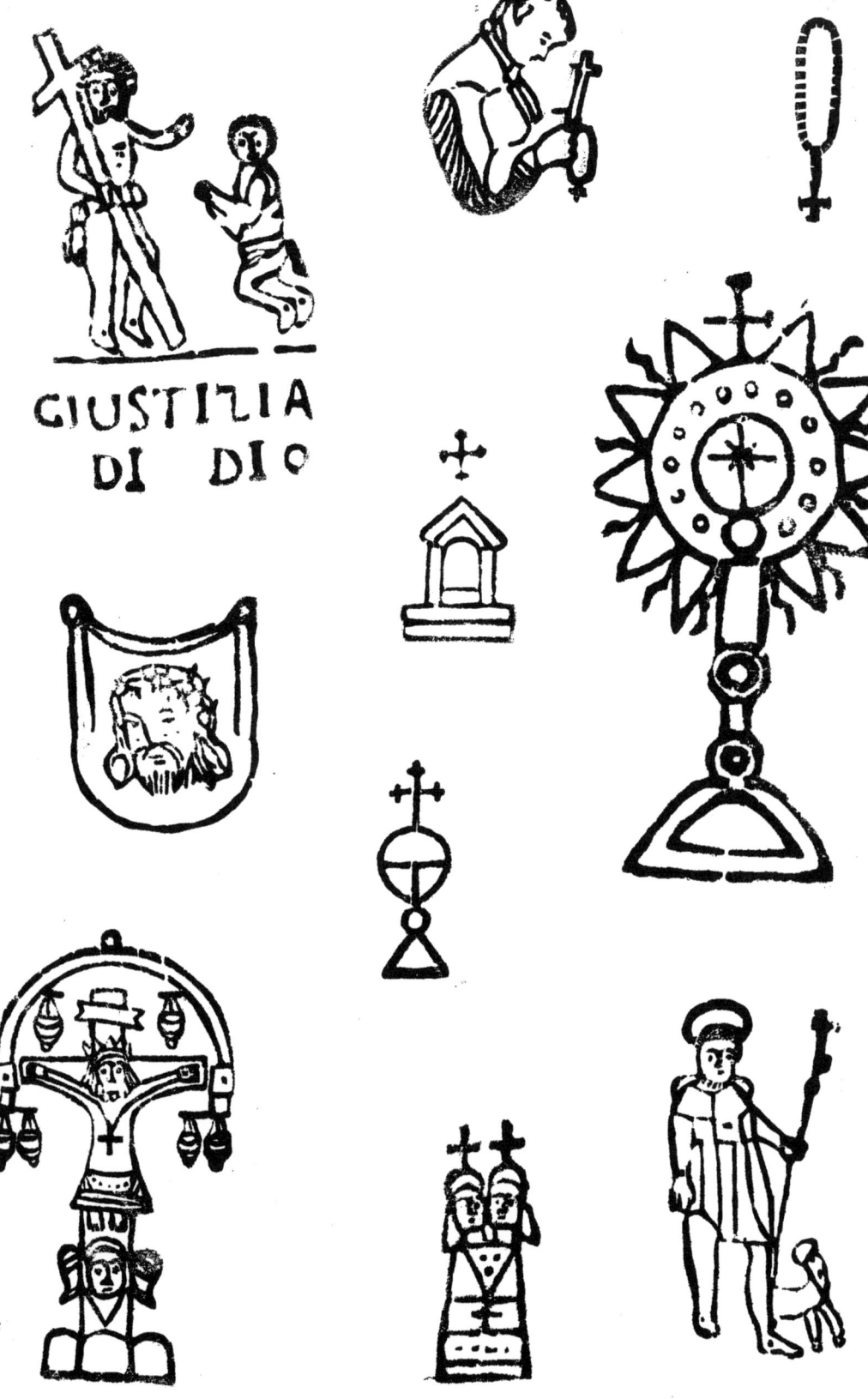

GIUSTIZIA
DI DIO

Prints from Loreto tattoo stamps, twentieth century. Rome, Museo delle Civiltà,
Popular Traditions and Arts Collection.

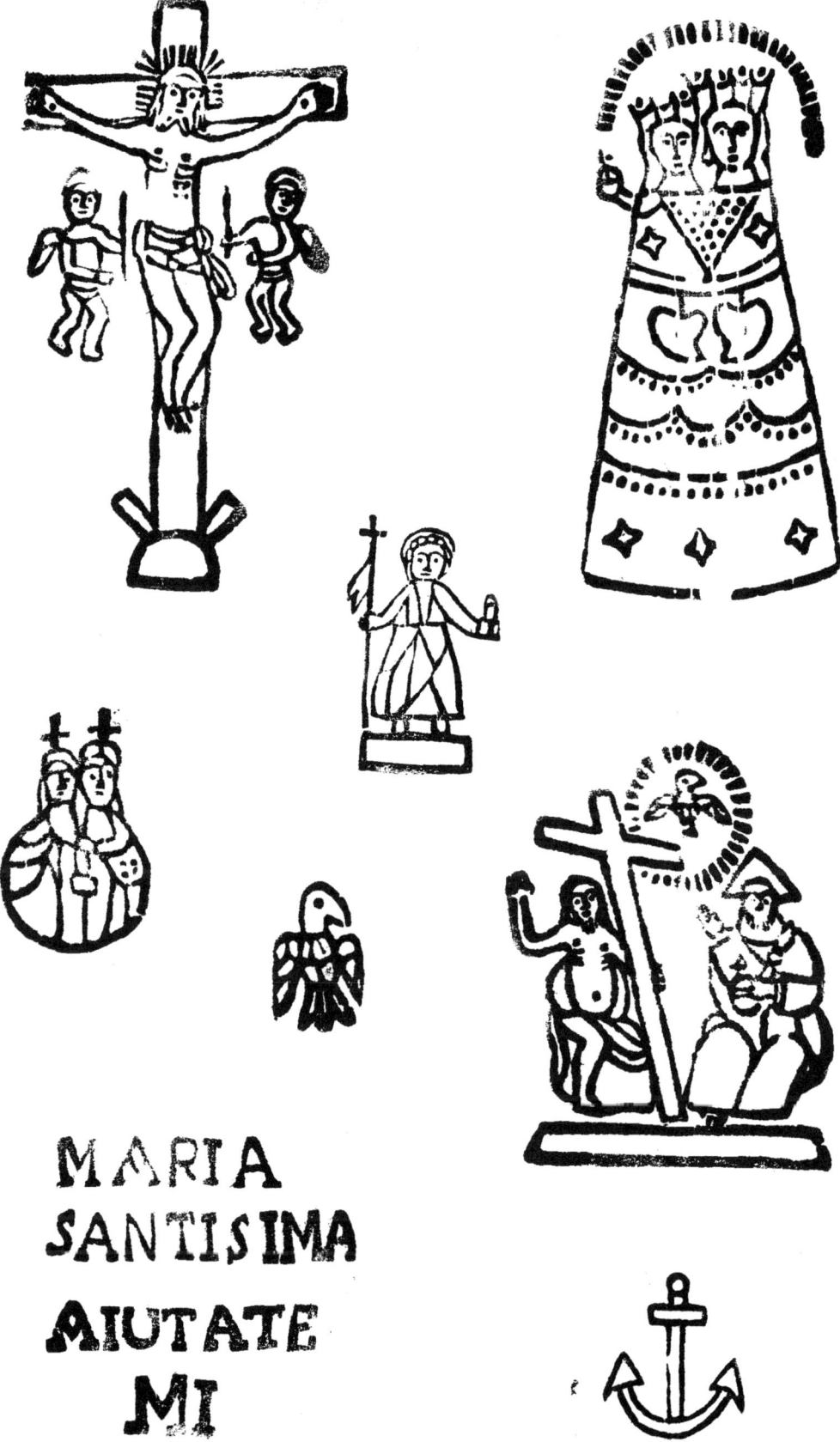

MARIA
SANTISIMA
AIUTATE
MI

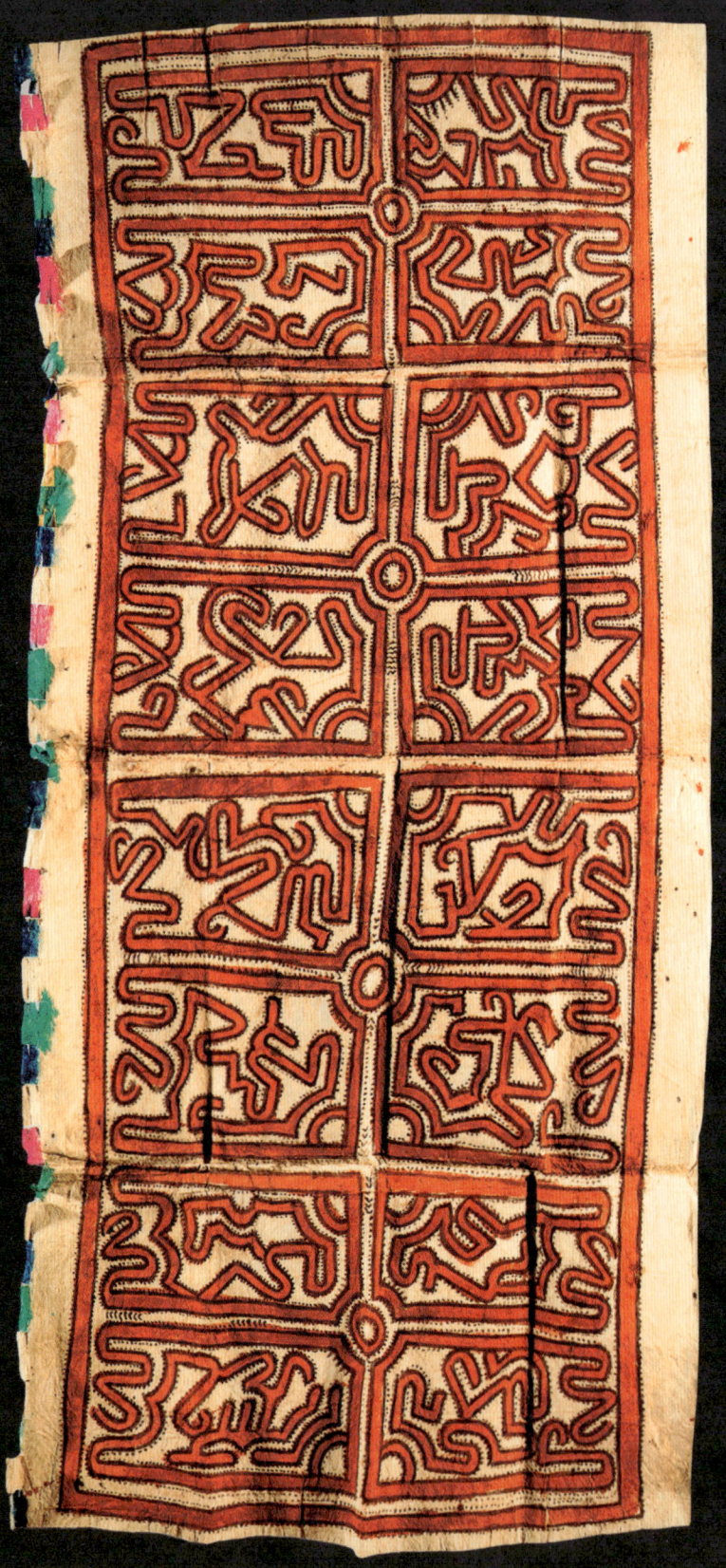

Tapa Korafe, Papua New Guinea, twentieth century. Milan, Tattoo Museo Gianmaurizio Fercioni

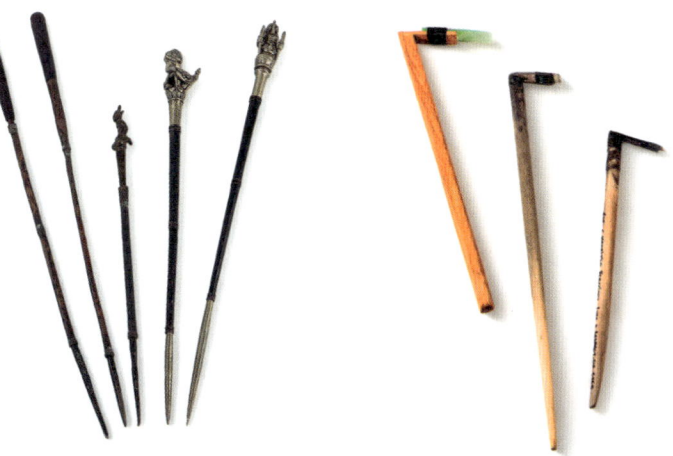

Left: Needles for tattooing, Burma, late nineteenth–early twentieth century. Milan, Tattoo Museo Gianmaurizio Fercioni.

Right: Rods with comb-shaped needles, Polynesia, late nineteenth–early twentieth century. Milan, Tattoo Museo Gianmaurizio Fercioni.

In the collective consciousness of the nineteenth century, which was Caucasian, colonial, and positivist, the multicolored marks that adorned the bodies and faces of the "rarely good" savages, more than possessing any intrinsic meaning, marked a general otherness from the Eurocentric value system, an inferiority that was even more moral than it was aesthetic.

Tattoos, which according to general historiographic consensus were supposedly introduced to Europeans by Cook in 1769, and Bougainville in 1771, thus marked the clear yet perilously crossable line between bourgeois righteousness and criminal deviance (eccentric aristocrats and restless travelers notwithstanding).

After all, the Italian word *tatuaggio* was derived from the Anglo-Saxon word "tattoo," which was in turn derived from the Tahitian word *tatau,* which according to the Royal Museums Greenwich appeared for the first time in English as "*tattaw*" in an account of the first voyage of Captain James Cook, which was published in 1769. Yet, the word had already become popularized by the Polynesian Omai, a talented young man discovered by the famous British explorer. While Cook was about to finish his second voyage on the HMS *Resolution*, in July 1774, the sister ship, the HMS *Adventure* (commanded by the faithful Tobias Furneaux), arrived in England. On board was a young Polynesian named Mai, also known as Omai, whose body was completely covered with tattoos. He was introduced to the king and to high British society as a member of a royal family, even though he actually came from a family of average lineage from the island of Raiatea. This was in contrast to his compatriot, Tupaia, the noble prince who had sailed with Cook during his first voyage in the Pacific and had left Tahiti in 1969, dying one and a half years later from malaria in Jakarta.

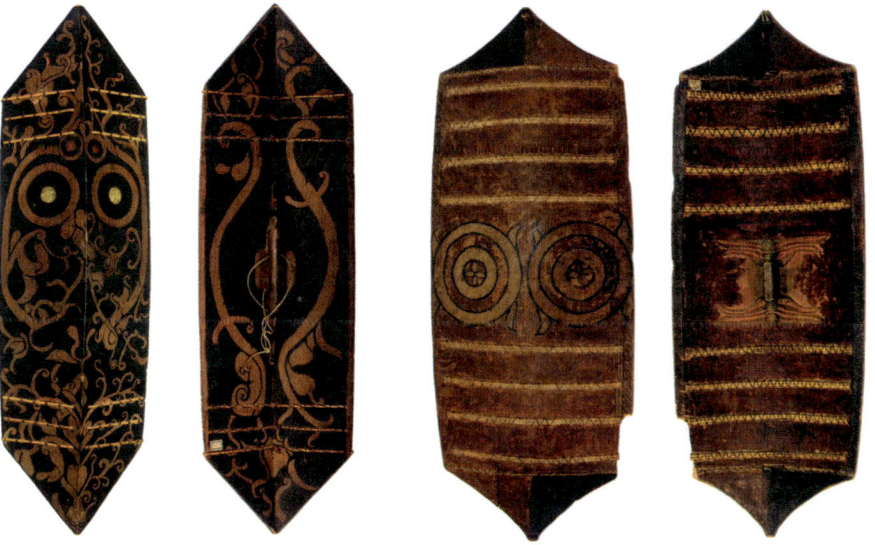

Shields (*kliau*) (front and back of each) from the Dayak people, Borneo, late nineteenth–early twentieth century. Capra Collection.

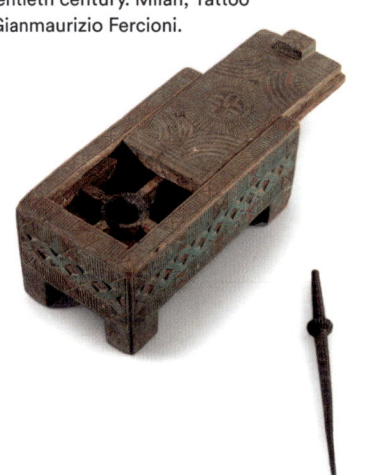

Bronze box for tattooing needle and equipment, India, late nineteenth–early twentieth century. Milan, Tattoo Museo Gianmaurizio Fercioni.

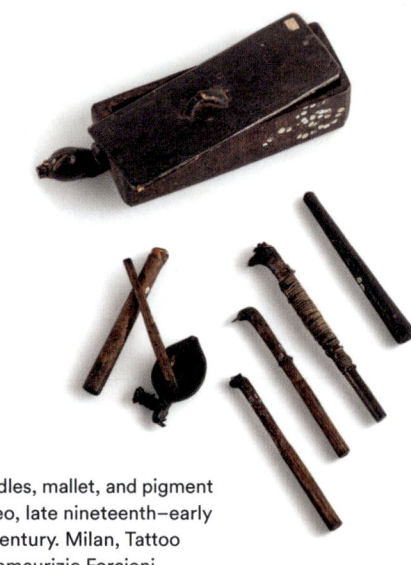

Box for needles, mallet, and pigment bowl, Borneo, late nineteenth–early twentieth century. Milan, Tattoo Museo Gianmaurizio Fercioni.

While he was not the first Polynesian to set foot in Europe (in 1769, Bougainville had introduced the Tahitian prince Ahutoru to King Louis XV and to French high society), Omai (also thanks to his tattoos) roused major curiosity and quickly became a celebrity. He was even immortalized in a well-known painting by Joshua Reynolds, the most famous British portrait painter of the eighteenth century. After two successful years in elite society, Omai returned to his country on the HMS *Resolution*, the ship that Cook took for his last expedition, which ended in 1779, when the British explorer died in a clash with the local people in the Hawaiian Islands.

Nevertheless, a few decades later, in the second half of the nineteenth century, the Austral Islands, which Omai had arrived from, were no longer the lost paradises of the South Seas that had inspired Jean-Jacques Rousseau and Benardin de Saint-Pierre's noble savages and the innocent primitivism of Eden of the late eighteenth century. According to the stereotypical pseudoscientific and imperial vision of the nineteenth century (the Iron Century), the islands of Oceania and the Pacific hid away incredibly ferocious cannibals. Criminal anthropologists asserted that tattoos marked the atavistic aggressiveness of cavemen, and it would take centuries to discredit this belief.

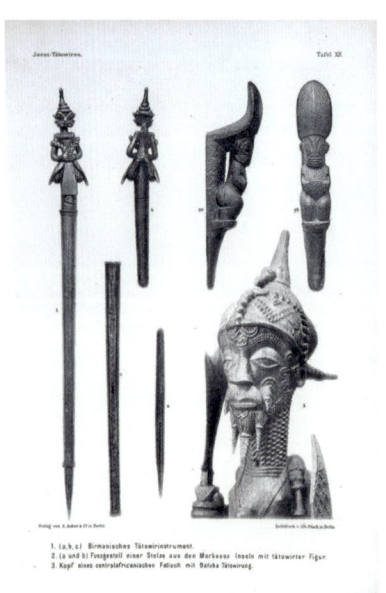

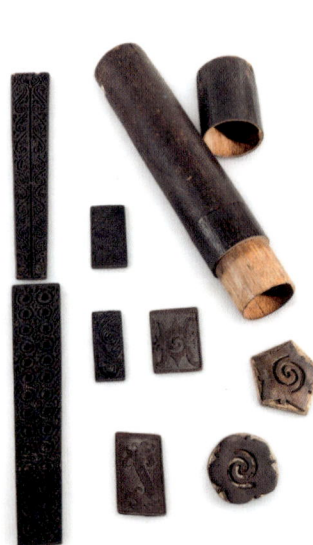

Box with eight wooden stamps to transfer a tattoo's design onto a person's skin before engraving with needles, Borneo, late nineteenth–early twentieth century. Milan, Tattoo Museo Gianmaurizio Fercioni.

Burmese tattooing instruments: Tattooed idols of the Marquesas Islands; central African Baluba sculpture with tattoos, in Wilhelm Joest, *Narbenzeichnen und Korperbemalen: Ein beittrag zur vergleichenden ethnologie* (Berlin: Asher, 1887), plate XII. Milan, Tattoo Museo Gianmaurizio Fercioni.

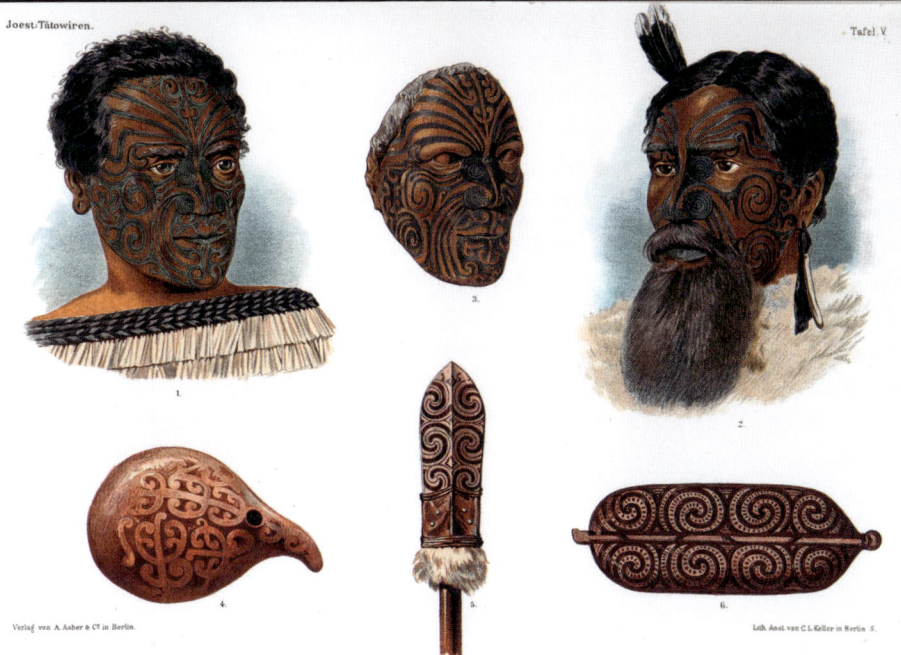

Portraits, Gypsmaske und ornamentirte Geräthe von Eingeborenen von Neuseeland.

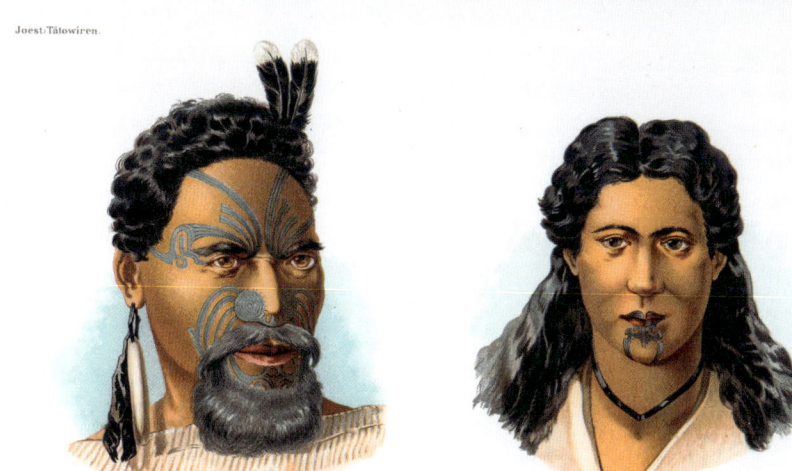

Mann und Frau von Neuseeland.

Top: Portraits, masks, and ornamental objects of the native people of New Zealand, *in Wilhelm Joest, Tatowiren; Narbenzeichnen und Korperbemalen; Ein beittrag zur vergleichenden ethnologie* (Berlin: Asher, 1887), plate V. Milan, Tattoo Museo Gianmaurizio Fercioni.

Bottom: Man and woman from New Zealand, *in Wilhelm Joest, Tatowiren: Narbenzeichnen und Korperbemalen; Ein beittrag zur vergleichenden ethnologie* Berlin: Asher, 1887), plate IV. Milan, Tattoo Museo Gianmaurizio Fercion

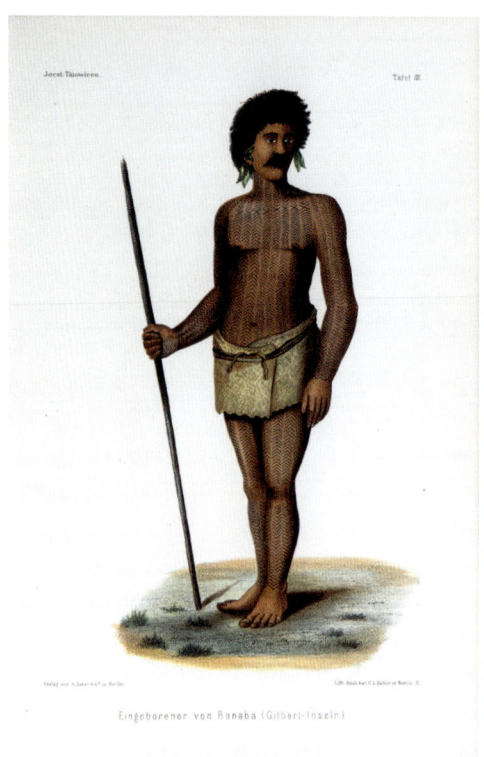
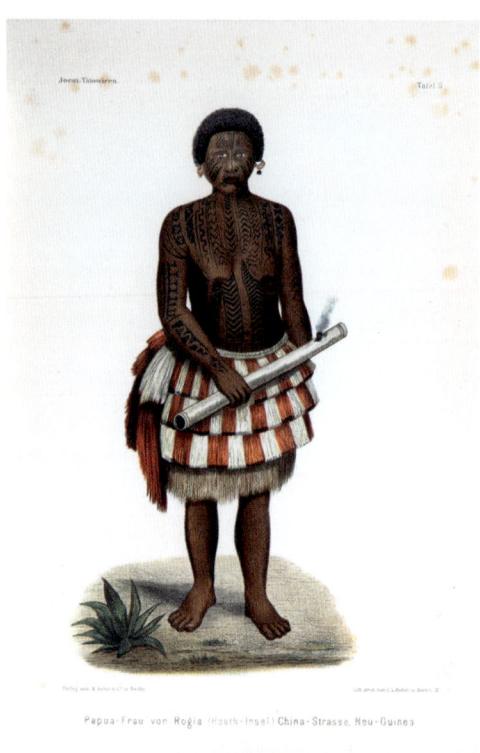

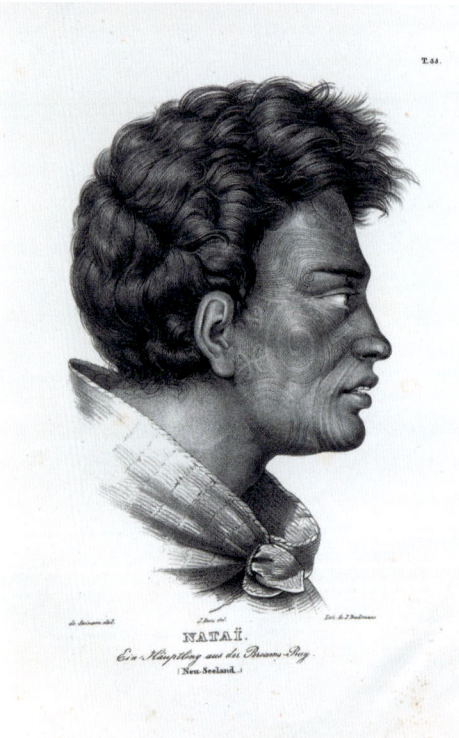
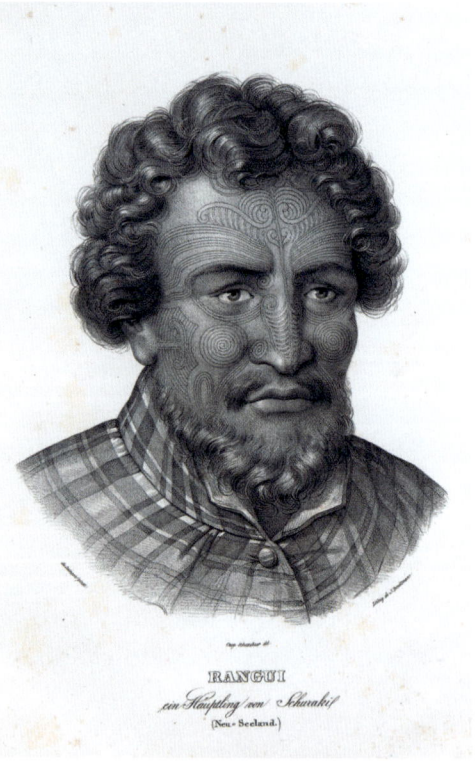

Top: Banaba man *(left)*, Papua woman *(right)*, in Wilhelm Joest, *Tatowiren: Narbenzeichnen und Korperbemalen; Ein beittrag zur vergleichenden ethnologie* (Berlin: Asher, 1887), plates III–II. Milan, Tattoo Museo Gianmaurizio Fercioni.

Bottom: Maori facial tattoos (New Zealand), in Jules Sébastien César Dumont d'Urville, *Entdeckungs-Reise der französischen Corvette Astrolabe unternommen in den Jahren 1826–29* (J. Brodtmann Schaffhausen, 1836), Plates 33–31, Milan, Tattoo Museo Gianmaurizio Fercioni.

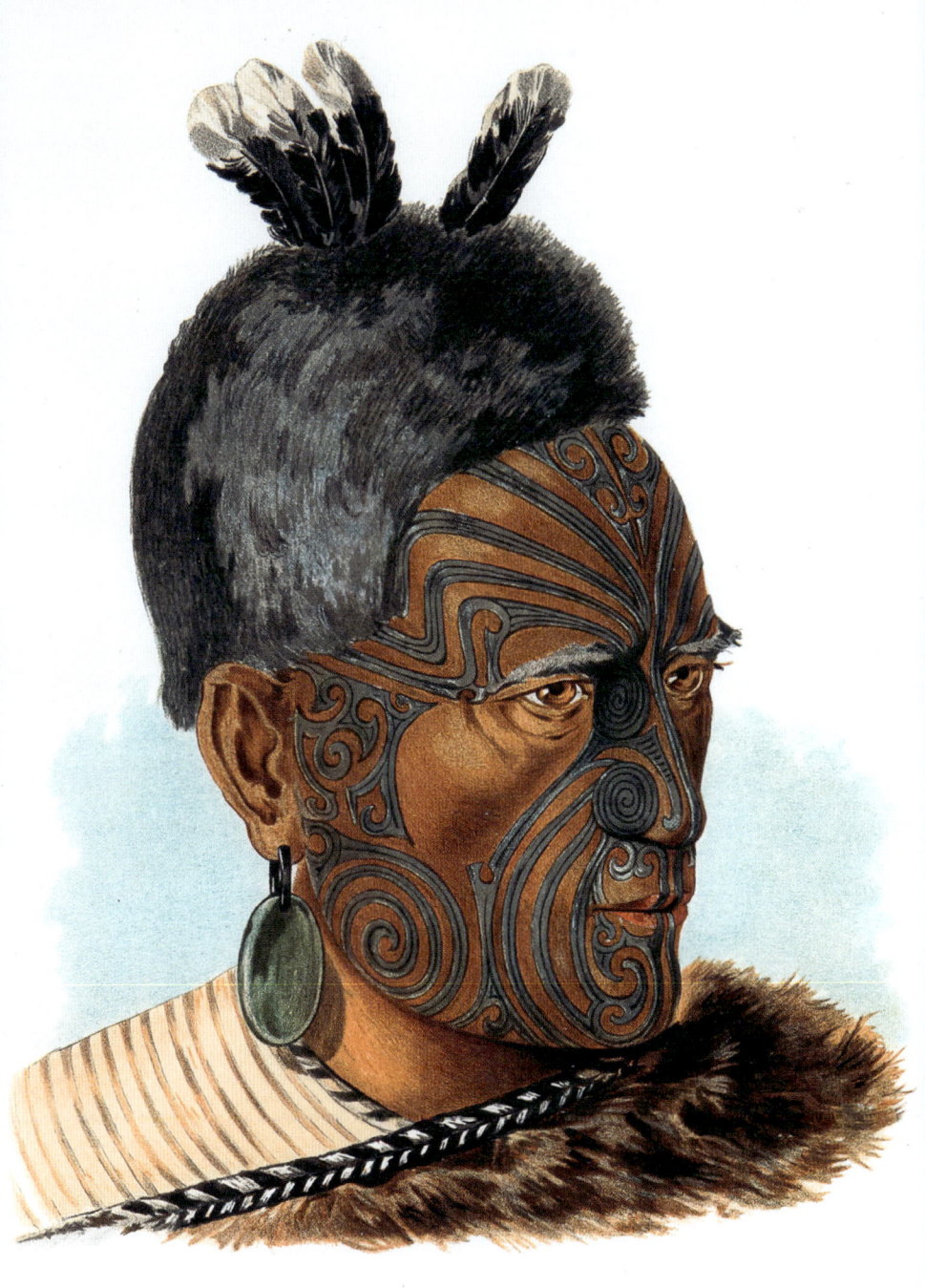

Unidentified author from the German school, *Moko, facial tattoo of a Maori chief* (New Zealand), 1894, color lithograph. Private collection.

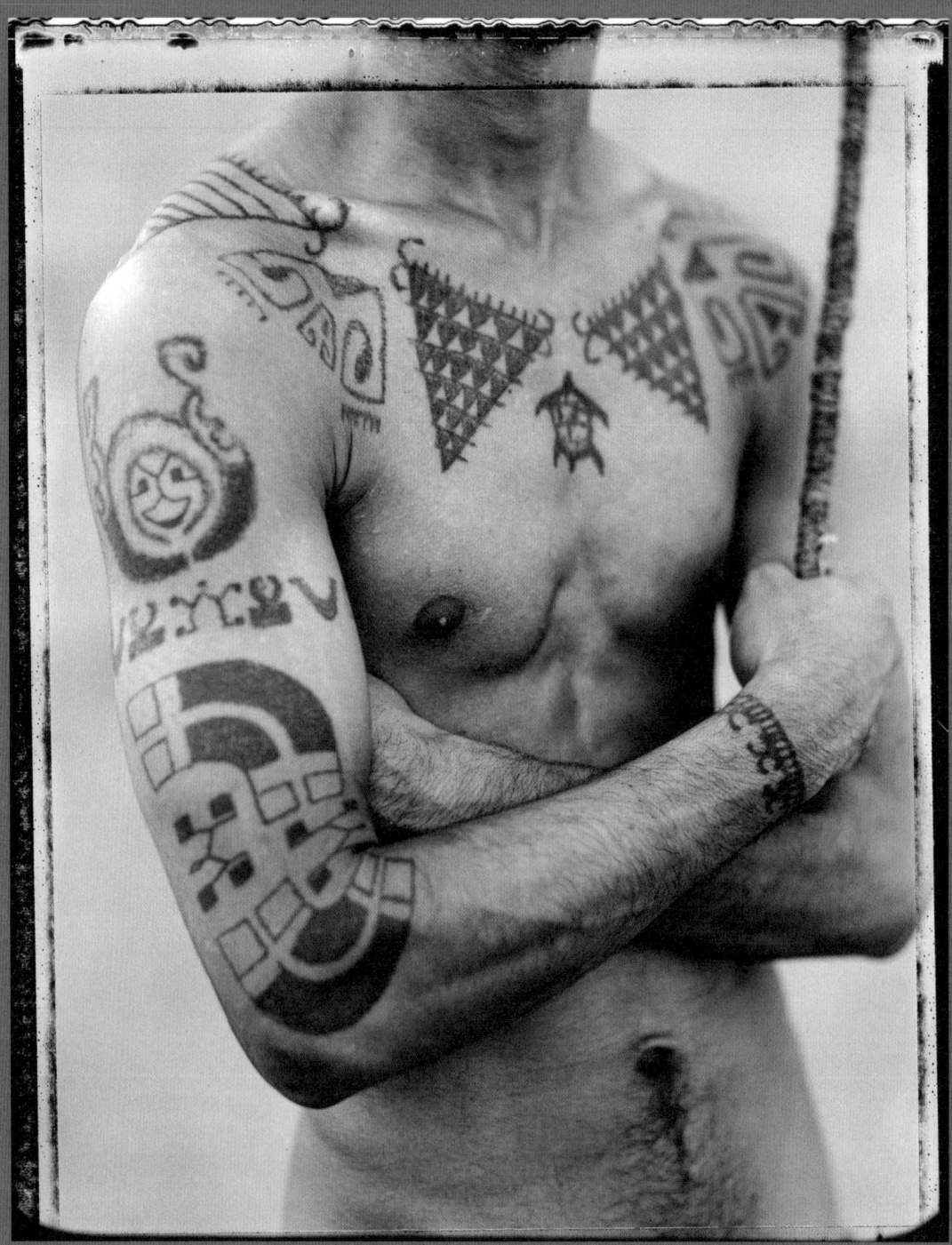

Gian Paolo Barbieri, *Tahiti*, 1989, analog photograph, salt print on emulsion-coated canvas. © Gian Paolo Barbieri, courtesy of the Fondazione Gian Paolo Barbieri.

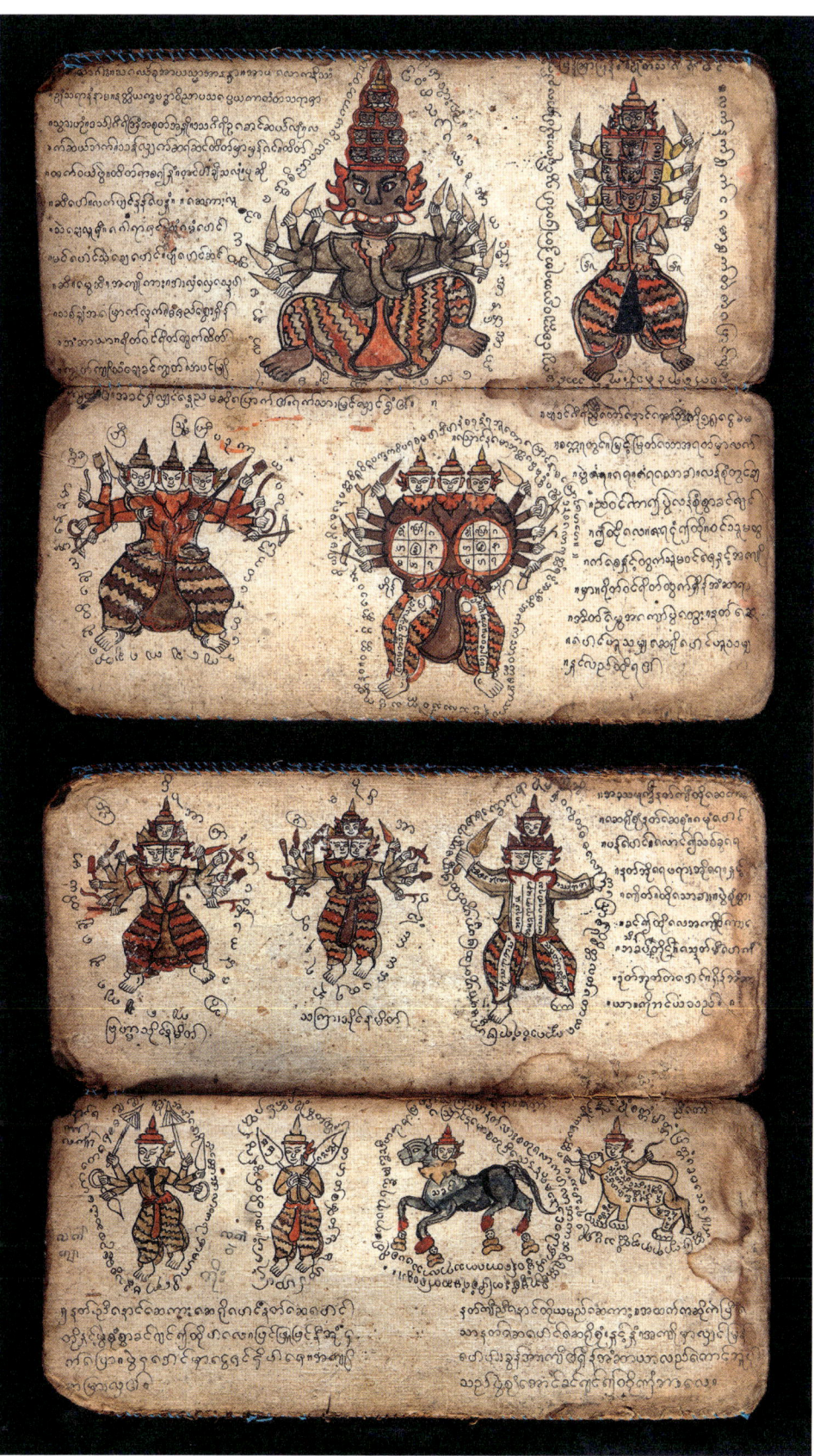

Index of tattoo designs, Burma, nineteenth century. Tattoo Museo Gianmaurizio Fercioni.

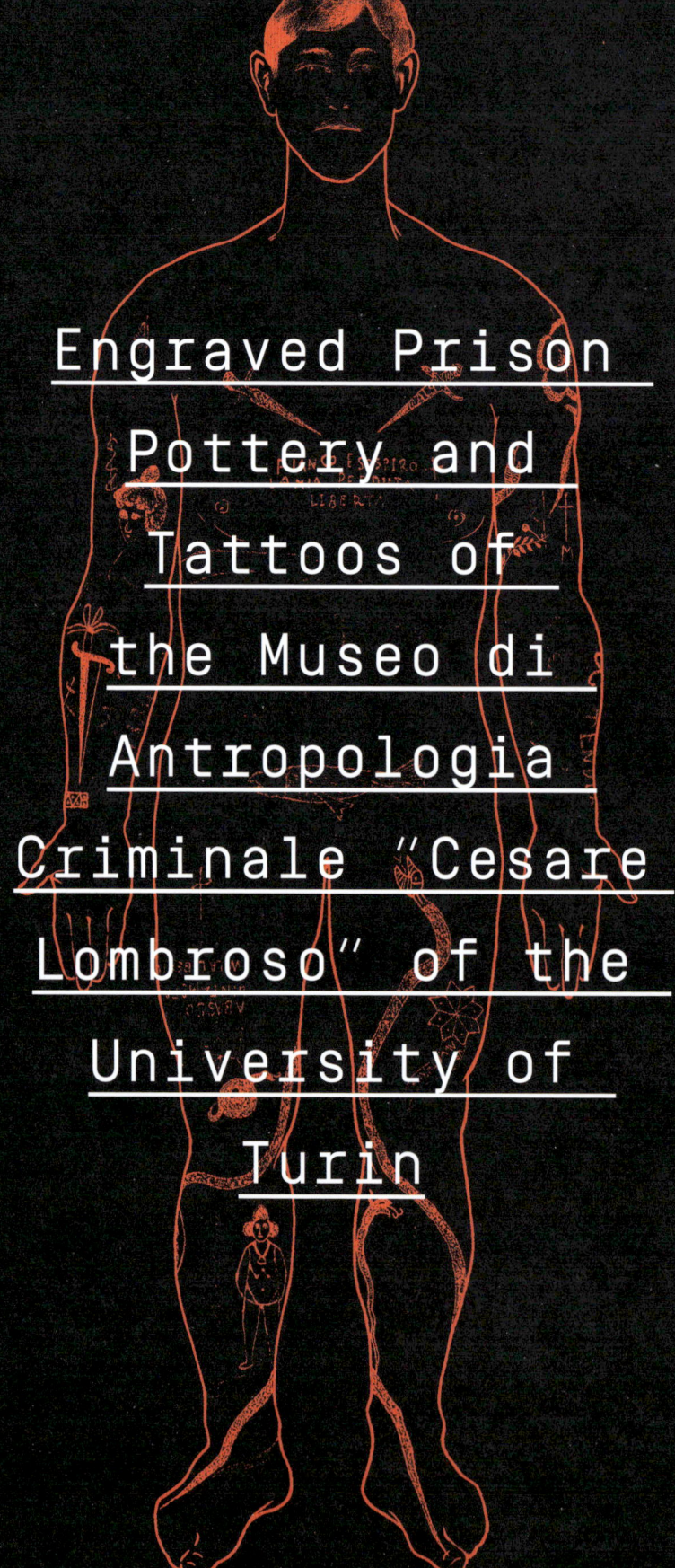

Engraved Prison Pottery and Tattoos of the Museo di Antropologia Criminale "Cesare Lombroso" of the University of Turin

— Cristina Cilli and Silvano Montaldo

Cesare Lombroso (born in Verona, 1835–died in Turin, 1909) became interested in tattoos during the 1860s, when, as a medical officer, he observed various examples of tattoos on the skin of 134 soldiers, who primarily belonged to the poorer classes and had no criminal records.[1] Ten years later, following his observation of thousands of individuals, Lombroso declared that tattoos were decreasing "among noncriminal men" while "expanding considerably among both the military and civil criminal populations." Through a comparison with the tattoos he saw on the bodies of Indigenous peoples, such as Australian Aborigines, which were documented in the anthropology books of the time, Lombroso drew a direct link between the "underdeveloped stages of civilization" and criminal behaviors. He used this connection to support the theory of criminal atavism, which he developed in 1871 after observing a third occipital dimple at the base of the skull of a prisoner who had died in Pavia. He went on to describe the concept in *L'Uomo delinquente* (*The Criminal Man*)[2] for which he became internationally famous. In the third chapter of the book, titled "Tattoos in Criminals," the anthropologist presents the results of a study of 7,114 individuals, 4,380 of whom were soldiers and 2,734 of whom were criminals. He argues that criminals, being incapable of higher forms of expression and unconcerned with pain (since they had dulled senses), were induced to permanently imprint designs, symbols, and sayings on their own bodies, expressing their otherness, and unconsciously repeating a practice that went back to the dawn of mankind. Lombroso thus began to gather reproductions of features and full-size drawings of the tattooed people he came into contact with in his activities as a physician in the prisons of Turin, and as an expert witness for the court.[3] The collections currently conserved at the Archives of the Museo di Antropologia criminale "Cesare Lombroso," as well as in museum storage, dating from 1870 to 1907, are a testament to his tattoo research methodology.

1. C. Lombroso, "Sul tatuaggio degli italiani"; letter from Dr. C. Lombroso to Dr. Zanini, in *Gazzetta medica italiana–Lombardia–Appendice medico-legale*, s. 1, 1/3, 1864, 3–5.

2. C. Lombroso, *L'uomo delinquente studiato in rapporto alla antropologia, alla medicina legale ed alle discipline carcerarie* (Milan: Hoepli, 1876), 43–56.

3. A. Petrizzo, *Fonti iconografiche sul tatuaggio, in Il Museo di Antropologia criminale Cesare Lombroso* (*Cesare Lombroso Museum of Criminal Anthropology*), University of Turin, curated by Montaldo S., in collaboration with C. Cilli (Cinisello Balsamo, Italy: Silvana Editoriale, 2015), 145–157.

There is a series of drawings, some loose, others bound in an album, along with a series of vellum papers that were used to copy a tattoo off the prisoner's body in person and then transfer it into the original position onto a drawing of a full-size complete human outline. This collection now consists of fifteen large panels (on average measuring 51 × 31 inches [130 × 80 centimeters]) and notably includes the completely tattooed body of Francesco Spiteri, a serial rapist and murderer, whom Lombroso considered to be the quintessential atavistic criminal. The fifth edition of *L'uomo delinquente* contained three pages meticulously describing his 106 tattoos, of which "10 were pictures of attractive women, 22 were first or last names thereof, 9 were hearts, and 8 were flowers." Lombroso also described "a fish that had seven little dots near its tail in the shape of a V, with the two letters M.S. in front alongside its head, positioned between two rosebuds. The fish with the seven dots tattooed on his penis signifies that from the time he was young his "fish" (penis) has been used to have anal sex with seven boys (the seven dots). Hence, I believe that the fish on his penis should also be considered a hieroglyph for pederasty. The two letters M.S. signify: My sister, whose virginity he attempted to take twice; thus, the two rosebuds next to the two letters." For the scientist, the obscene figures in erotic tattooed scenes were proof that Spiteri was to be considered a "born criminal."

Another noteworthy drawing is the large panel depicting a full human figure completely covered with tattoos, done in pencil and gray watercolor by Luigi Frigerio— a psychiatrist who worked with Lombroso. The title appears at the top in block letters: "Tattoo copied from the real person by Dr. Frigerio at the Alessandria Penitentiary." This drawing was presented in the section on criminal anthropology at the 1889 *Exposition universelle* in Paris.[4] Another panel reproduces a copy of the same individual, with partial tattoos. In this case, the anonymous illustrator colored the tattoos cobalt blue and on the lower right wrote, "Mullé Giovanni, deserter of the French navy (already appeared before a disciplinary board, we don't know why) October 1887." Lombroso published a more stylized drawing of the same individual under plate LXVIII in *L'Atlante dell'Uomo delinquente,*[5] with the following caption: Mullé Gio., French sailor, deserter, already convicted by the French Council of War, cause unknown. His forehead is tattooed with the inscription "*Pas de change*" ["No change"] and his chest with the words "*Le passé me tourment, le present me . . . , l'avenir m'épouvant*" ["The past torments me, the present . . . the future terrifies me"), which, together with the dagger, the corpse head on his chest, and the cluster of grapes tattooed on his penis, demonstrates his criminal tendencies. The pansy flowers that appear all over his body are quite common in pederasts. The letter M on his chest is the initial of his name; the epaulettes and ship are professional symbols; we also see the portrait of a woman and the words "*Souvenir de la Martinique*" ["A keepsake from Martinique"].

The archives also contain two posters which look somewhat like a collage, with pieces of fabric that contain the tattoos studied by

---

4. Ibid.

5. C. Lombroso, *L'uomo delinquente studiato in rapporto alla antropologia, alla giurisprudenza ed alla psichiatria* (Turin, Italy: Bocca, 1897).

Alexandre Lacassagne, a well-known French forensic pathologist who assembled another collection on tattoos of criminals in Lyon in the late 1800s. Lacassagne conversely considered tattooed criminals to be "degenerate" rather than "atavistic."[6]

The storerooms of the Museo Lombroso also contain thirty-six fragments of dried tattooed skin, and one strip of skin preserved in liquid. There is also an artifact showing one of the rare cases of a tattoo that belonged to a woman.[7] Some of these pieces of tattooed skin were assembled into a picture and framed so that Lombroso could show the tattoos to the public at national and international exhibitions. The Turin museum also contains photographs documenting tattoos ranging from 1906 to 1927.[8]

The study of the culture and psychology of criminals owes its existence to a second collection of the Museo Lombroso—prison jugs. Having become the doctor of the Le Nuove prison, Lombroso collected all written traces left by the inmates. He combined all the material in his 1888 *Palimsesti del carcere.* While there were inscriptions everywhere (on walls, beds, books, packages of medicines or cigarettes, clothing), Lombroso used the white enameled ceramic carafes used to hold drinking water in prisoners' cells to deepen his analyses. The inmates would use random objects such as forks or bent nails to make engravings on them. For Lombroso, the inscriptions and drawings—which were autobiographical, self-congratulatory, religious, or pornographic in nature, were "signs," or even "monuments" of a state of archaic civilization and of the primitive mentality of Turin criminality, most often done by semi-illiterate criminals.

Today, the collection consists of eighty drinking jugs, twelve plates, four bowls, one chamber pot, and one medallion from the Le Nuove jail, and of eleven carafes and one mug from the La Generala jail for minors in Turin. The main producer of these prison objects was defendant Buzzo, from whom we have a jar, a chamber pot, a medallion, two plates, and two bowls done in bas-relief and painted in color. Nicknamed Bersagliè d'Vanchija for the tough look and provenance of his namesake Turin working neighborhood, Buzzo was the leader of a band of criminals who were arrested and brought to trial in 1900. His artistic work revealed a deep resentment of society, which he considered at fault for the disadvantaged living conditions that had pushed him toward a life of crime.[9]

---

6. A. Lacassagne, *Les tatuages: Etude anthropologique et médico-légale* (Paris: Librerie J.-B. Baillière et fils, 1881).

7. E. Petrizzo, "Tatouages de prostituées en Italie (fin du XIXe-début du XXe siècle): Lectures d'une écriture subalterne," *Revue d'Histoire di XIXe siècle* 65 (2022): 127–146.

8. G. Dilettuso, "Le fotografie dei criminali tatuati nell'archivio del Museo di Antropologia criminale 'Cesare Lombroso,'" University of Turin, level I diploma thesis. School of Communications and Promotion of Contemporary Artistic Heritage, Albertina Academy of Fine Arts of Turin, 2018.

9. L. Spanu, *Gli orci in terracotta: La parola ai detenuti,* at Museo di Antropologia Criminale, Cesare Lombroso of the University of Turin, curated by Montaldo S., in collaboration with C. Cilli (Cinisello Balsamo, Italy: Silvana Editoriale, 2015), 139–141.

— **Cristina Cilli and Silvano Montaldo**

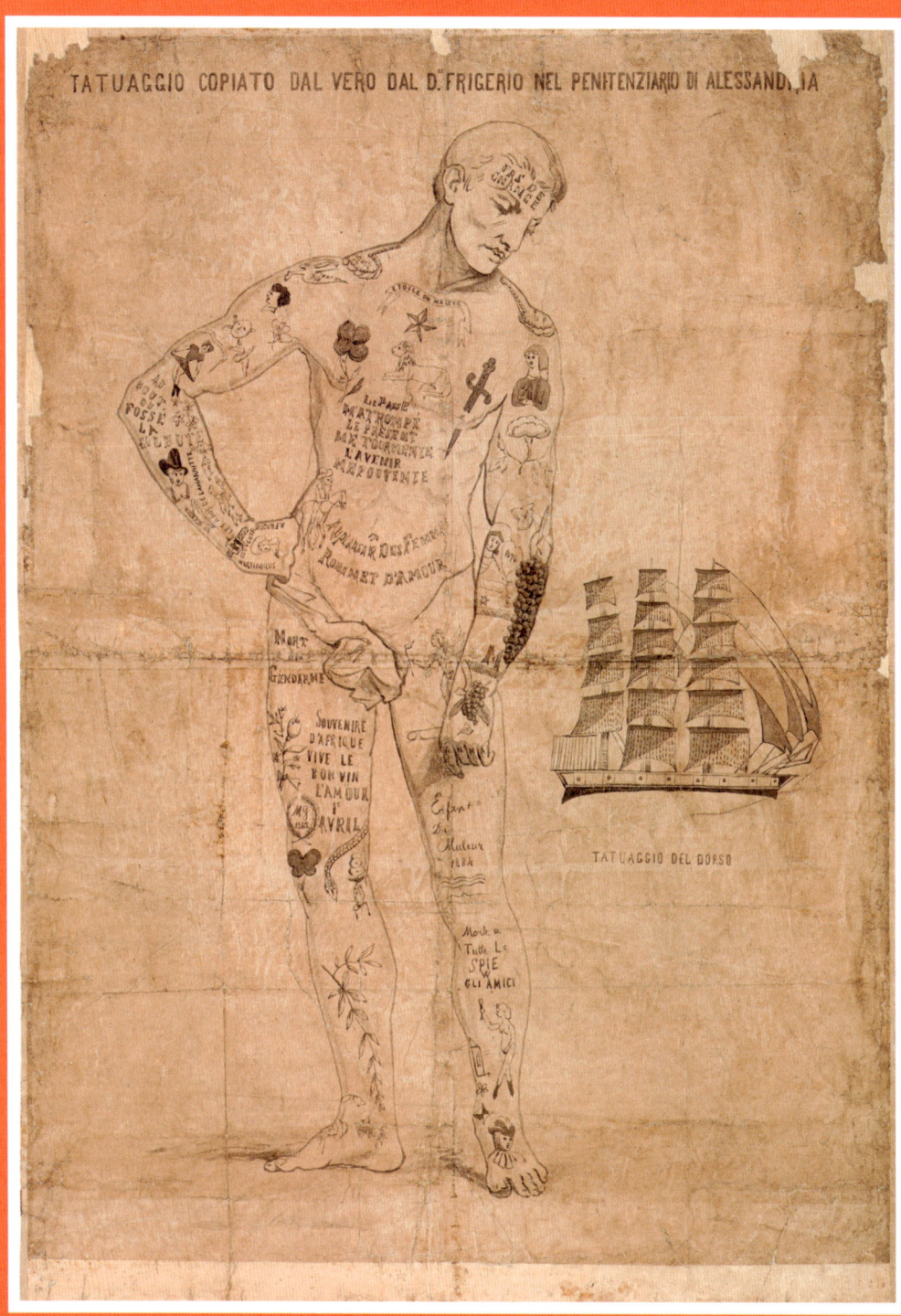

Luigi Figerio, drawing of tattoos copied from Giovanni Mullé at the Alessandria penitentiary; pencil, black and red watercolor on canvas-backed paper, prior to 1889. (312), Archives of the Museo di Antropologia Criminale "Cesare Lombroso" of the University of Turin.

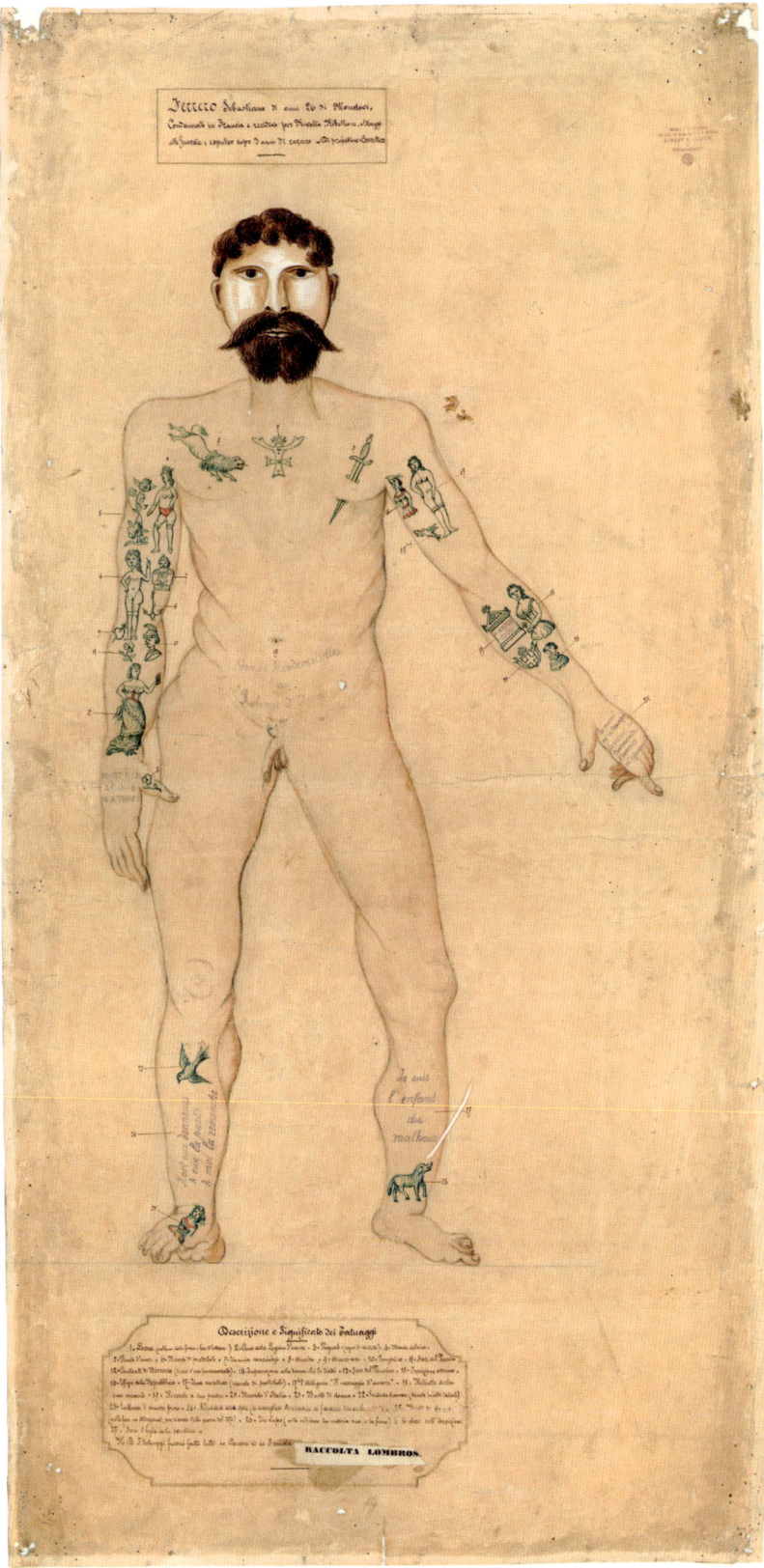

Anonymous, drawing of the tattooed Sebastiano Ferrero; pencil, tempera, and watercolor on canvas-backed cardboard, mid-nineteenth century. (317), Archives of the Museo di Antropologia Criminale "Cesare Lombroso" of the University of Turin.

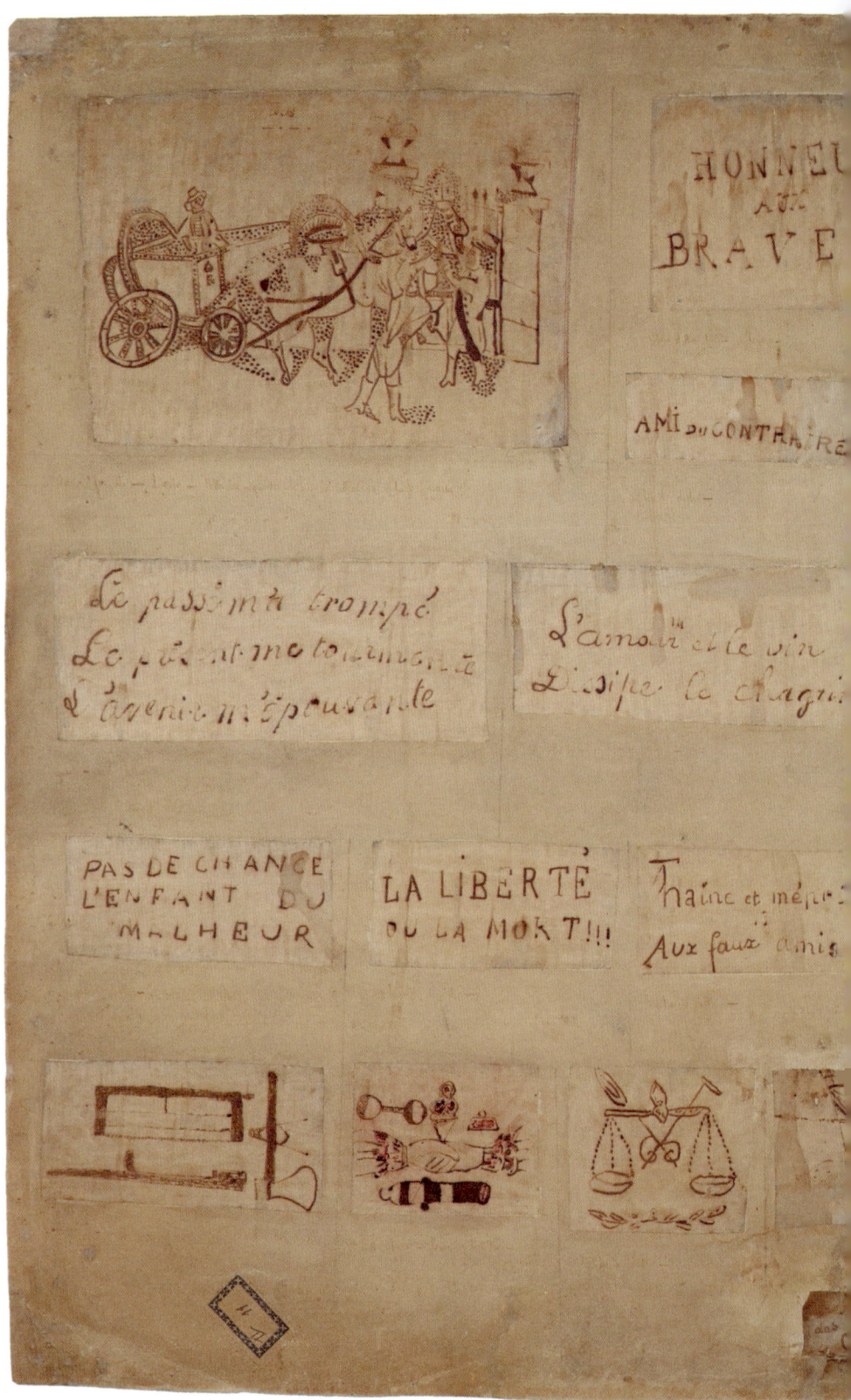

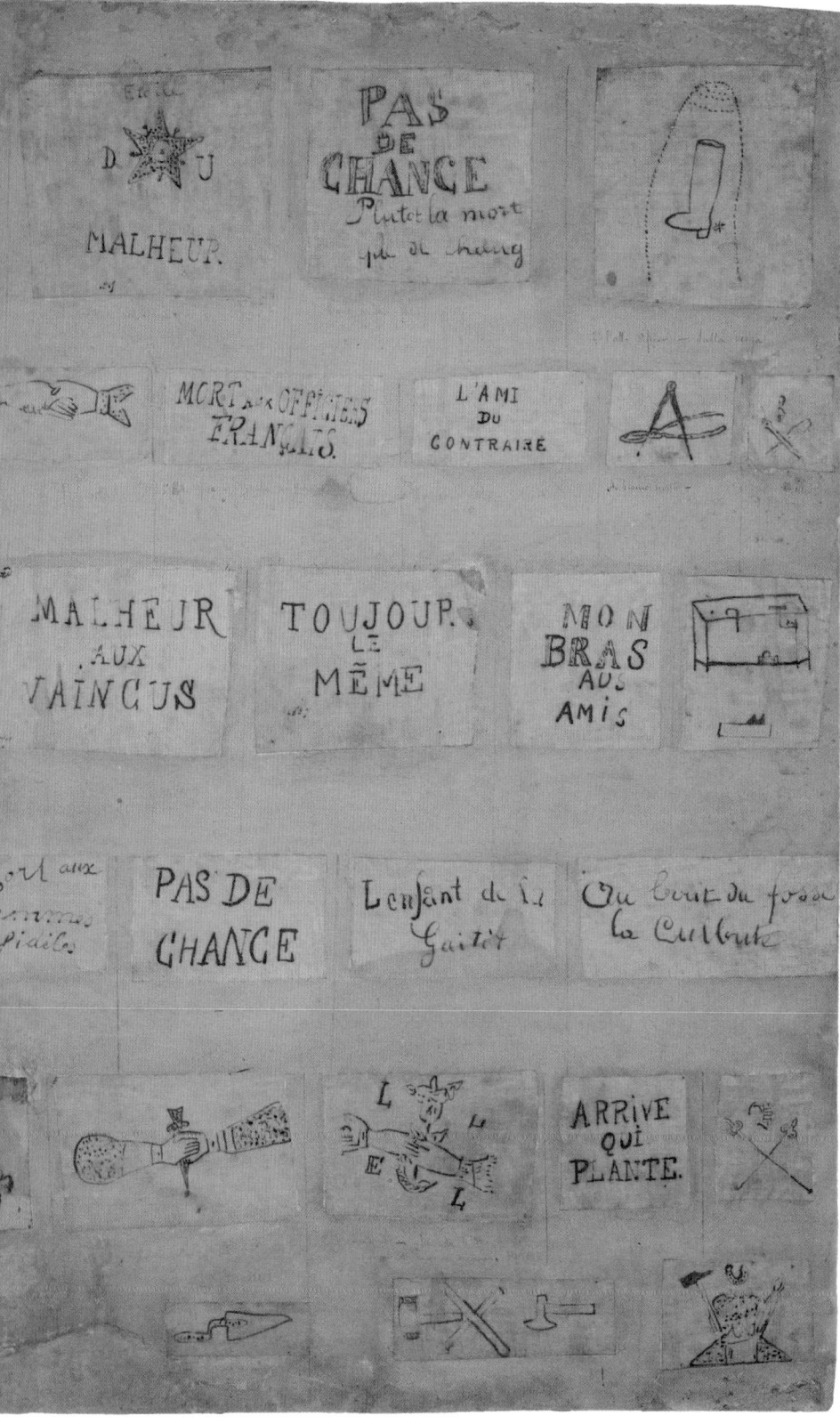

Anonymous, panel with square cutouts on light canvas-backed paper with drawings of the tattoos from the Lacassagne collection; black and red ink, second half of the nineteenth century. (310) Archives of the Museo di Antropologia Criminale "Cesare Lombroso" of the University of Turin.

Anonymous, drawing of four tattooed people; pencil, brown ink, colored pencil, crayon on canvas-backed paper, second half of the nineteenth century. (315), Archives of the Museo di Antropologia Criminale "Cesare Lombroso" of the University of Turin.

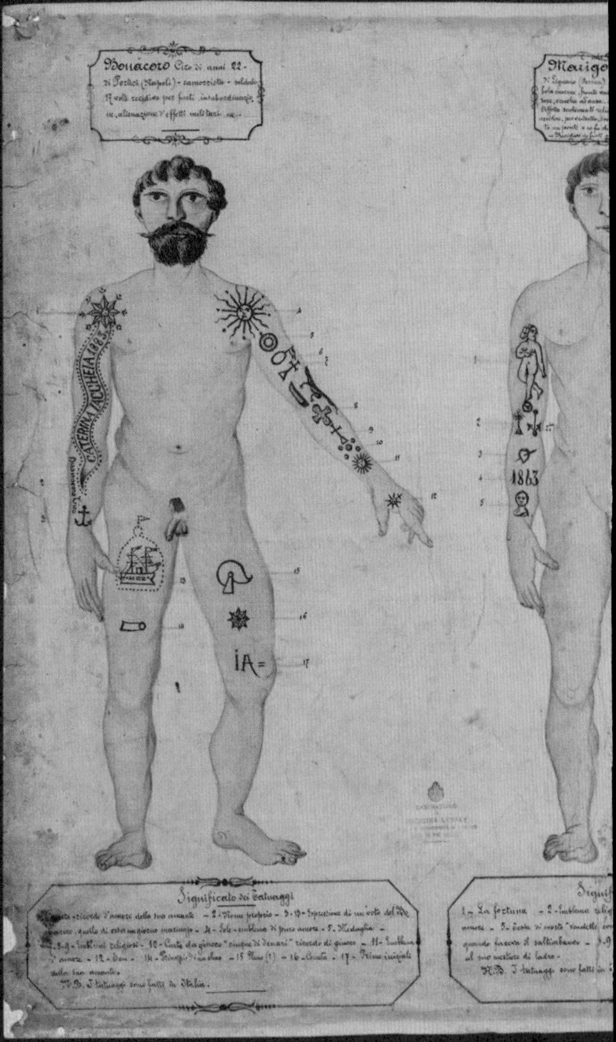

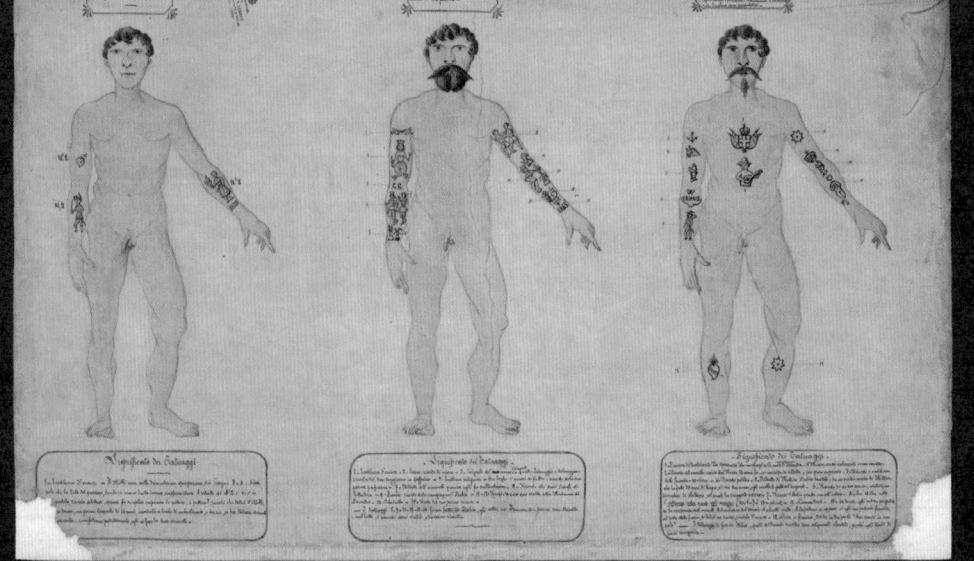

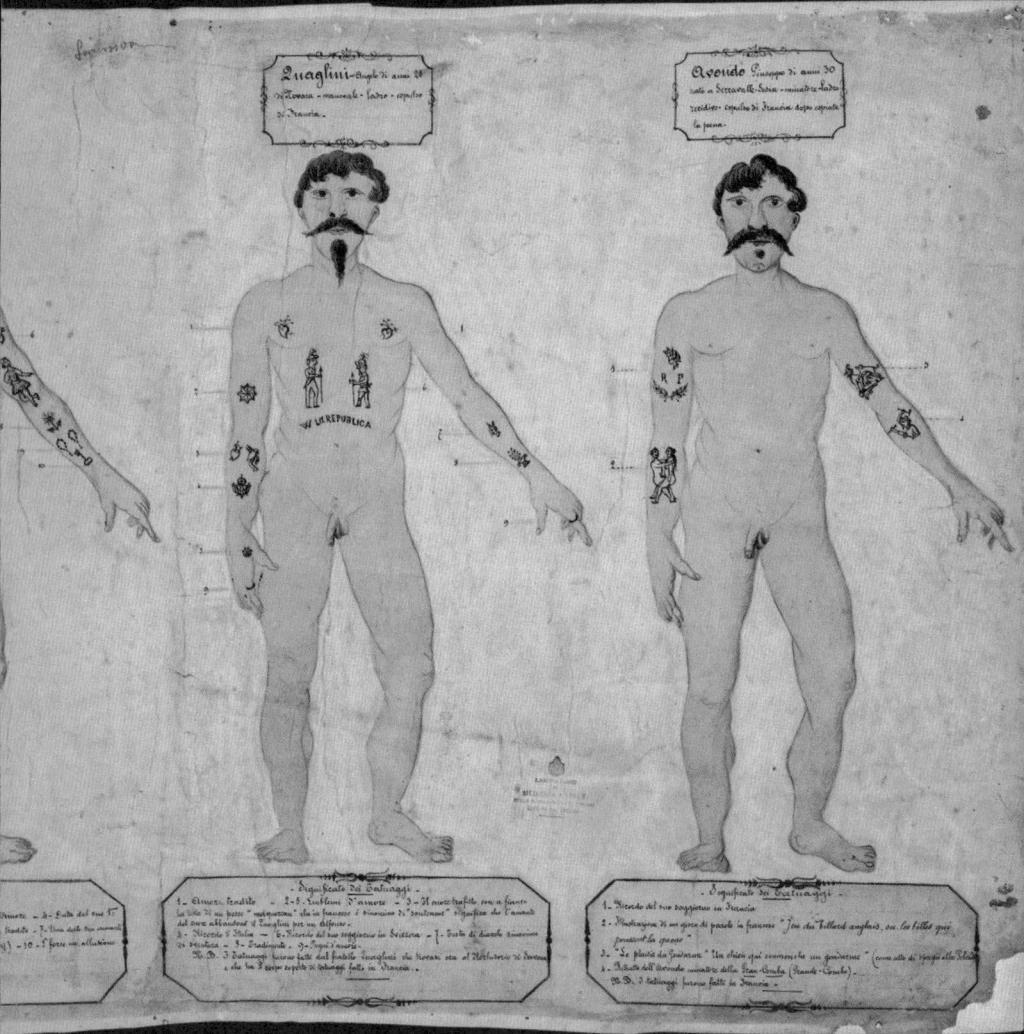

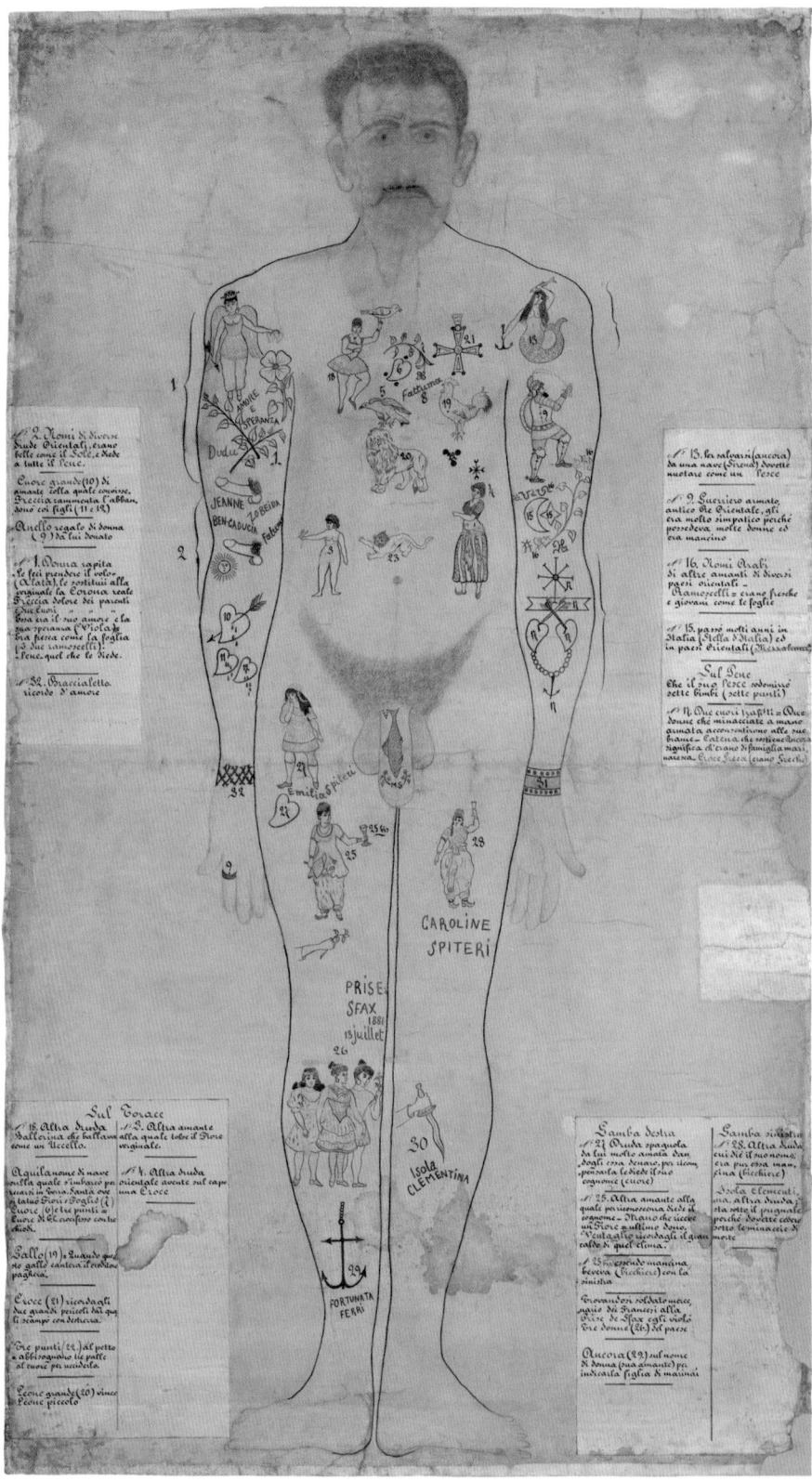

Anonymous, drawing with tattoos of Francesco Spiteri; pencil, tempera, and watercolor on beige canvas-backed paper, second half of the nineteenth century. (323), Archives of the Museo di Antropologia Criminale "Cesare Lombroso" of the University of Turin.

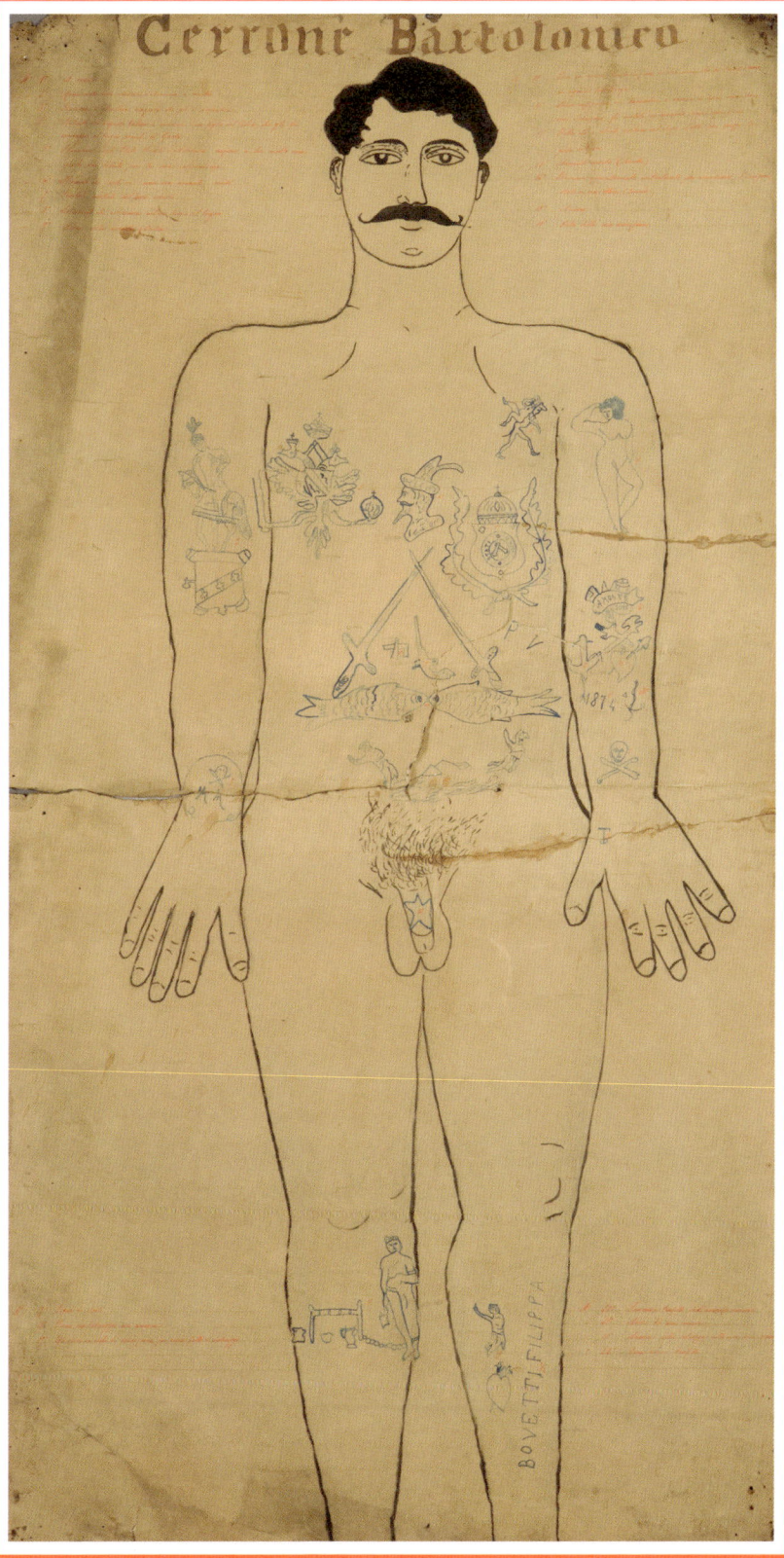

Anonymous, drawing with tattoos of Bartolemeo Cerrone; pencil, black and blue tempera on brown paper, second half of the nineteenth century. (318), Archives of the Museo di Antropologia Criminale "Cesare Lombroso" of the University of Turin.

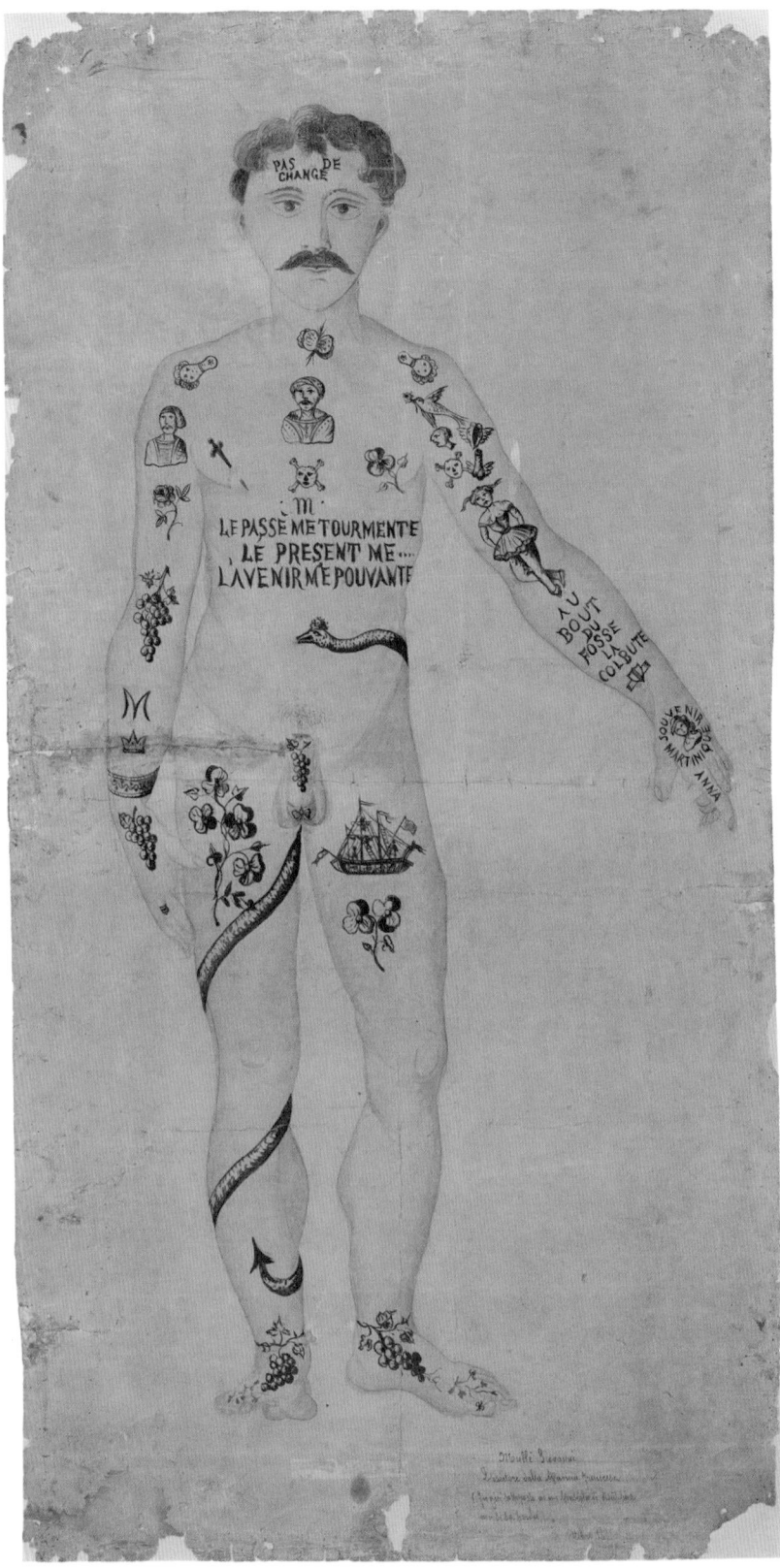

Anonymous, drawing with tattoos of Giovanni Mullé; pencil, tempera, and watercolor on canvas-backed paper, second half of the nineteenth century. (313), Archives of the Museo di Antropologia Criminale "Cesare Lombroso" of the University of Turin.

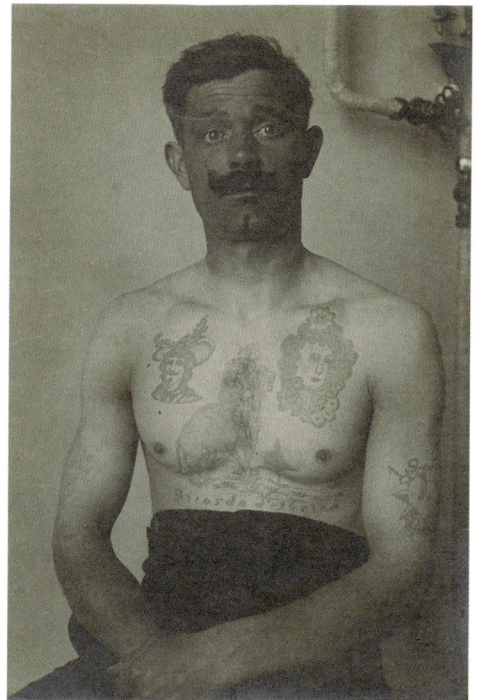
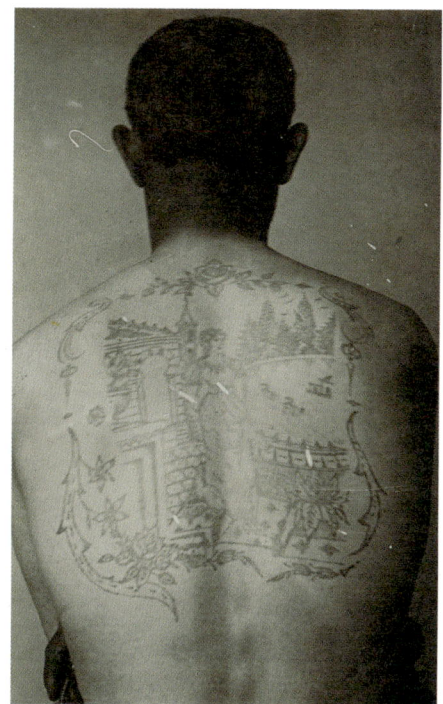

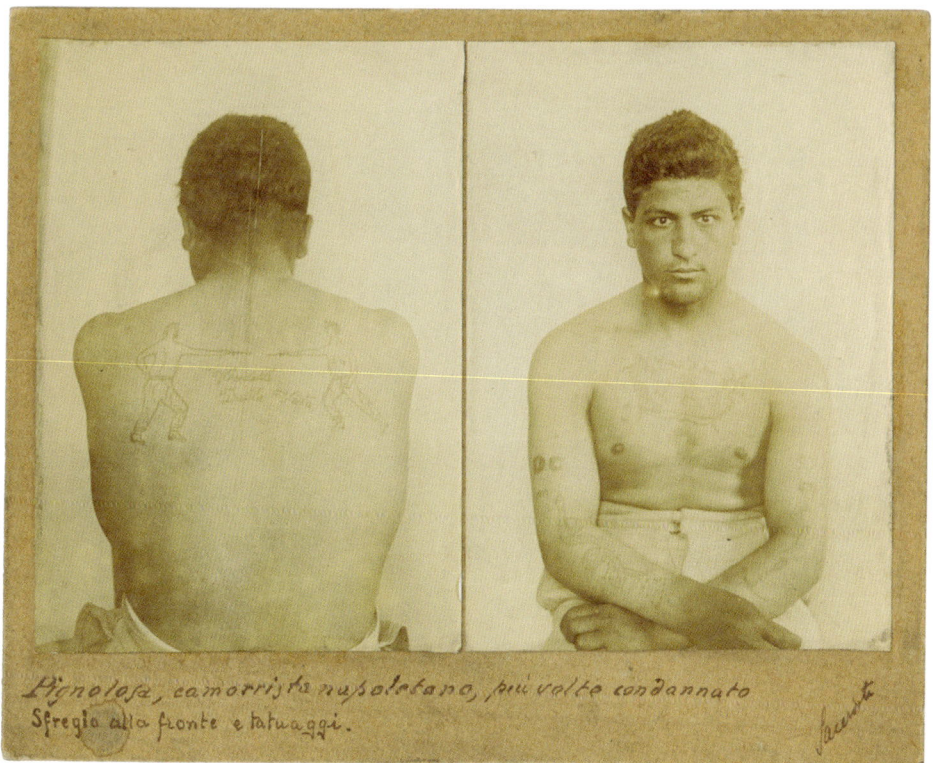

Top: Unidentified photograph, *Ricordo d'Africa*, gelatin silver print on cardboard, late nineteenth–early twentieth century. (CCN 0100407803 and CCN 0100407804), Archives of the Museo di Antropologia Criminale "Cesare Lombroso" of the University of Turin.

Bottom: Unidentified photograph, *Pignolosa camorrista napoletano*, gelatin silver print on cardboard, late nineteenth–early twentieth century. (CCN 0100407744), Archives of the Museo di Antropologia Criminale "Cesare Lombroso" of the University of Turin.

— Cristina Cilli and Silvano Montaldo

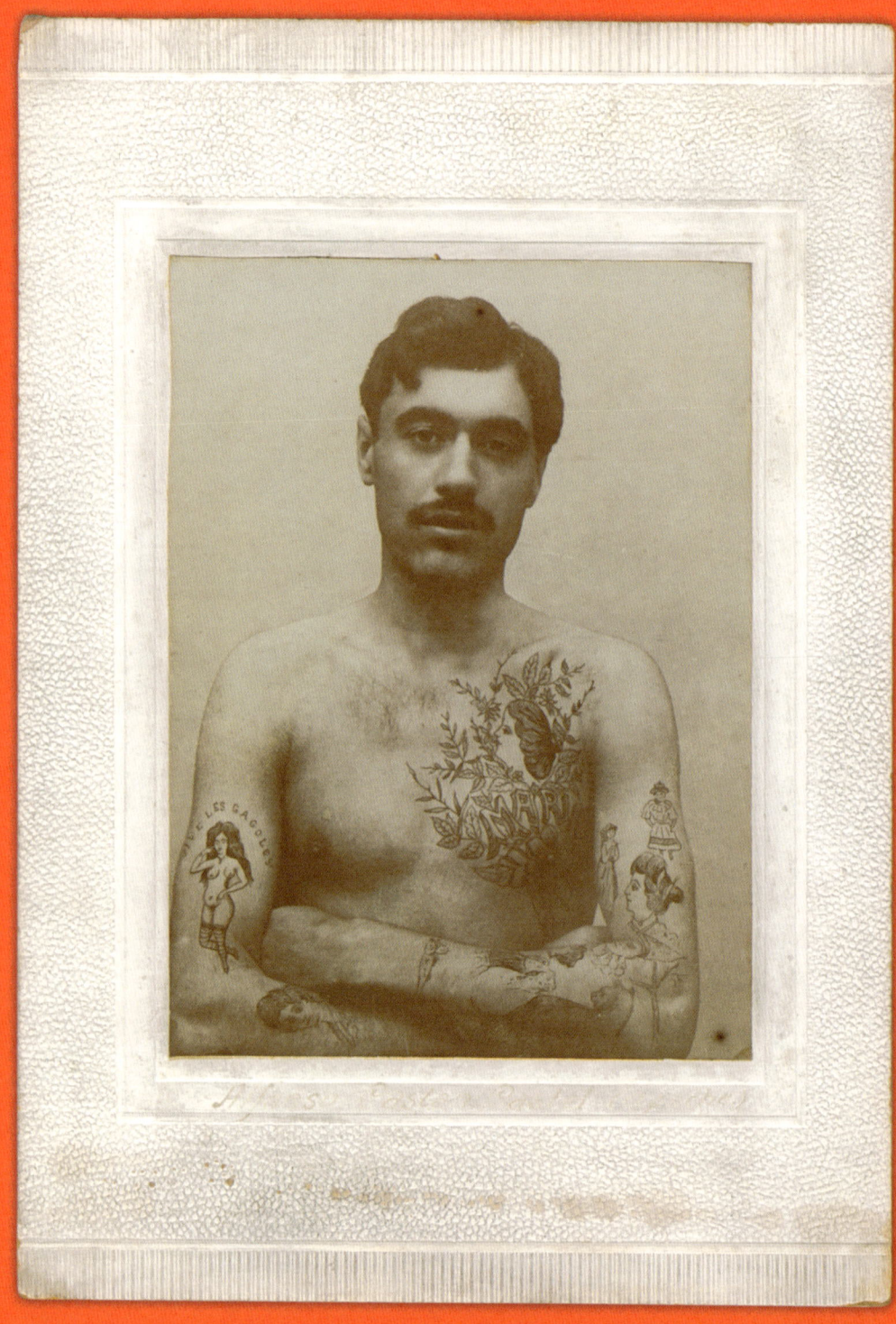

Unidentified photograph, *Alfonso Castan Castel,* aristotype on cardboard with India ink touch-ups, before 1906. (CCN 0100407737), Archives of the Museo di Antropologia Criminale "Cesare Lombroso" of the University of Turin.

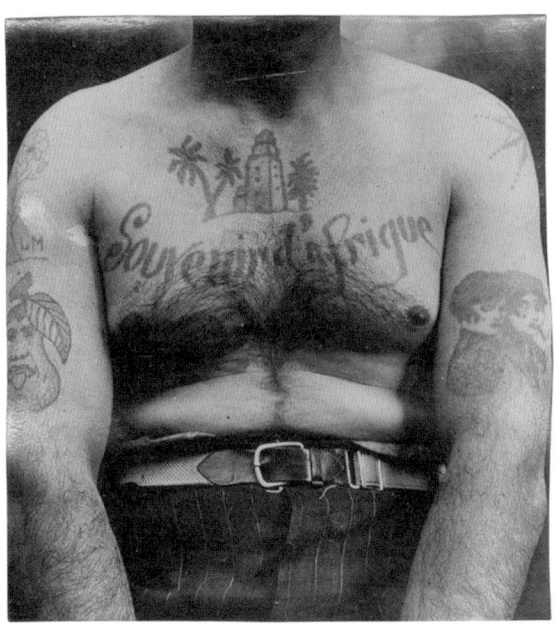

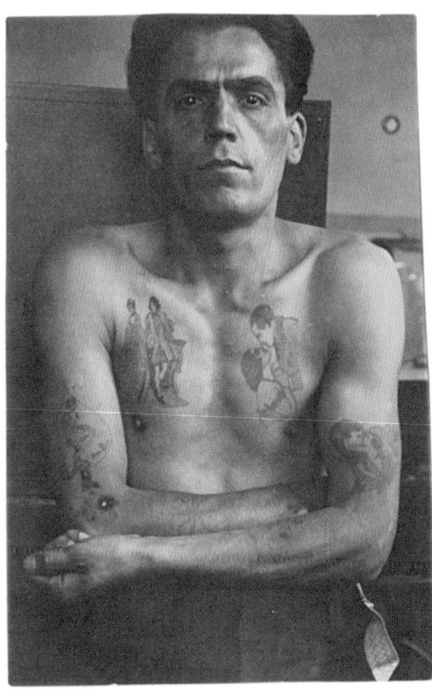

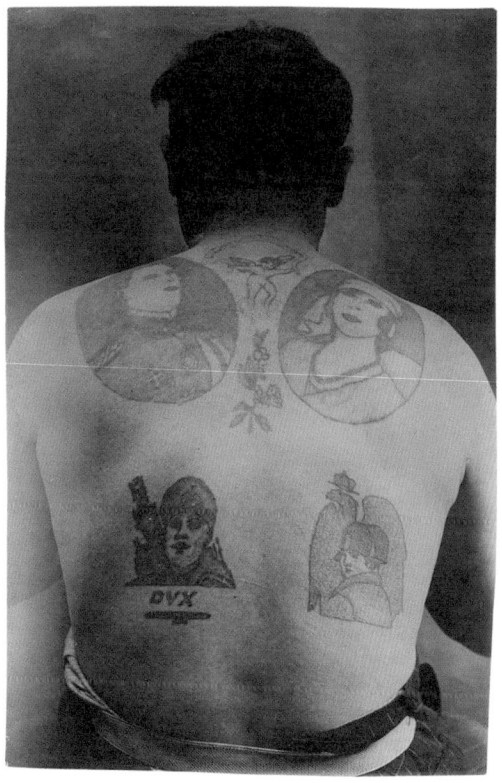

Top: Unidentified photograph, *Souvenir d'afrique*, gelatin print on cardboard, late nineteenth–early twentieth century. (CCN 0100407784), Archives of the Museo di Antropologia Criminale "Cesare Lombroso" of the University of Turin.

Bottom: Unidentified photograph, *Pandini Carlo,* gelatin print, 1920–1937. (CCN 0100407801), Archives of the Museo di Antropologia Criminale "Cesare Lombroso" of the University of Turin.

Unidentified photograph, *Schiena tatuata,* gelatin print, 1930–1937. (CCN 0100407787), Archives of the Museo di Antropologia Criminale "Cesare Lombroso" of the University of Turin.

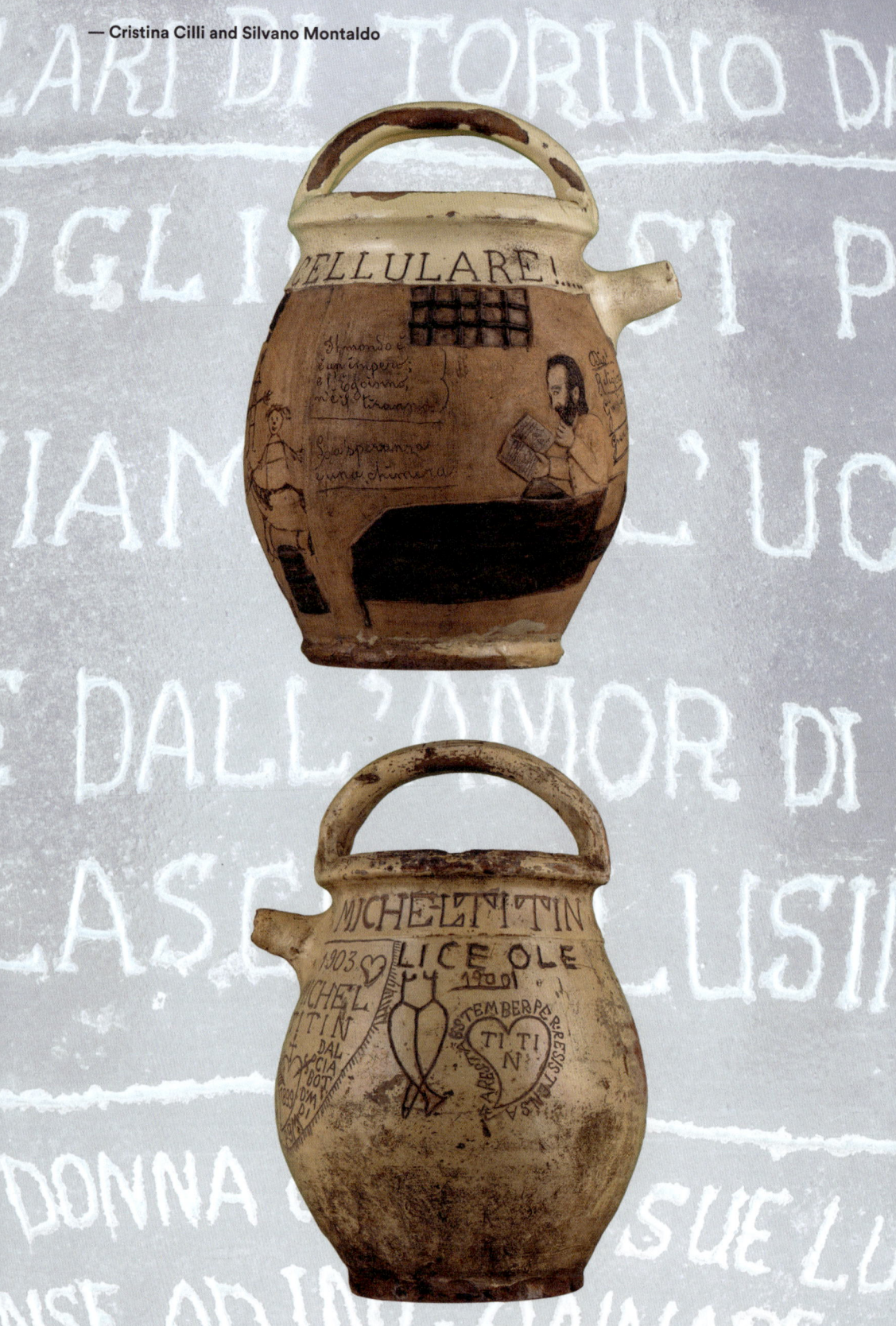

— Cristina Cilli and Silvano Montaldo

Top: Defendant Buzzo, drinking jug, engraved and colored ceramic, Le Nuove jail in Turin, ca. 1900. (19), Museo di Antropologia Criminale "Cesare Lombroso" of the University of Turin.

Bottom: Anonymous, drinking jug, engraved ceramic, Le Nuove jail in Turin, 1899. (78), Museo di Antropologia Criminale "Cesare Lombroso" of the University of Turin.

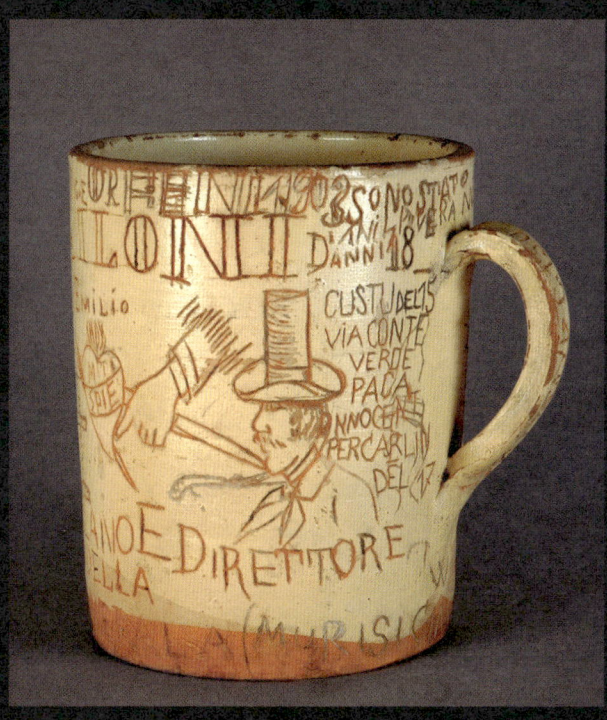

Anonymous, mug, engraved ceramic, La Generala prison for minors in Turin, second half of the nineteenth–early twentieth century. (183) Museo di Antropologia Criminale "Cesare Lombroso" of the University of Turin.

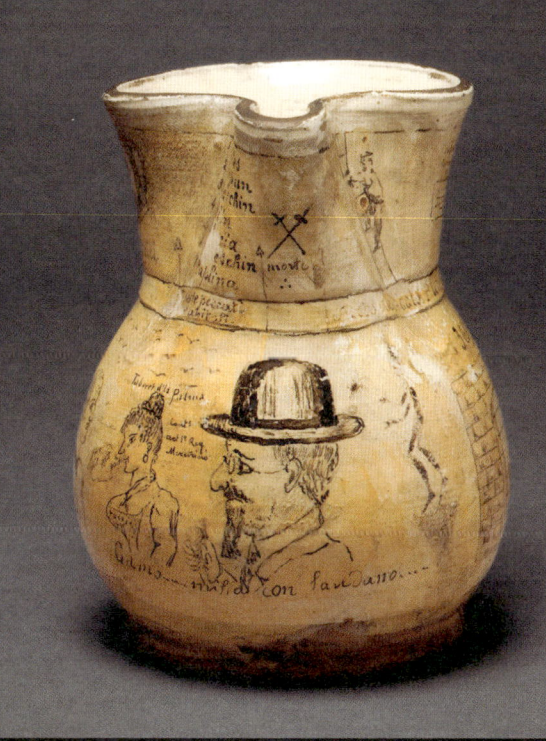

Anonymous, carafe, ceramic, engraved and painted with India ink, La Generala prison for minors in Turin, second half of the nineteenth–early twentieth century. (177), Museo di Antropologia Criminale "Cesare Lombroso" of the University of Turin.

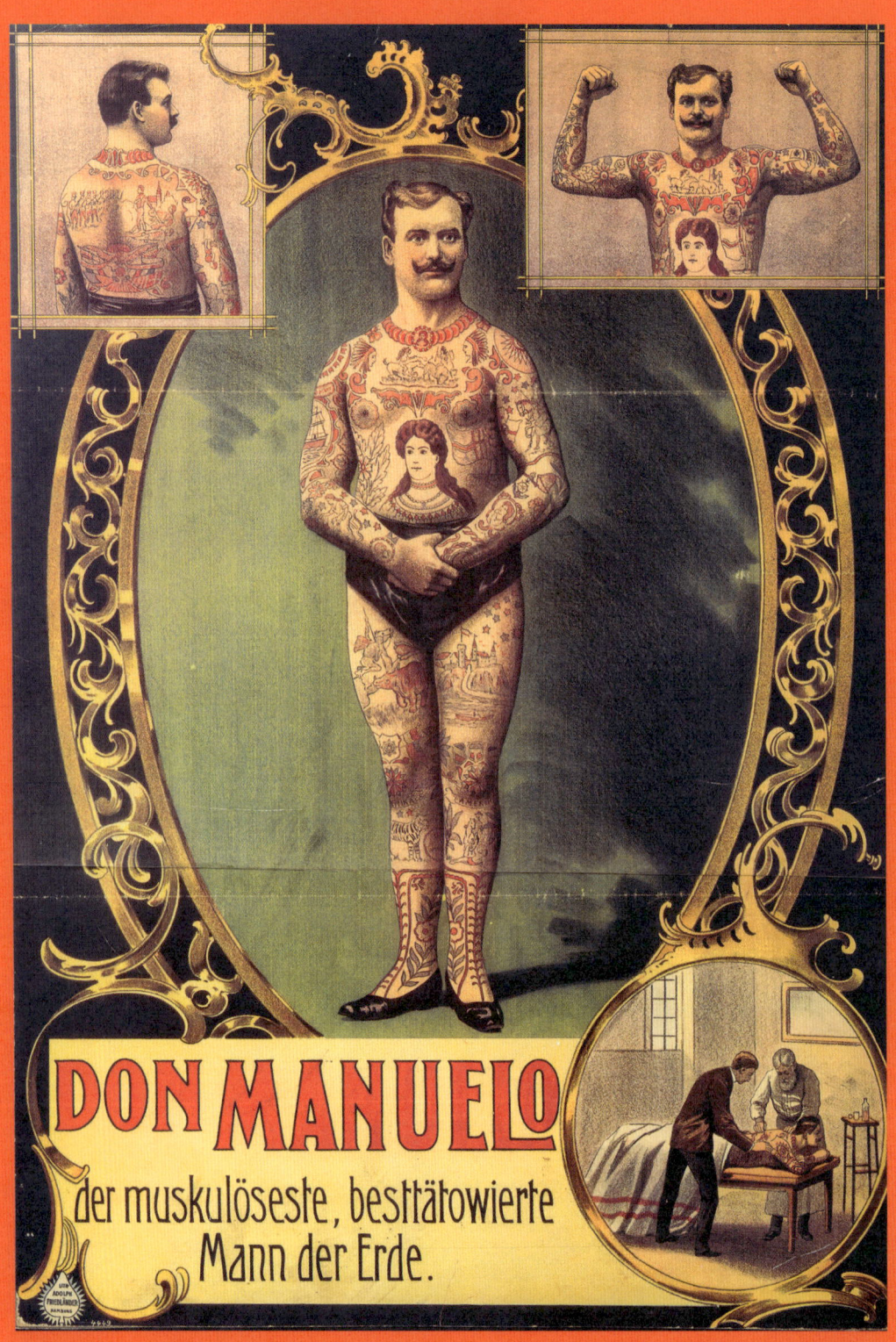

Anonymous, *Don Manuelo*, ca. 1908. Milan, Tattoo Museo Gianmaurizio Fercioni.

Circus

The popularity of modern tattoos in Europe and the United States is due in large part to the circus. Indeed, while tattoos were imported by seamen who, having returned from their travels in the East, opened the first tattoo shops in the major European and American ports, it was actually circuses that made them well known in the interior regions of United States and Europe. For more than seventy years beginning in the mid-nineteenth century, the most-important circuses in the world had male and female artists who flaunted the most-extensive, the most-numerous, the strangest, and the most expertly executed tattoos.

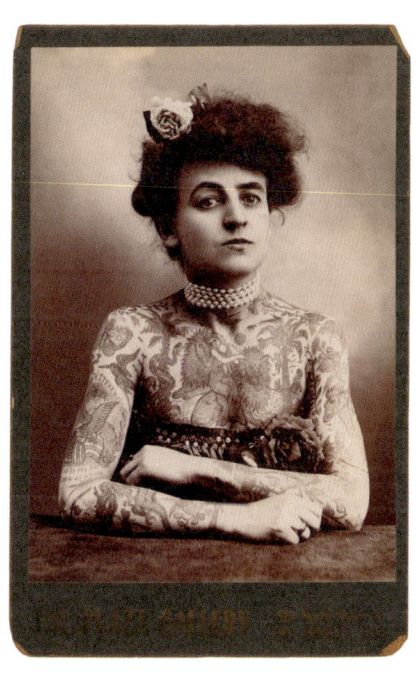

Unidentified photograph, *Maud Stevens Wagner,* 1907, gelatin print. Washington, DC, Library of Congress.

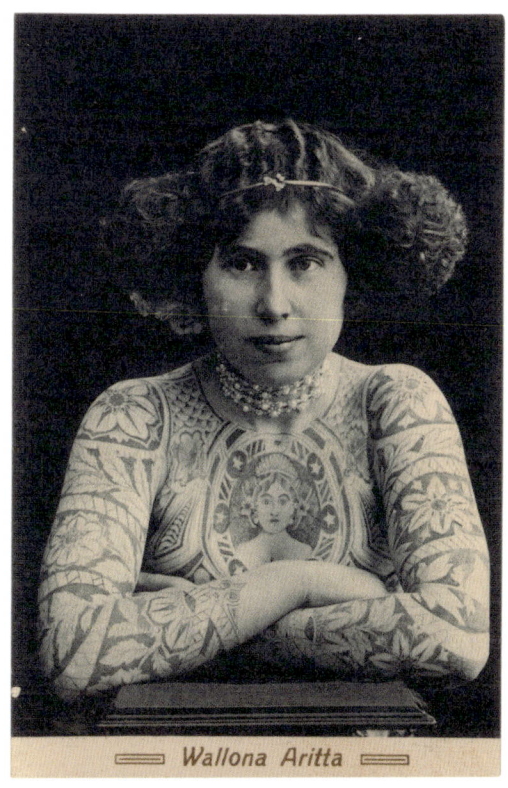

Unidentified photograph, *Wallona Aritta,* 1913. Melbourne, Australia, State Library of Victoria.

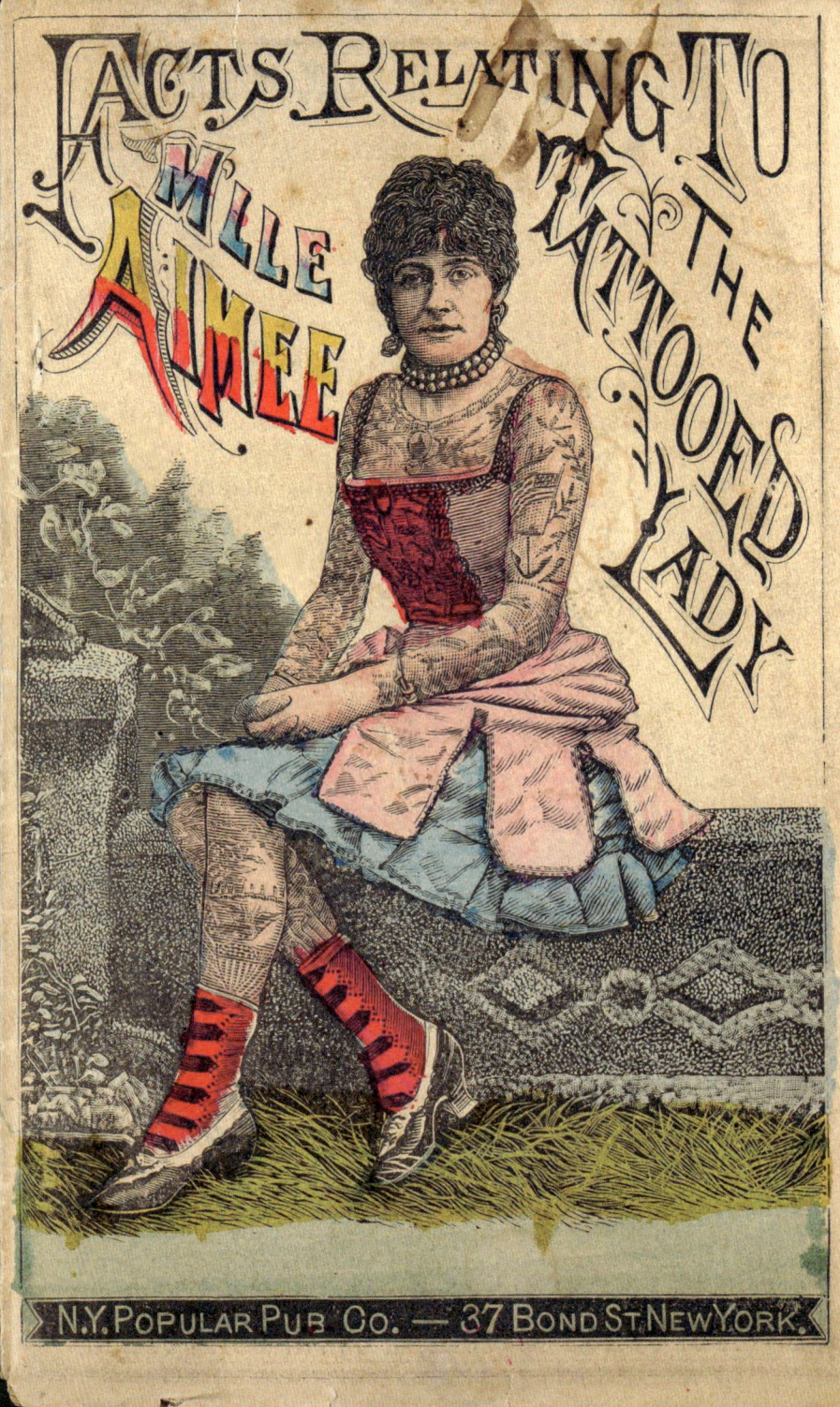

FACTS RELATING TO THE TATTOOED LADY

MLLE AIMEE

N.Y. POPULAR PUB CO. — 37 BOND ST. NEW YORK.

A cover with Irene Woodward, for *Facts Relating to the Tattooed Lady, M.elle Aimee* (New York: Popular Publications Company, 1986). New Haven, Connecticut, Yale University Library, Beinecke Rare Book and Manuscript Library.

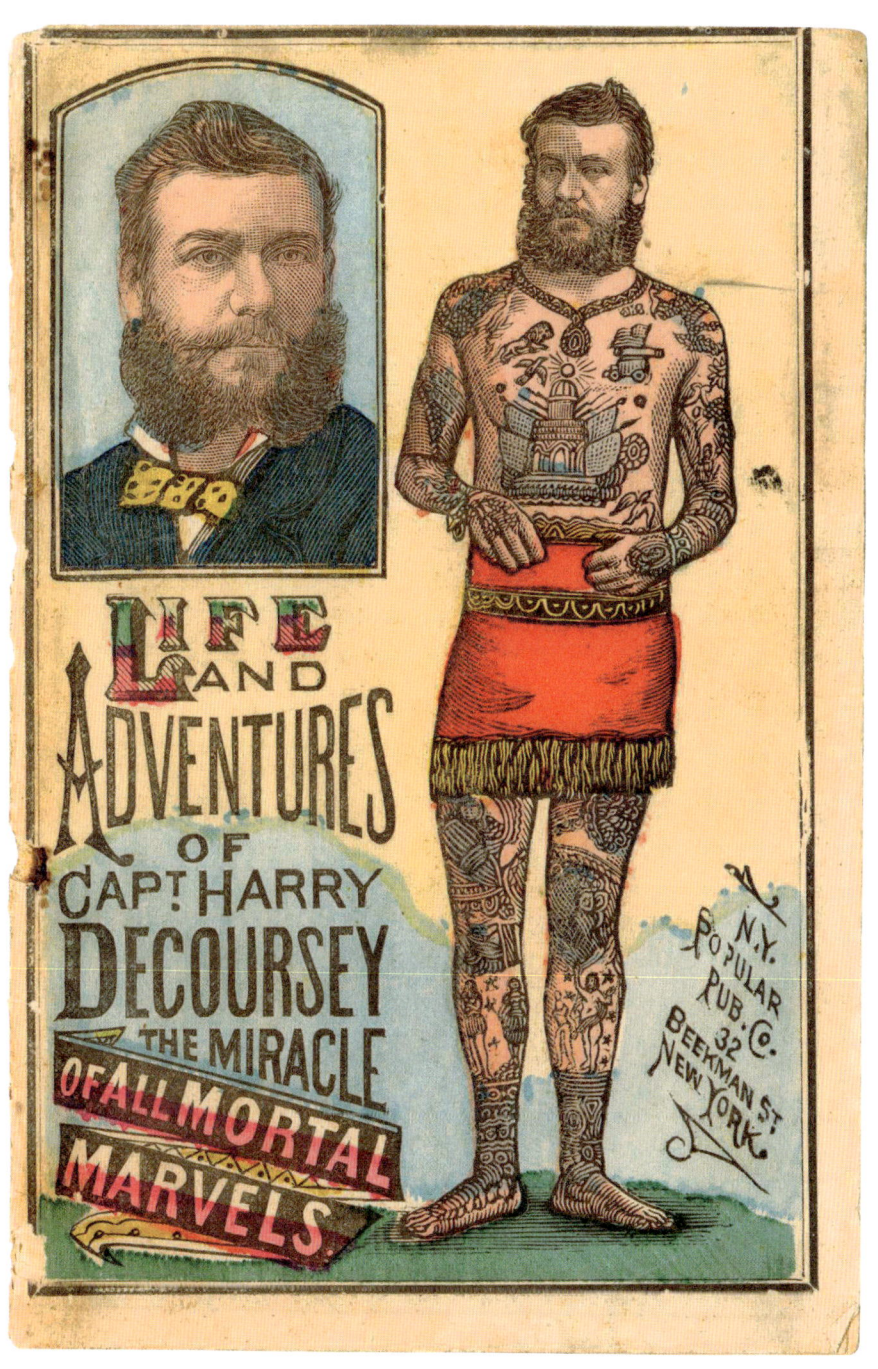

Cover of *Life and Adventures of Capt. Harry Decoursey, the Miracle of All Mortal Marvels* (New York: Popular Publications Company, 1892). Private collection.

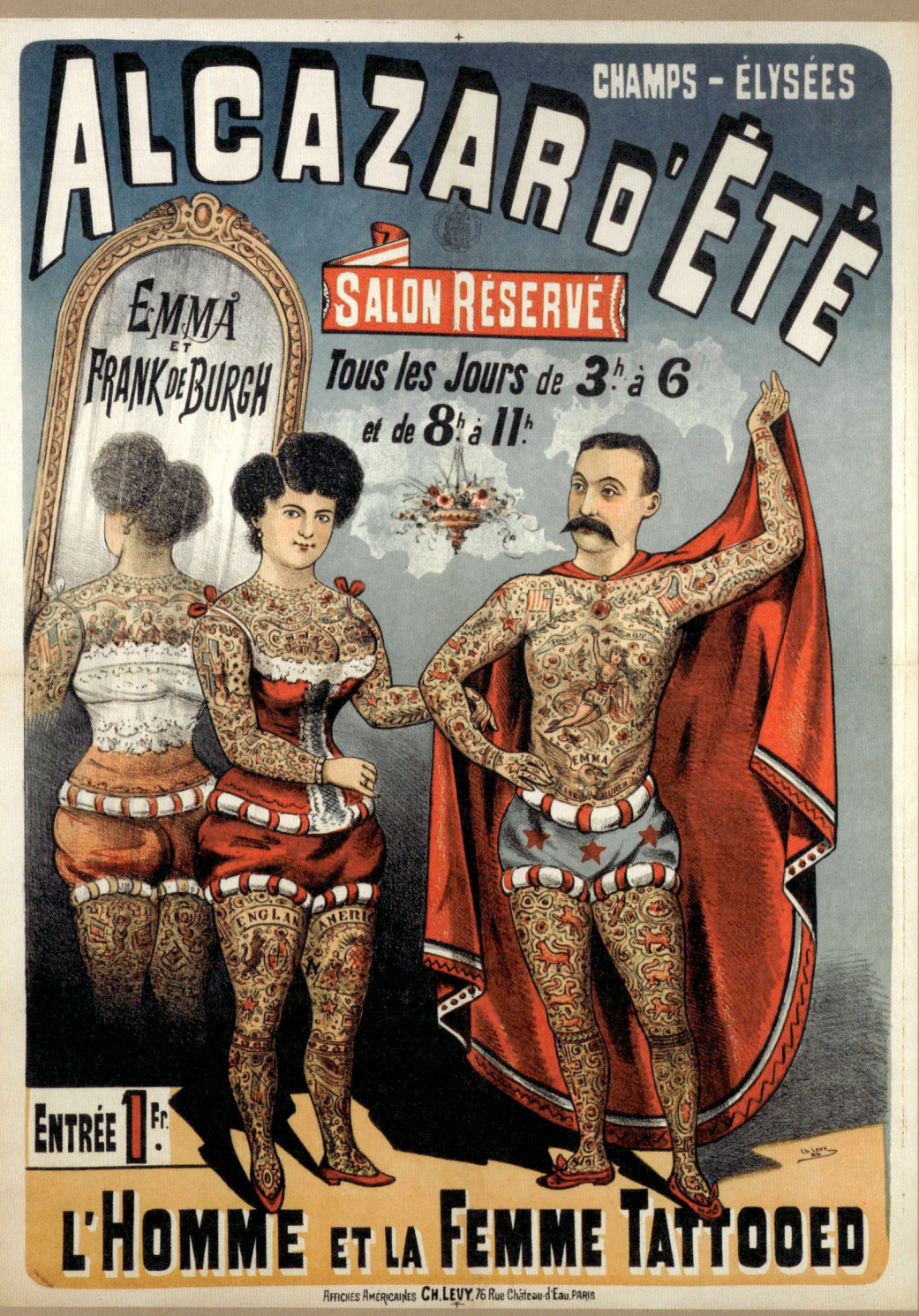

Anonymous, *Alcazar d'Eté. L'homme et la femme tattooed* (Paris: Edition Charles Lévy, 1886). Private collection.

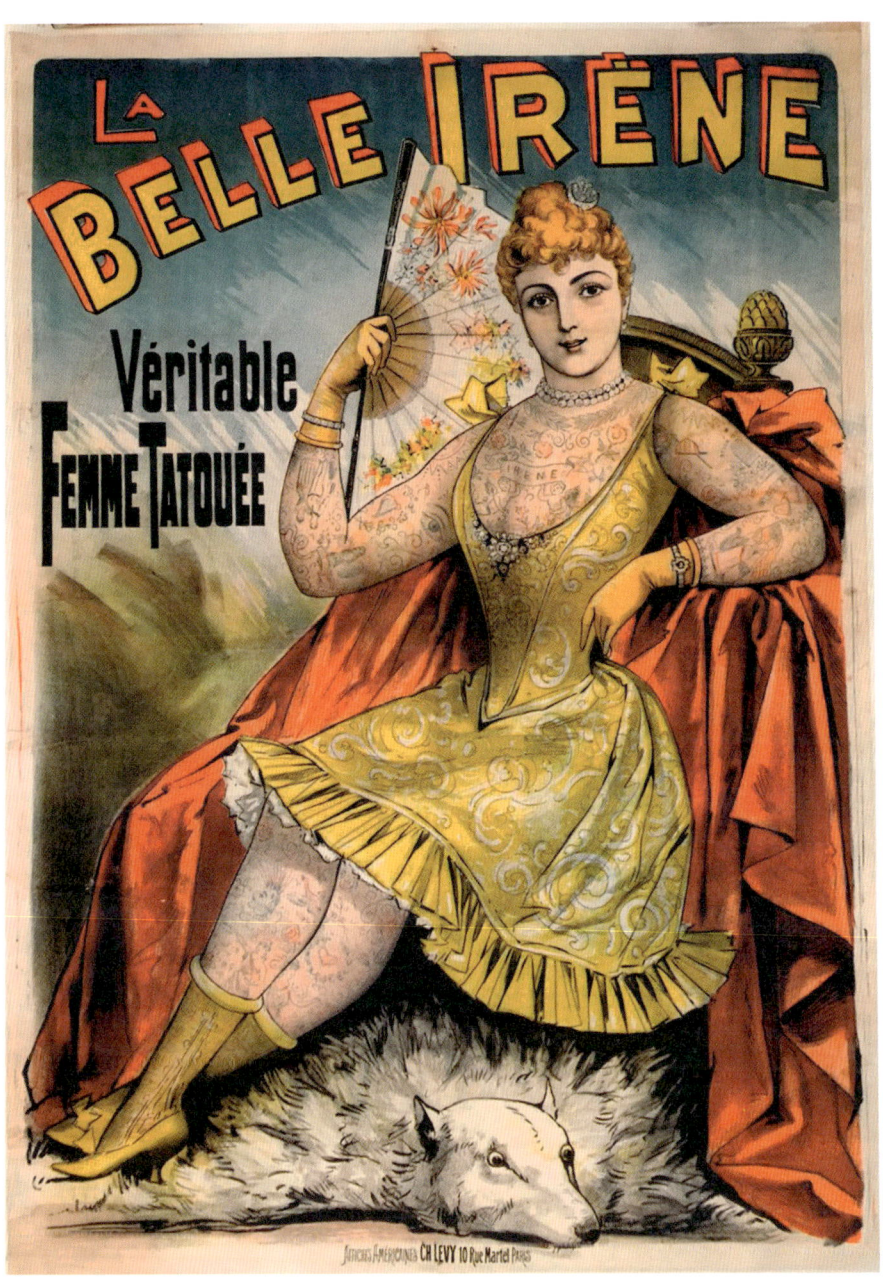

Anonymous, *La belle Irène (Paris:* Edition Charles Lévy, 1886). Paris, Musée Carnavalet–Histoire de Paris.

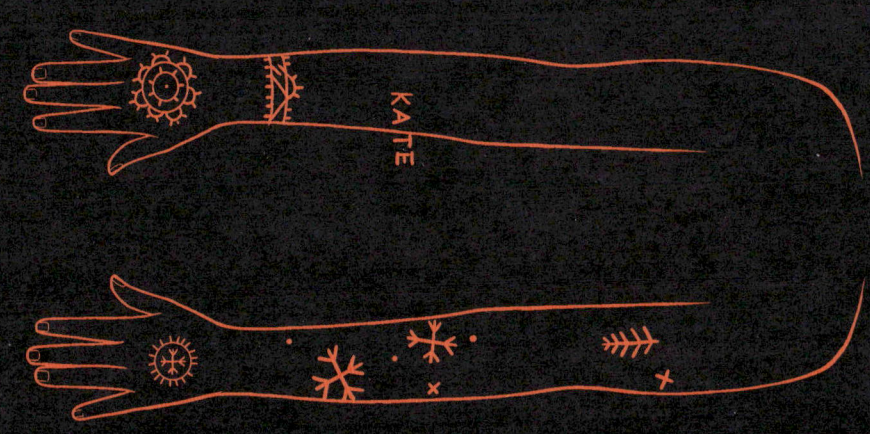

Traditional Tattoos of Women in the Balkans: Jajce, a Case Study in Bosnia and Herzegovina

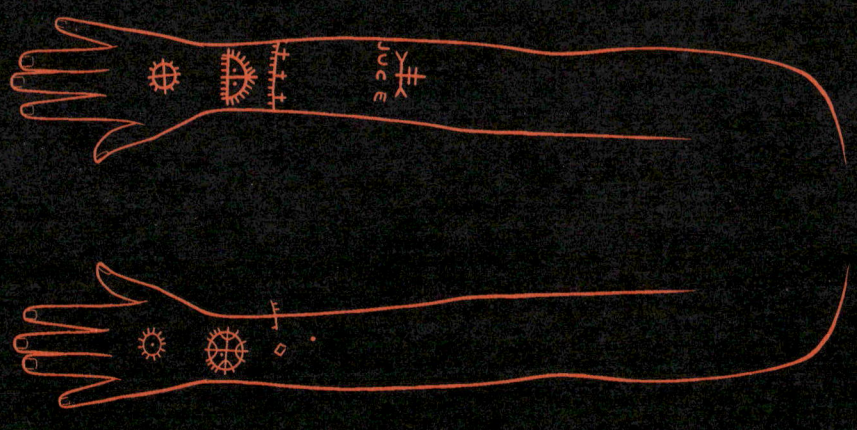

— Nataša Ilinčić

In the rural villages of the mountainous areas of Bosnia and Herzegovina, and in the Croatian hinterland, you can still find elderly women with faded, deep-blue inscriptions on the skin of their hands, arms, and sometimes chests. What they share in common is their belonging to the Catholic religion and their now-advanced age. Almost all of them are older than seventy, and they are the last bearers of this tradition, which gradually began to disappear after World War II.

The practice of traditional tattoos among the Catholic population of these regions is locally known as *bocanje* or *sicanje* ("puncturing, pricking").

Archeological and historical sources have confirmed that this is a tradition that is thousands of years old. It was already present among the native Illyrian people, as may be observed from their painted Greek vases and other classical sources, and it is possible that its roots go back to even more remote times.

These tattoos are a display of pre-Christian symbolism, linked to the natural realm. The symbols can be subdivided into five main categories: schematic representations of crosses (called *križ*), circular elements with rays (*kolo,* wheel), semicircular elements (*ograda,* fence), plant motifs (*grančica*, *grain*, *jelica*: twig, branch, and spruce, respectively), and bracelets (*narukvica*).

The tradition continued during and after the Slavic migrations of the seventh century and Christianization, preserving its original form but adapting to a new context. During the Ottoman occupation, which began in the middle of the fourteenth century and went on for three centuries, tattoos were used both as a sign of distinction and ethnic-religious recognition and as decoration. These two functionalities continued even after the annexation of the Austro-Hungarian Empire.

A determining factor for the purposes of preservation was certainly the unique geography of the Balkan Peninsula. The area was not easy to access, and its high altitudes have often had a protective function over the course of history.

Direct sources pertaining to this practice in more-recent centuries have revealed that girls began to get tattoos at prepuberty or puberty. Tattoos were in many cases cyclical: New designs were often added each year, depending on the wishes of the tattooed women, who usually stopped getting tattoos once they were married.

This was an almost exclusively female practice, although there are also rare examples of tattooed men. Women had a set repertoire of symbols, and tattoos that covered a larger surface area of the body, and engaged in a cyclic and systematic application, whereas the occasional male tattoo was generally limited to a simple sign (often a cross).

The body's spring corresponded to the earths' spring, and women would get tattoos after the winter months, when nature began to reawaken.

Tattoos were generally done during the spring period preceding Easter ("when the trees flower"), when young people were going up the mountains to tend to their flocks of sheep. Many communities chose to tattoo themselves for a very specific festival, close to the spring equinox. One of the most common days was that of Sveti Josip (Saint Joseph, March 19).

These elements lead me to speculate that the tradition was linked not only to the rites of passage of becoming an adult, but also to the celebration of nature's cycles.

Tattooing was a community practice. People would go to the same house, and girls would tattoo one another, often guided by the older, expert women.

The most commonly used tattooing tool was a single sewing needle. The most widespread technique consisted of preparing a dense mixture with the coloring substance and various other ingredients. This was used to draw the desired symbol, which was then punctured into the skin.

Generally, the base of the mixture seems to have been the same everywhere: *čađa* (soot) or, rarely, *ugljeni prah* (carbon dust). These substances were combined with other ingredients to create a paste. These included, depending on local customs, water, saliva, breas milk, animal milk, honey, *rakija* (fruit brandy), or fat.

The Balkan tattooing tradition has been disappearing since the middle of the twentieth century. Causes can be traced back to the overall internal dynamics linked to the changed political, economic, and social situation, rather than to outside forces. The Yugoslavia of the 1950s was indeed headed toward a new political landscape of a socialist bent, which was poorly prepared to address ethnic and religious particularisms. Likewise, there were new dynamics introduced by schooling and the gradual abandonment of agrarian rhythms, as well as the occupations linked to sheep farming, which in the history of traditional tattoos had had an important role.

In my work, I've combined historical-archeological inquiry with ethnographic field research. The latter was conducted in the summer of 2016 in the territory of Jajce, in central Bosnia, on the occasion of the celebration of Sveti Ivo Krstitelj (St. John the Baptist) in Podmilačje. There I had the opportunity to talk with the last bearers of this tradition and collect photographic material firsthand.

In the Jajce area, girls would get their first tattoo between the ages of ten and fifteen. A girl would independently decide whether or not to do so. This period coincided with an increase in her own independence, as attested by the power she had to leave the house alone to go out in the pastures. The tattooing continued cyclically: Each spring, new symbols could be added. The enhancement of the decoration of her skin mirrored her developing body.

Tattoos were applied in a community environment during an event known as *prelo* (from the verb *presti,* to spin, which is not dissimilar to the word *filò* of Venetian farming tradition). Originally linked to the activity of sheep farming, *prelo* was also a social gathering. It was held in a fairly large house that could host a reasonable number of people, usually in cold periods during the year, when people were taking a break from the fields. *Prelo* combined work activities (spinning, carpentry, basketweaving) with opportunities for socialization and leisure (such as storytelling, sharing songs, courtship, and indeed, also, tattoos). Girls tattooed one another, but their first tattoo was done by a more expert woman.

Here too, tattoos were done on the eve of the spring equinox (Sveti Josip).

The mixture was prepared with soot from the wood of a fir tree, extracted using a *sač* (portable stove that was already in use among the ancient Illyrians), then mixed with honey and applied using a sewing needle. "Light hands" were appreciated (for less painful tattoos), and traditional plant therapy and health knowledge was used to prevent the tattoos from getting infected (thanks to the medicinal properties of the resin of Pinaceae and honey, for example).

The women with whom I spoke affirmed they did not know the meaning of the symbols, and that to them they seemed to be mere decorations that at one time also served the purpose of ethnic-religious distinction and as a defense against the forced conversions to Islamic religion during the period of the Ottoman occupation.

The interviewed women mentioned as reasons for stopping this type of tattooing the fact that the practice had grown obsolete (being viewed as a *starina,* something from another time), the reluctance of openly showing one's own ethnic-religious affiliation due to the new political system, the influence of schooling, and teachers' disapproval of this practice.

Political and sociocultural changes had led to the end of an era, and with it the end of this particular tradition.

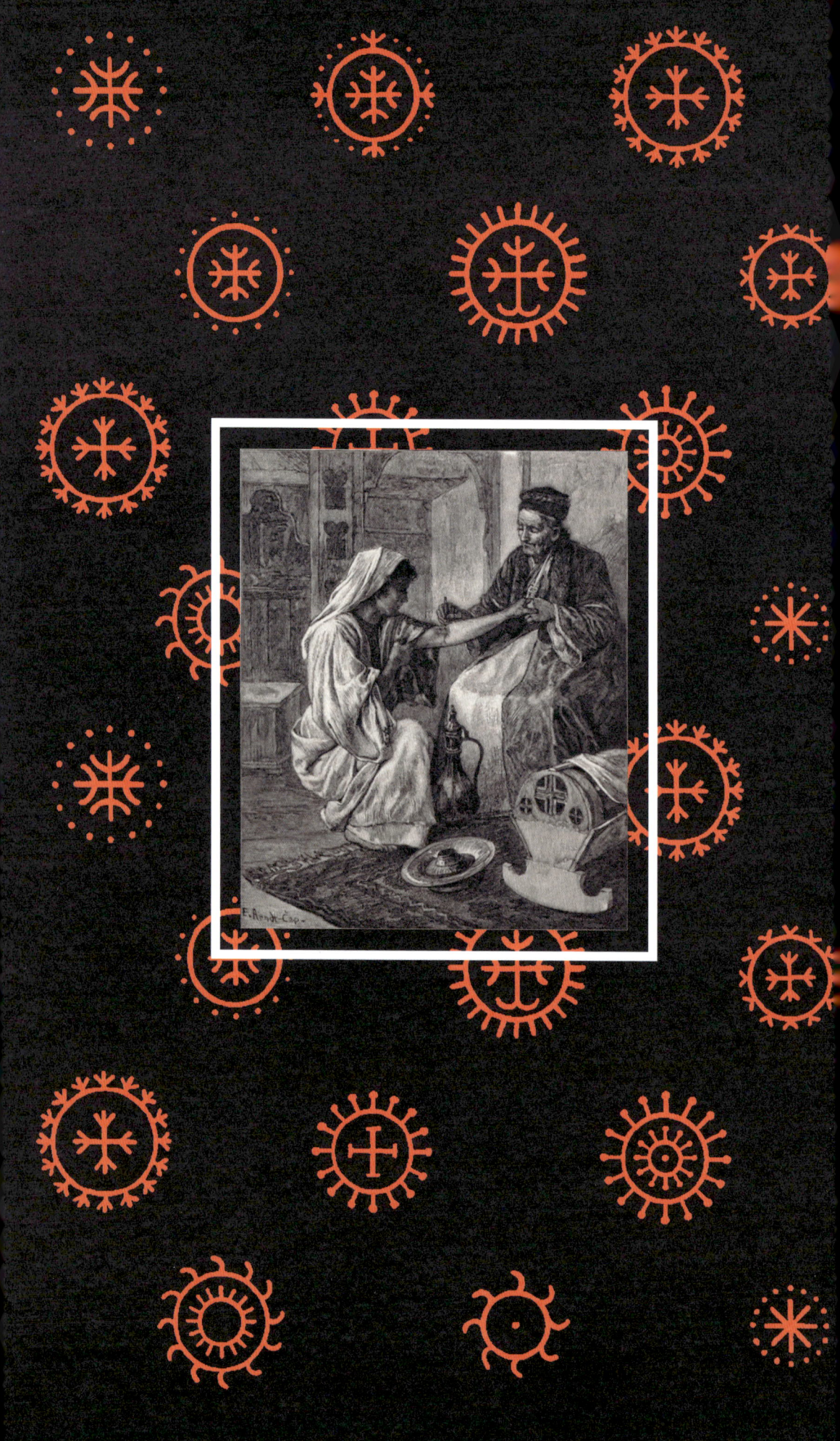

On opposite page:
Applying a tattoo, from "Die oesterreichisch-ungarische Monarchie," in *Wort und Bild, Bosnien und Hercegovina* (Vienna: k.k. Hof-und Statsdrueckerei, Alfred von Hoelder, 1901), vol. 22. Volksleben, by Čiro Truhelka.

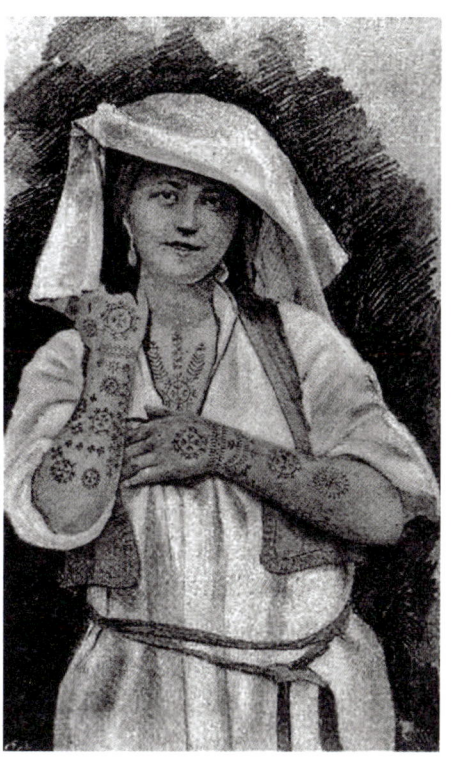

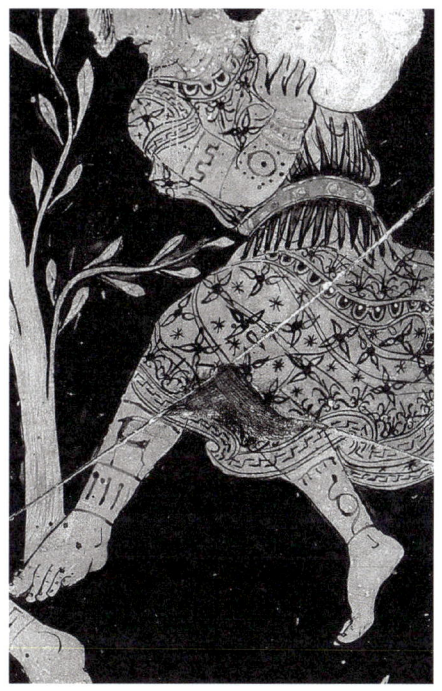

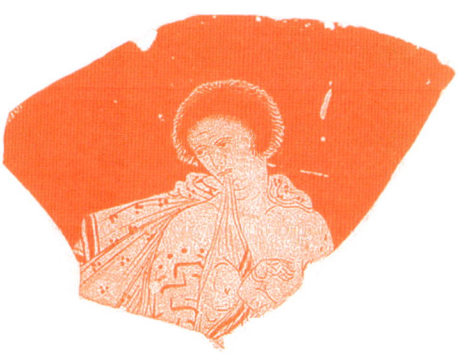

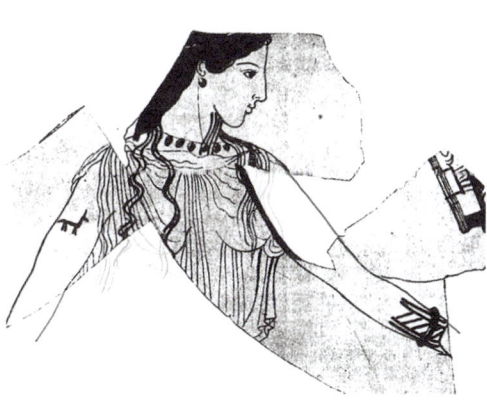

Top right: Woman from Bila Valley, by Čiro Truhelka

Bottom: Thracian tattoos on Greek vases

Križ [cross]

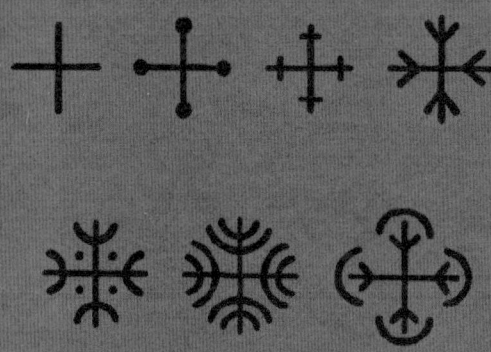

Kolo [ring]

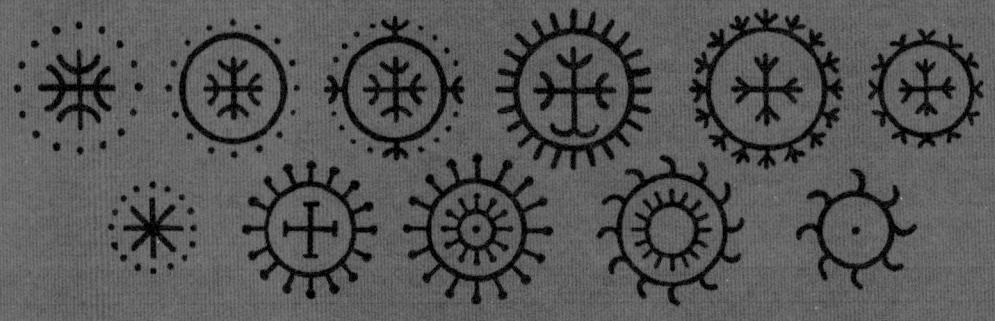

Narukvica [bracelet]

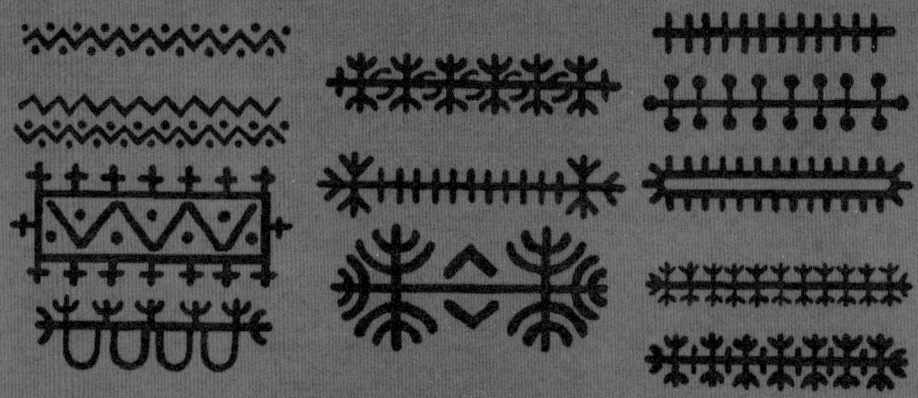

Ograda [fence]

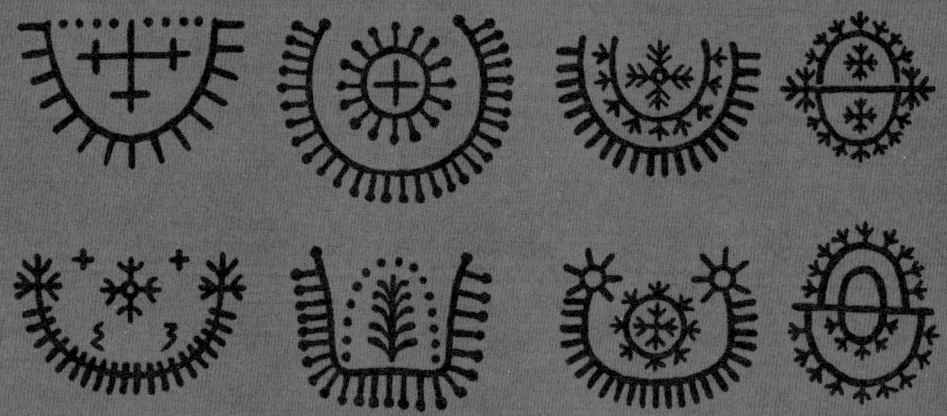

Grančica [twig]

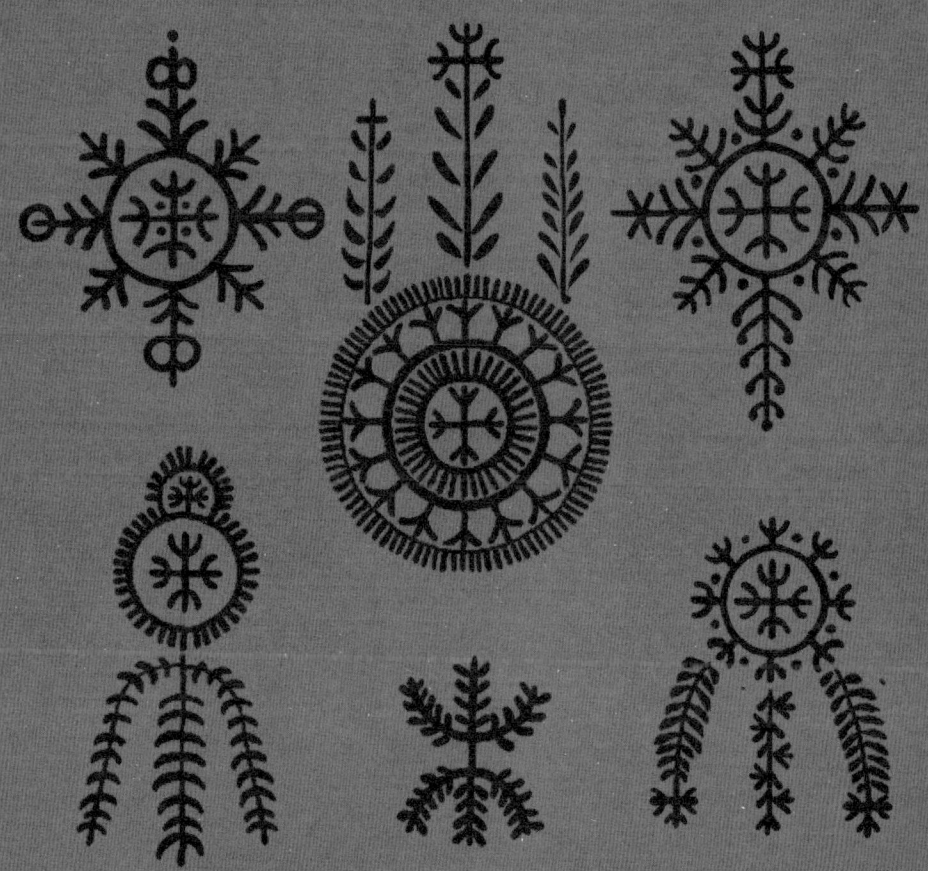

128

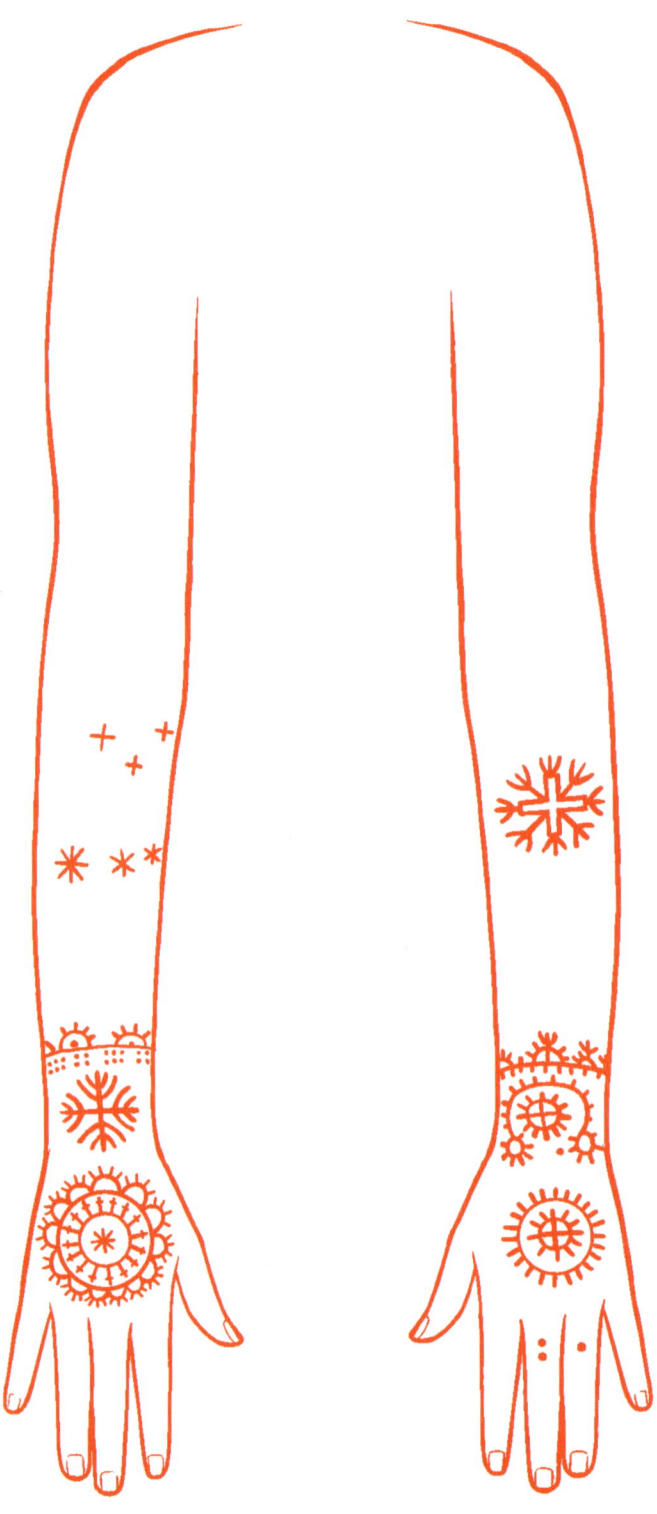

Anđela Jakovljević and her tattoos, Jajce 2016

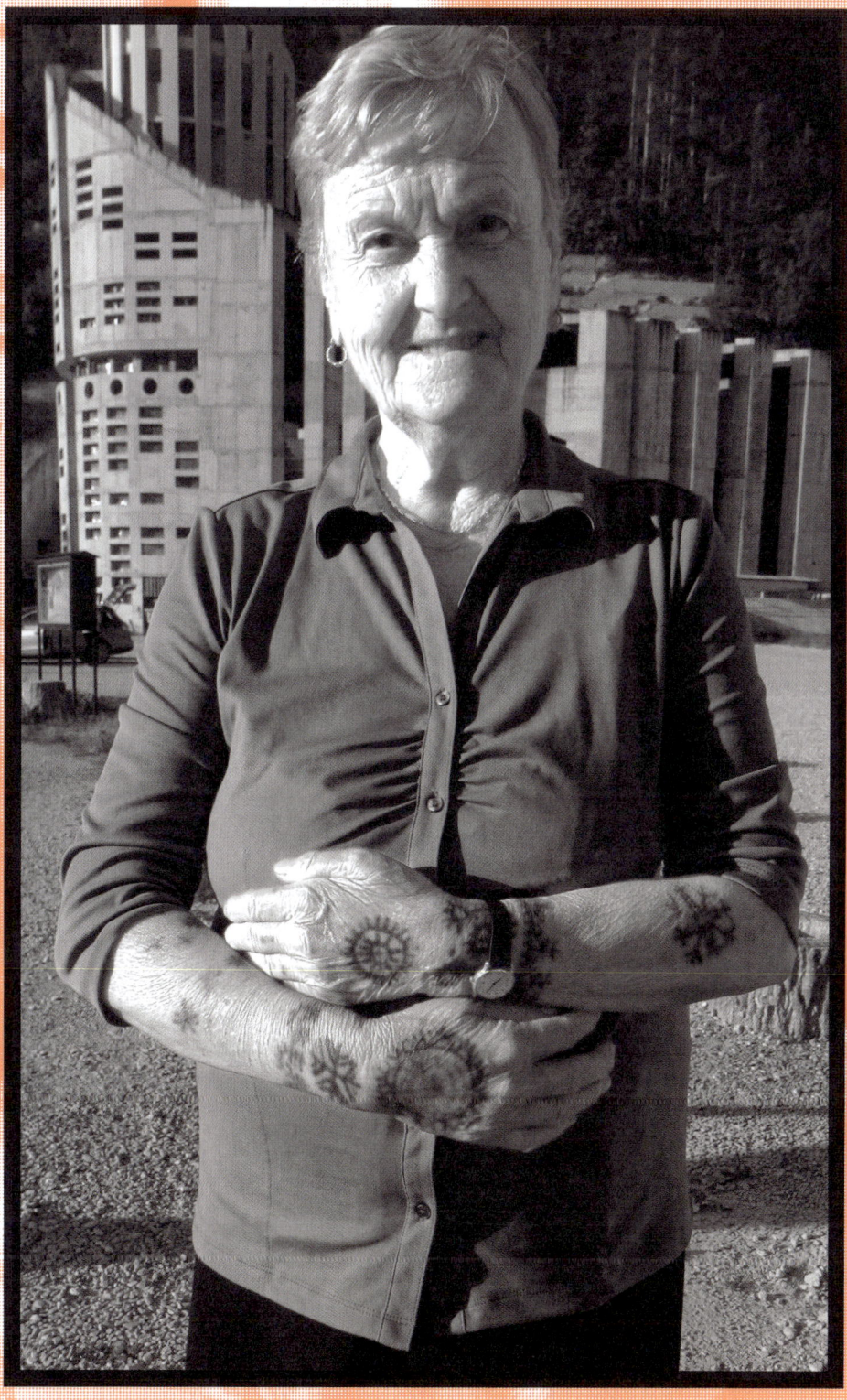

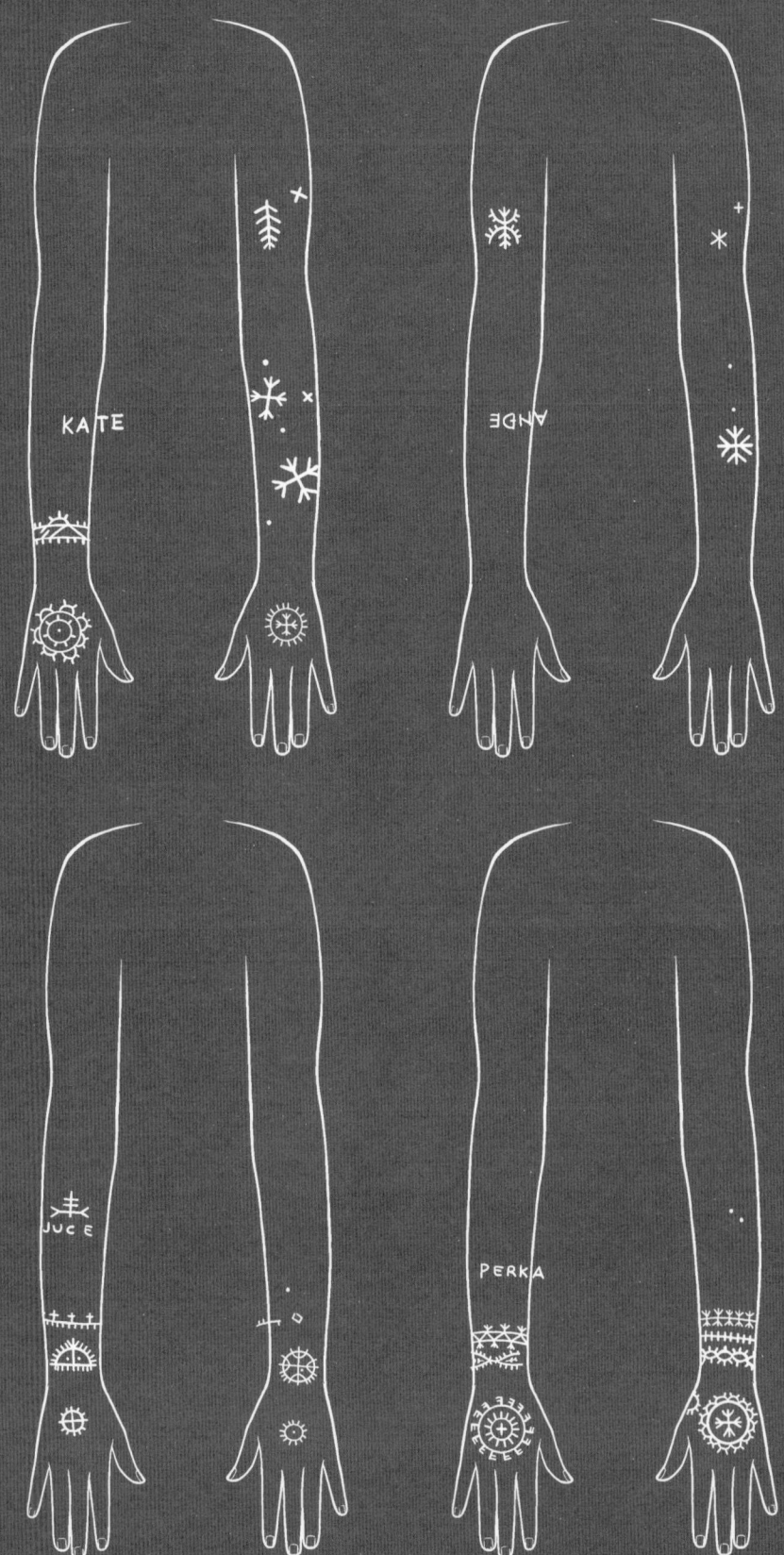

From top left: The tattoos of Kata Petrović, Andja Klarić, Luce Jezečić, and Perka, Jajce 2016

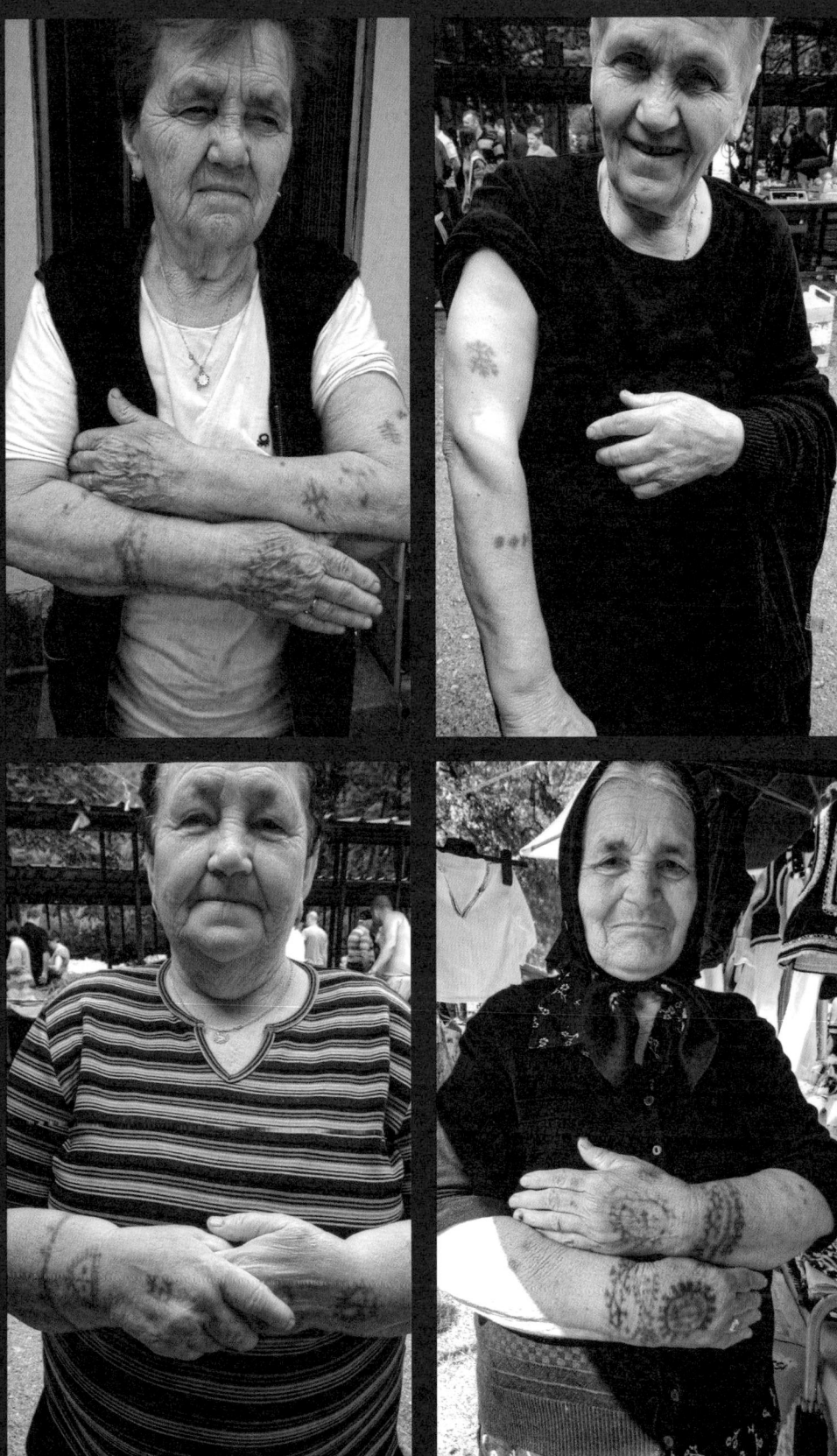

From top left: Kata Petrović, Andja Klarić, Luce Jezečić, and Perka, Jajce 2016

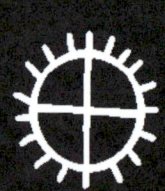
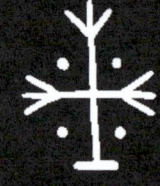
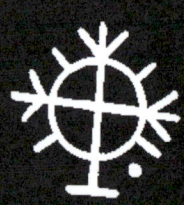
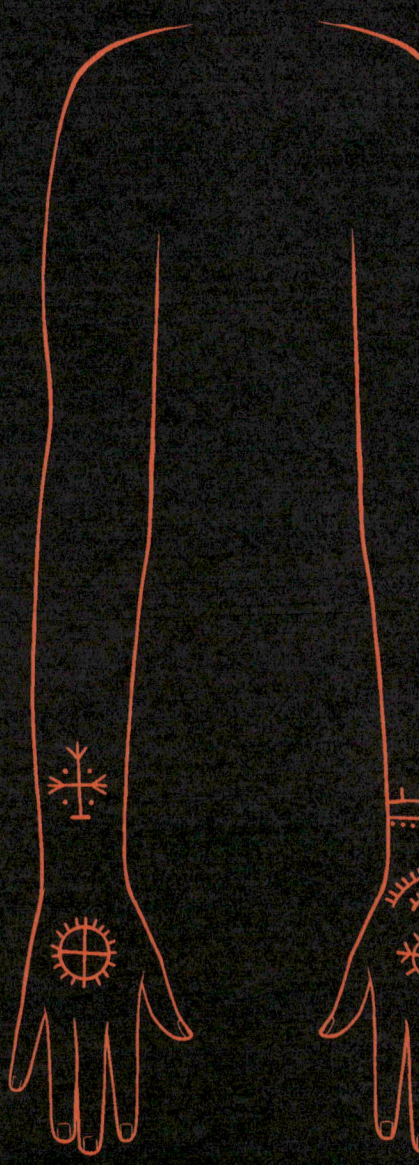
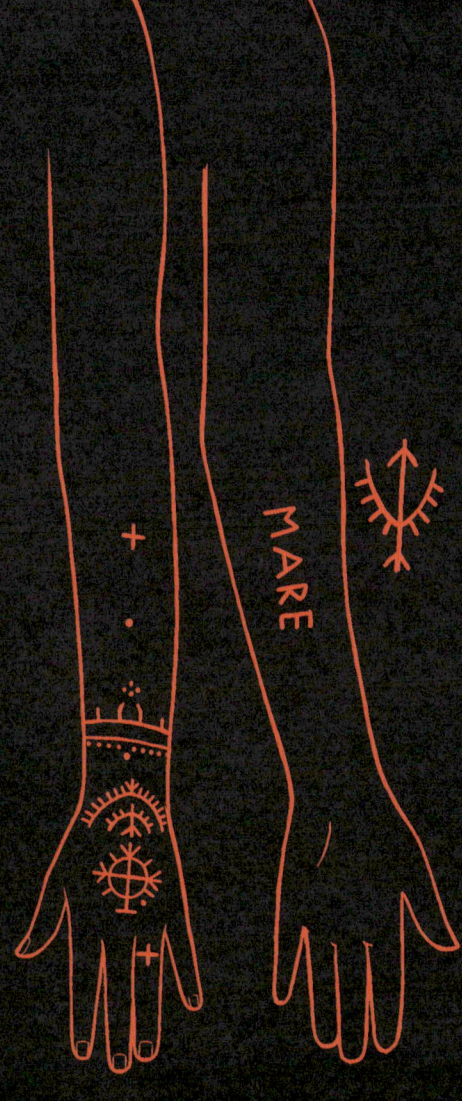

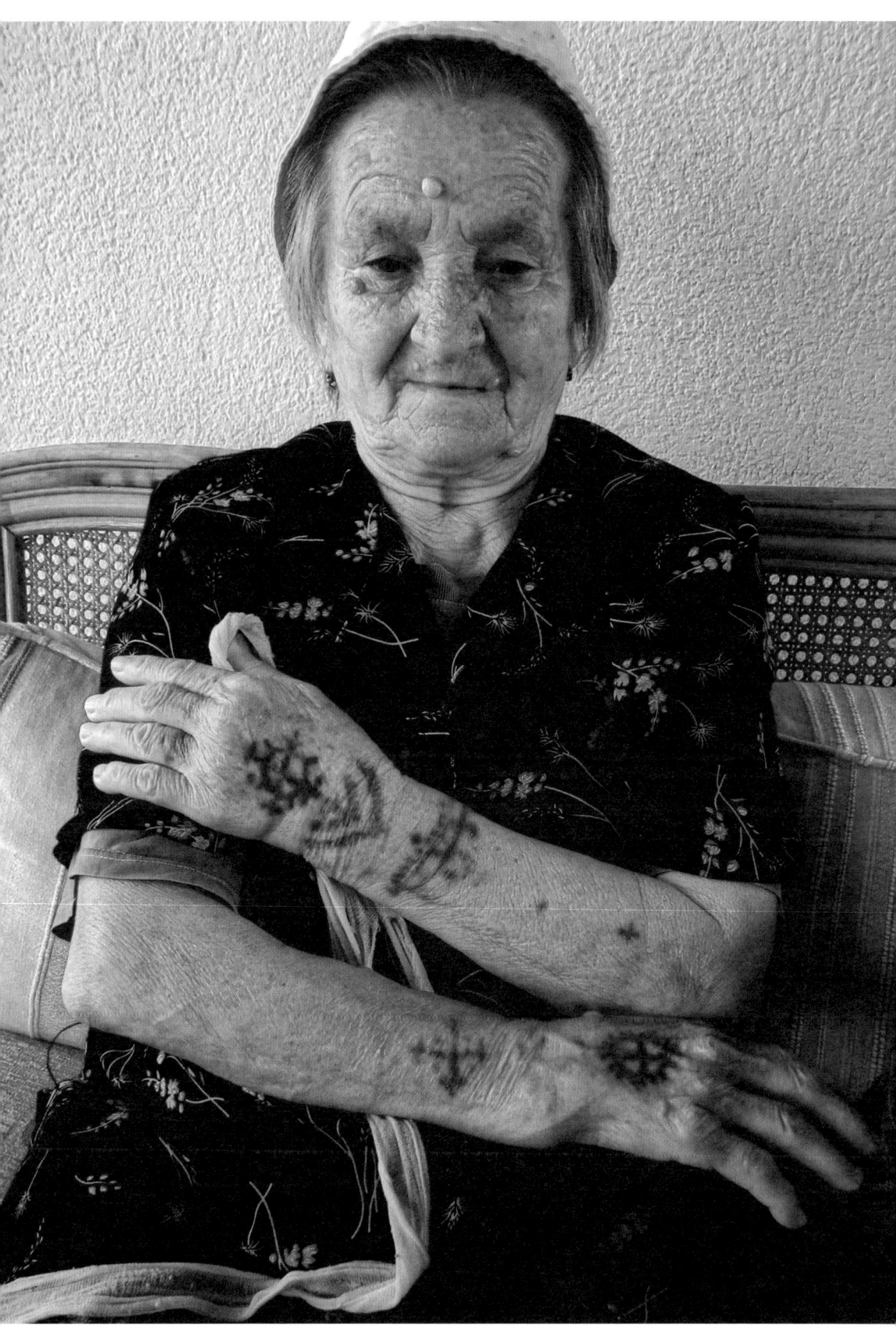

Marija Ladan and her tattoos, Jajce 2016

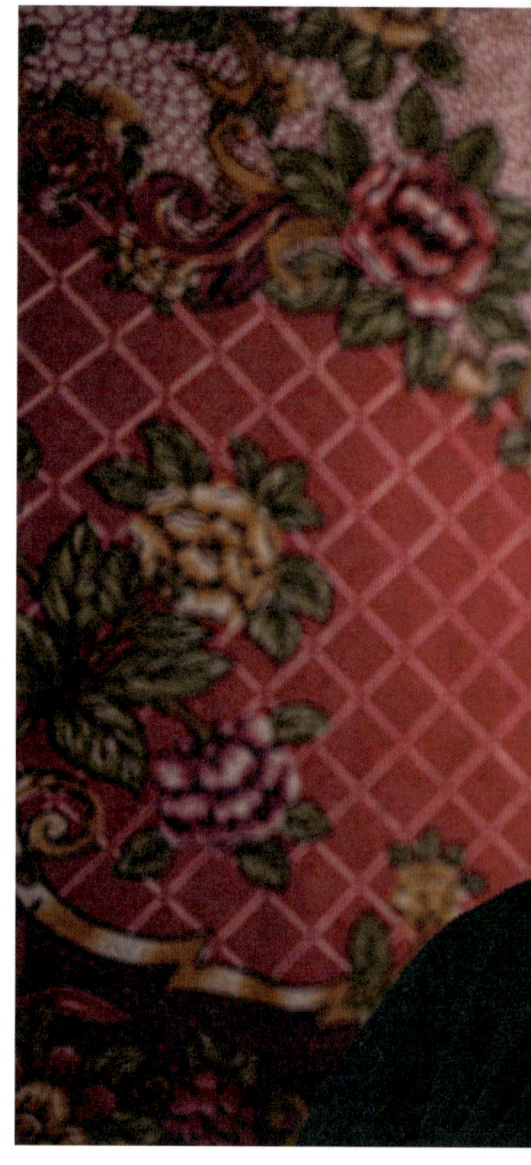

Algeria

Zohra Bensemra is an Algerian photojournalist. She began her career at the paper *El Watan* as the first female photojournalist in Algeria and joined Reuters in 1997 to document the Algerian Civil War.

The project *Algeria's Tattoos of Beauty* was completed in 2015 among the Chaouia of the Aurès Mountains, a mountain range in eastern Algeria. In these communities, a woman's beauty was judged on the basis of her tattoos. Traditionally, the more tattoos a woman had, the more she was admired by the local men.

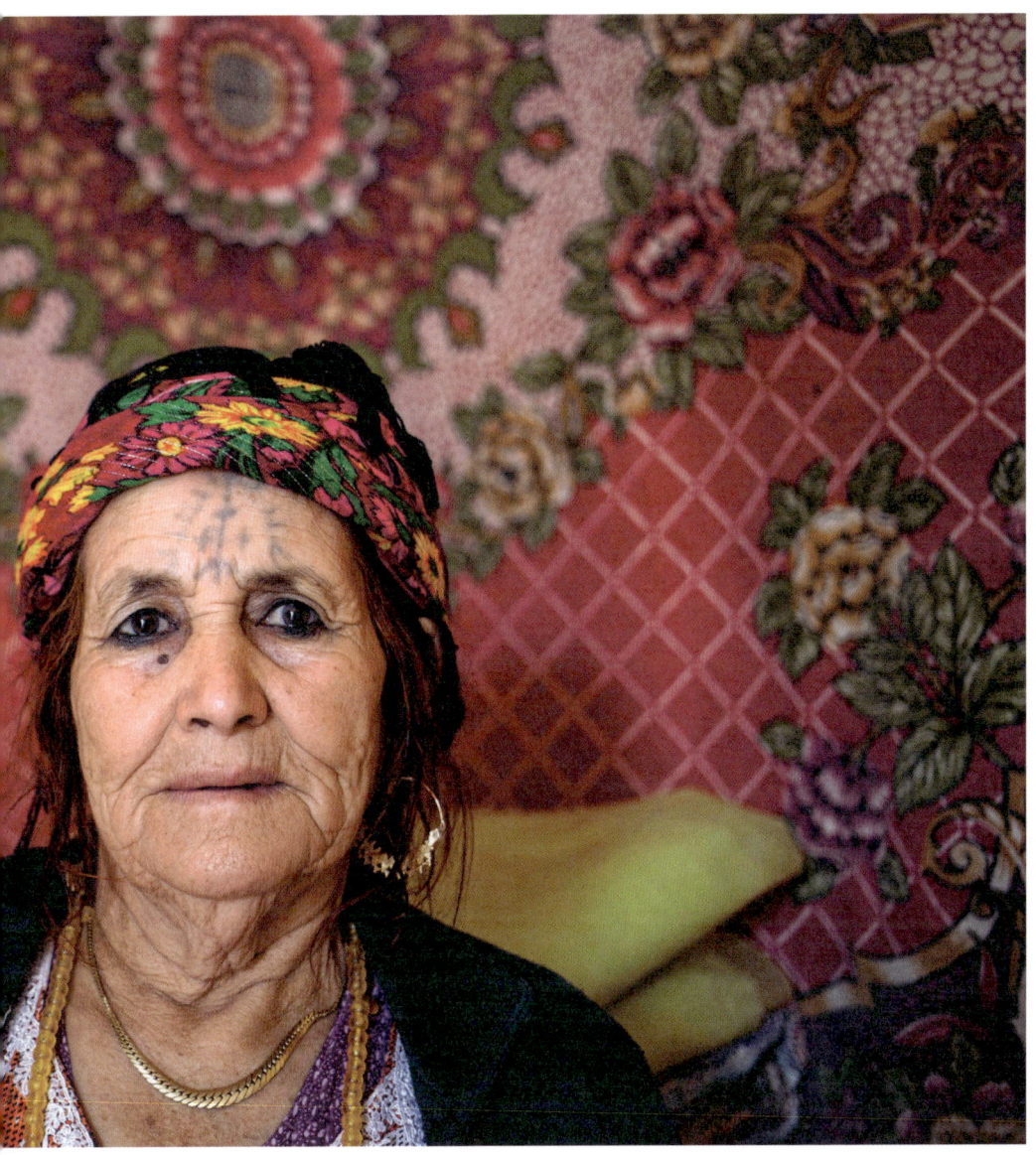

Fatma Haddad

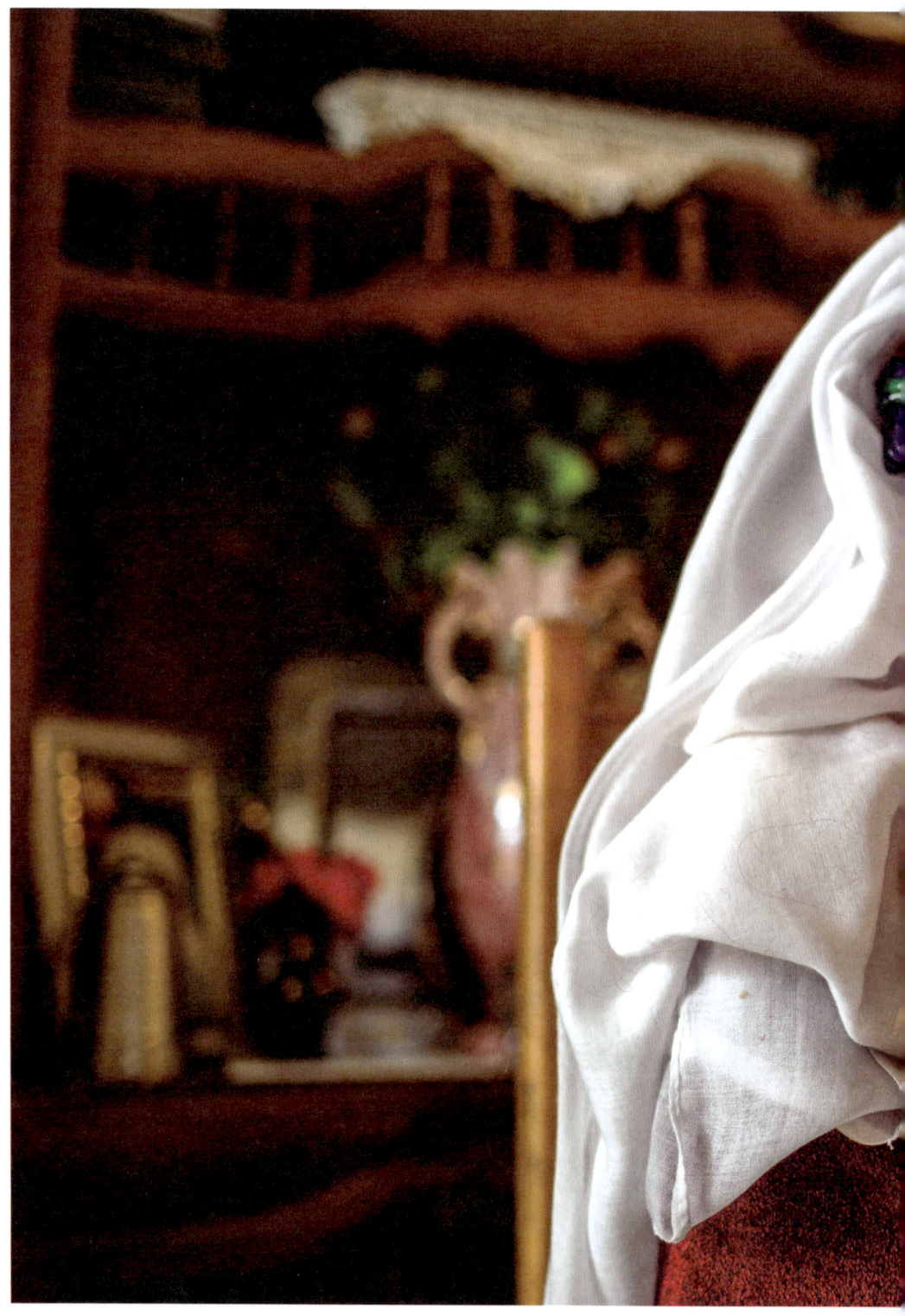

Fatma Badredine

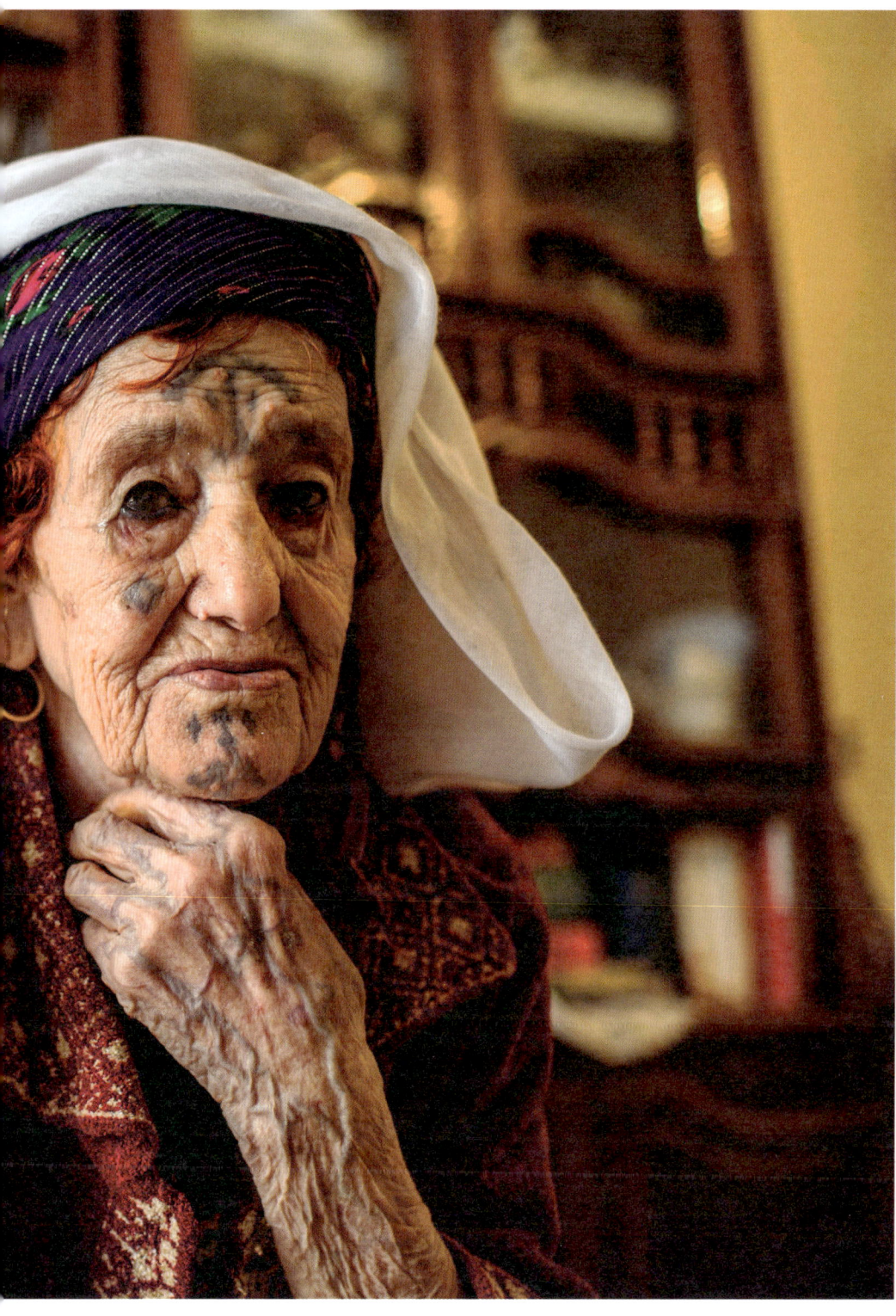

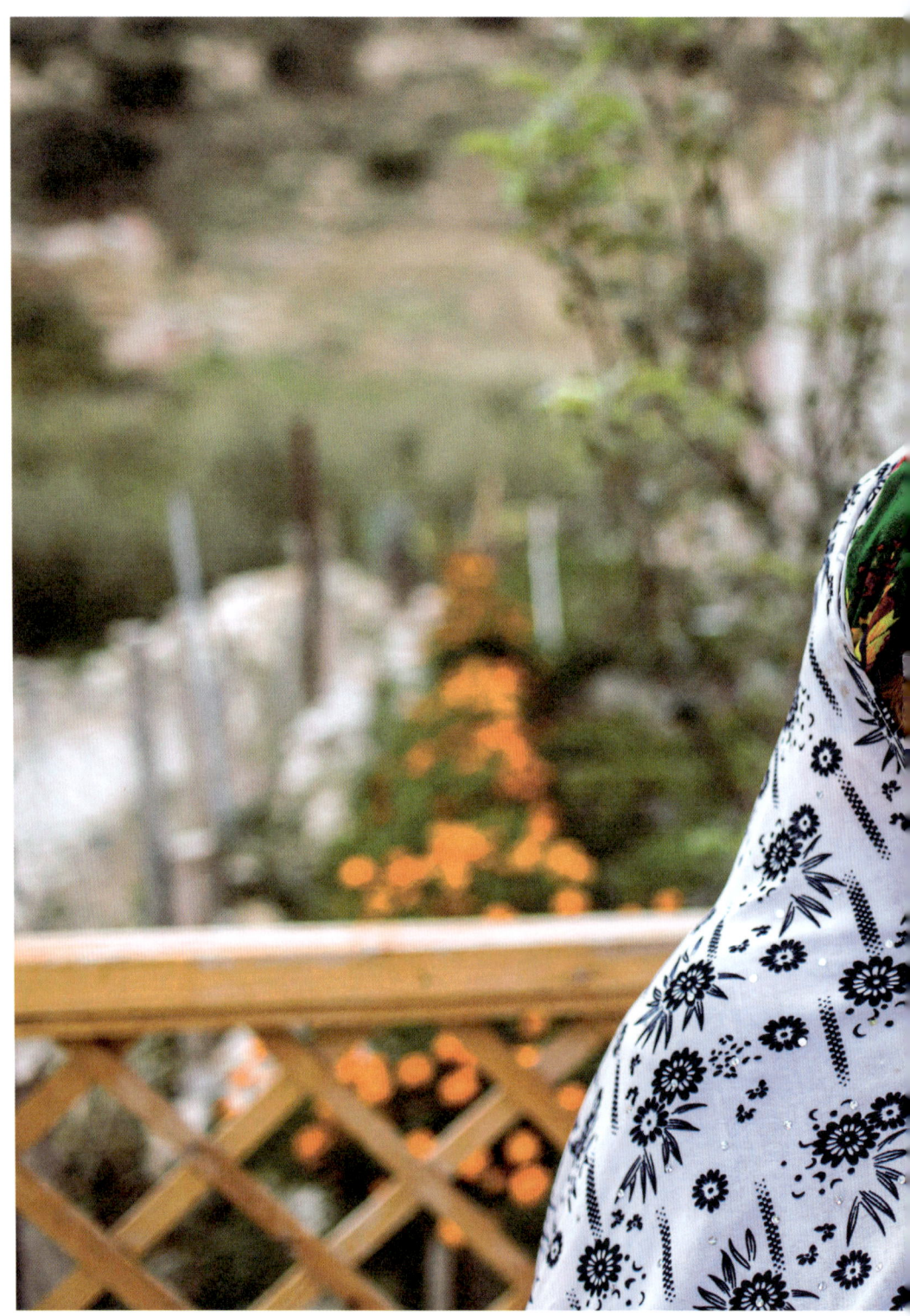

Djemaa Daoudi

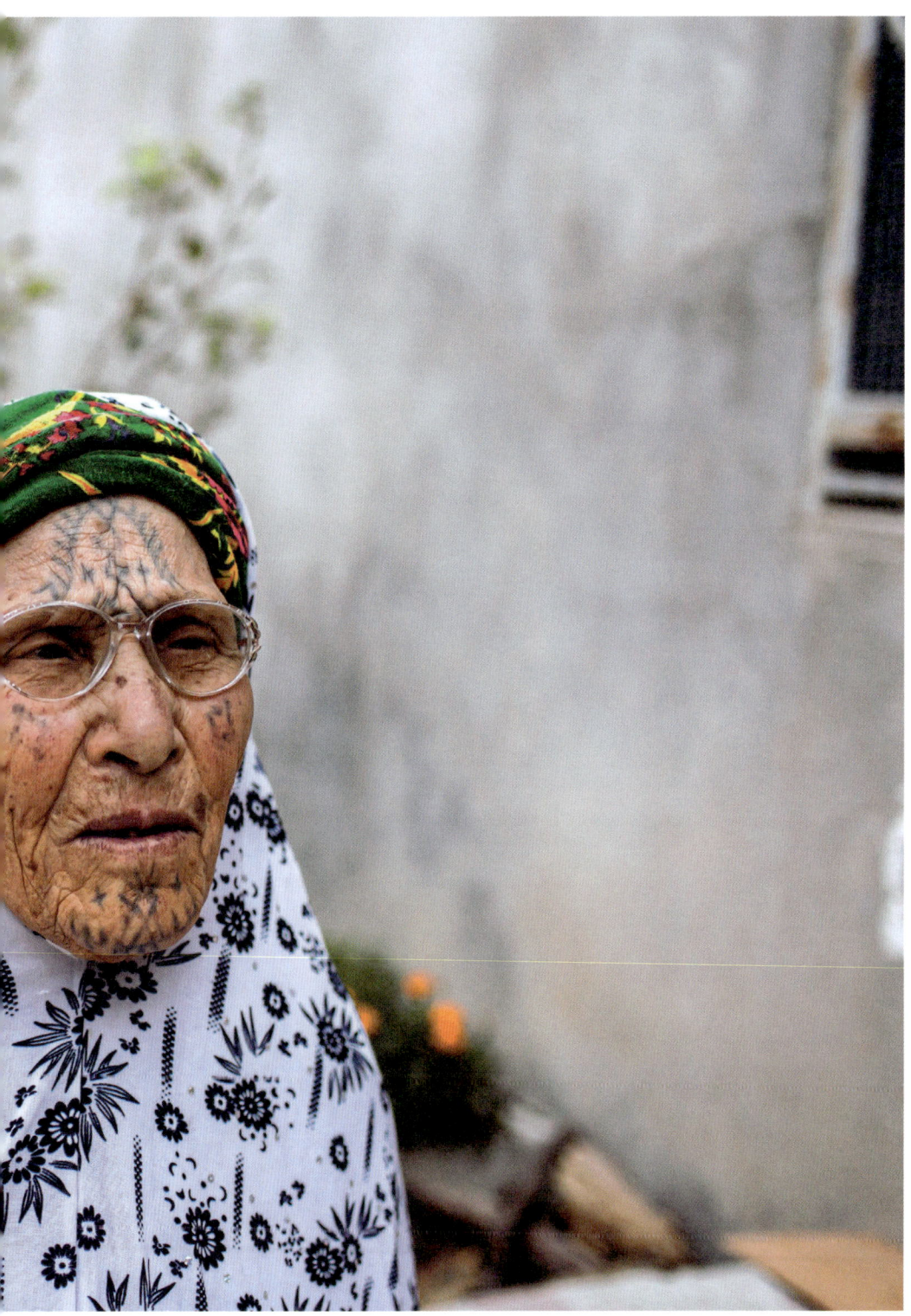

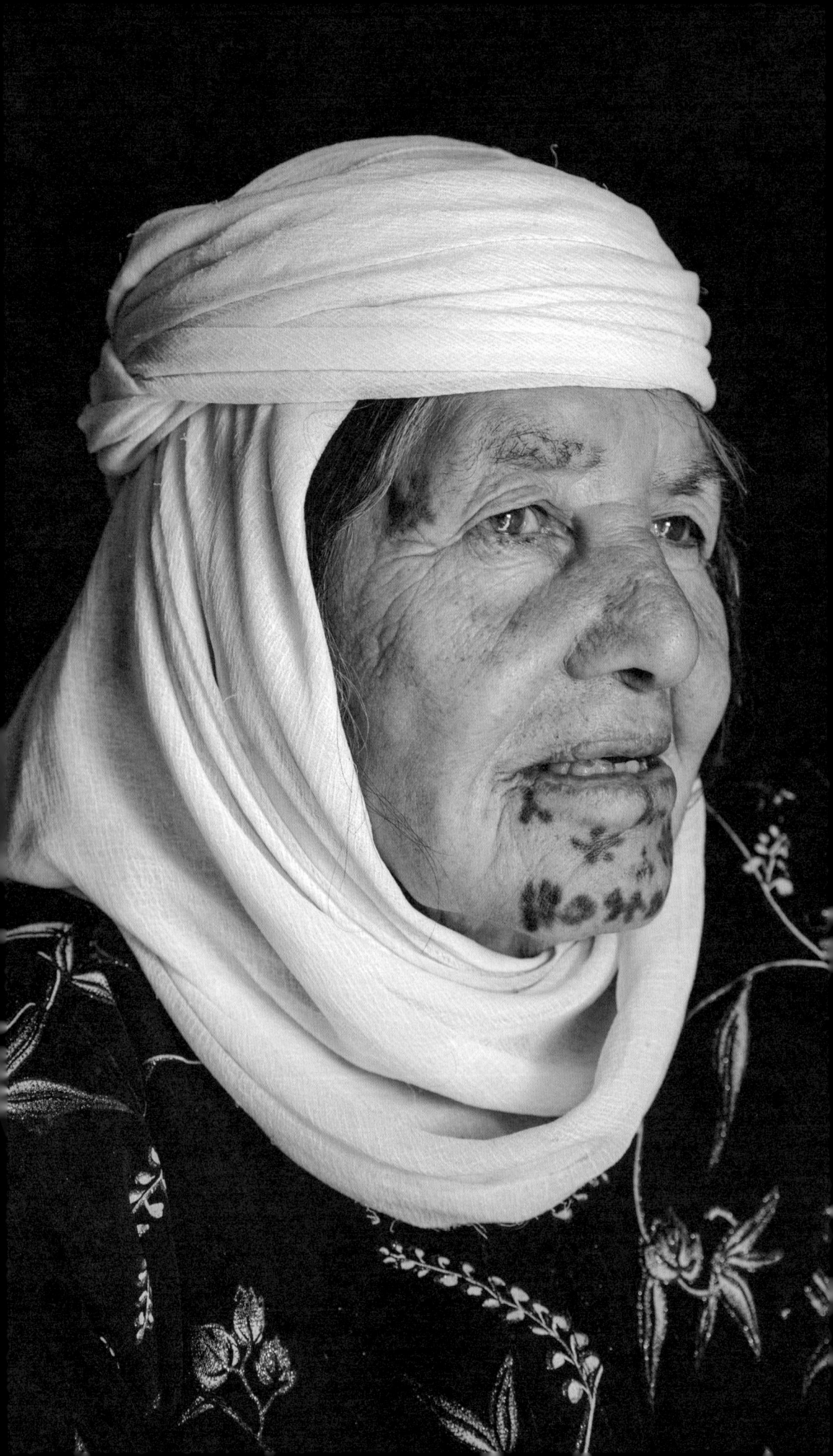

Turkey

Photographer Jodi Hilton, visiting the refugee camps in Turkey on the border with Kobane in Syria and Iraqi Kurdistan, has photographed certain older women who had the *deq* tattoo on their face. This form of tattooing is now disappearing. *Deq* tattooing was traditional not only among Kurdish women but was also widely practiced among Arabs and by women in general throughout the Islamic world. It was originally considered an element of great beauty.

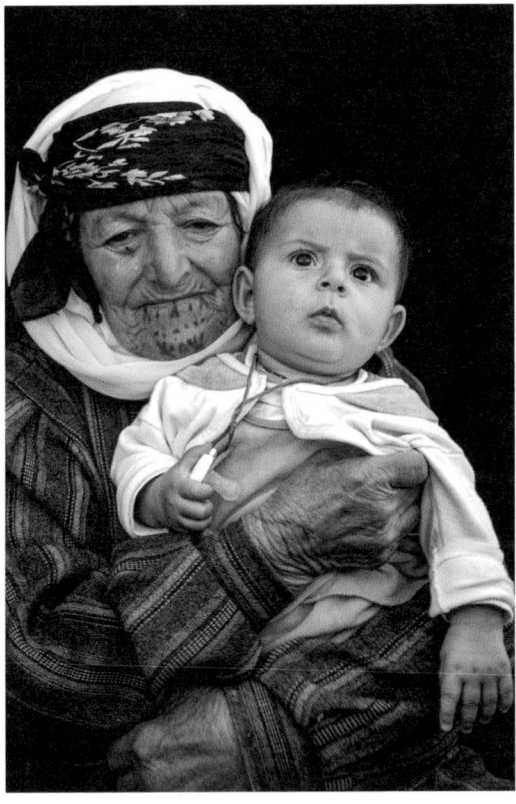

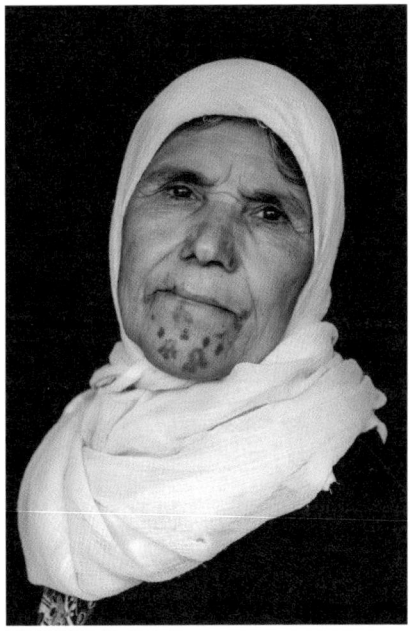

Suruç, province of Şanliurfa, Turkey. Noyle Muzlem, fifty-five years old, from the village of El Ajak near Kobane, in the Rojava refugee camp in Suruç, Turkey. "It's an old tradition. I actually don't like my tattoos."

Suruç, province of Şanliurfa, Turkey. Adule Imam Sheik Muhamad, sixty years old, from Kobane. "I didn't want the tattoos," she said, "because they are very painful, but when I saw the result, I liked them. Back then, people used to say they were beautiful, but not anymore."

On opposite page: Suruç, province of Şanliurfa, Turkey. Meliha Omer, approximately eighty years old, from the village of Girik near Kobane. She remembers getting her first tattoo when she was ten or eleven years old. "All of the women had tattoos," she recalls. "But when we understood it was *haram* [against Islam], we stopped doing it."

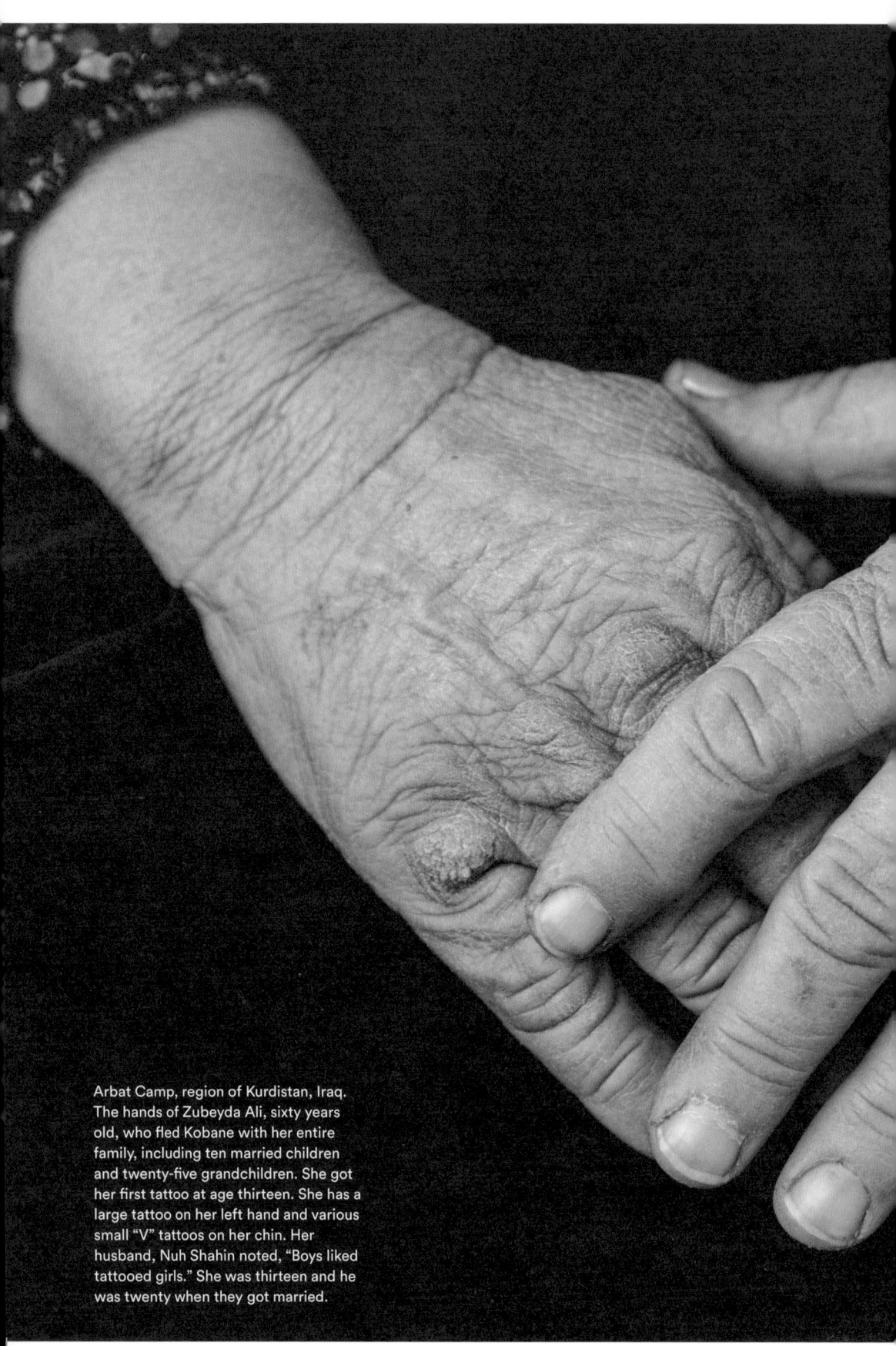

Arbat Camp, region of Kurdistan, Iraq.
The hands of Zubeyda Ali, sixty years
old, who fled Kobane with her entire
family, including ten married children
and twenty-five grandchildren. She got
her first tattoo at age thirteen. She has a
large tattoo on her left hand and various
small "V" tattoos on her chin. Her
husband, Nuh Shahin noted, "Boys liked
tattooed girls." She was thirteen and he
was twenty when they got married.

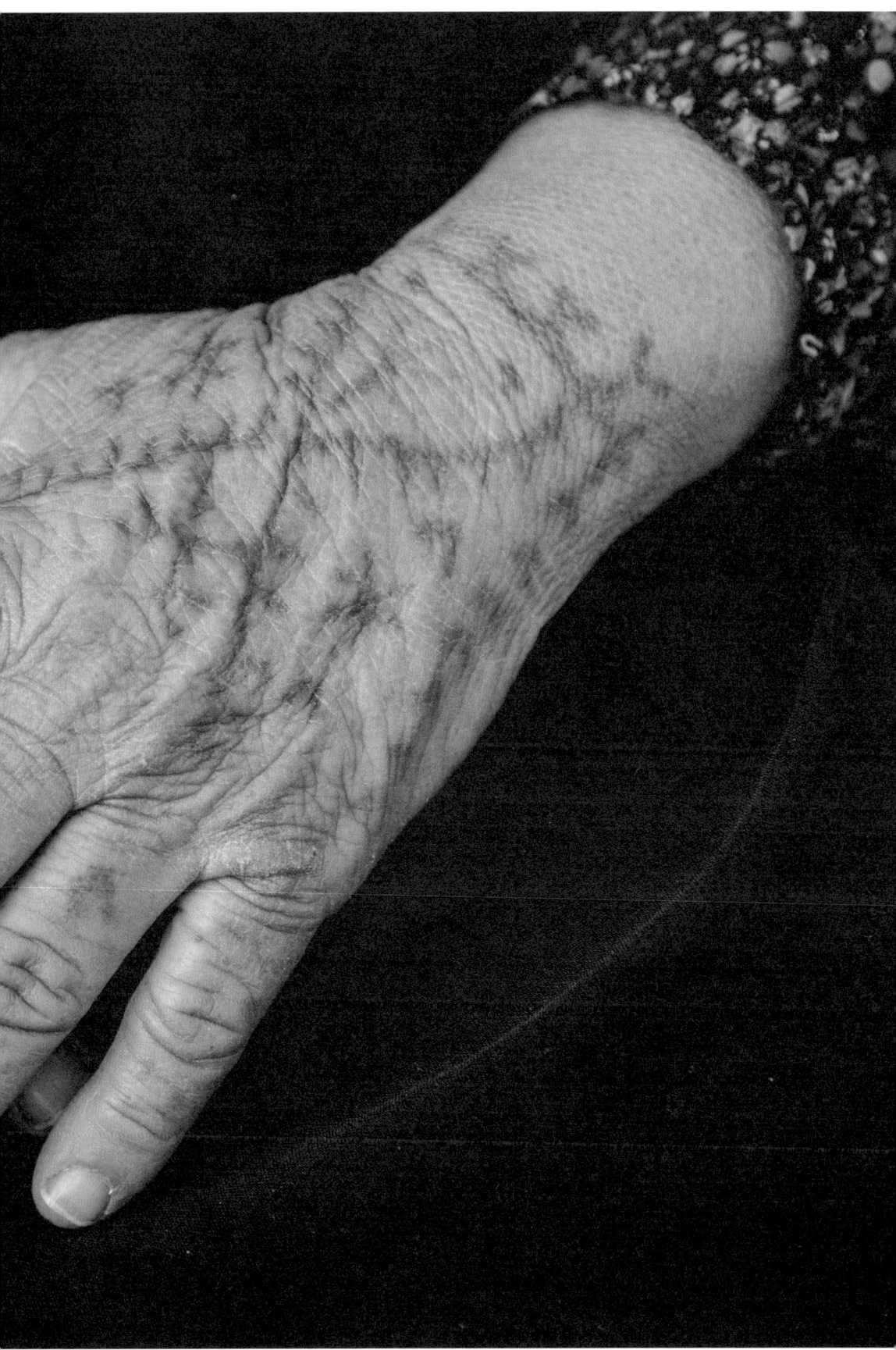

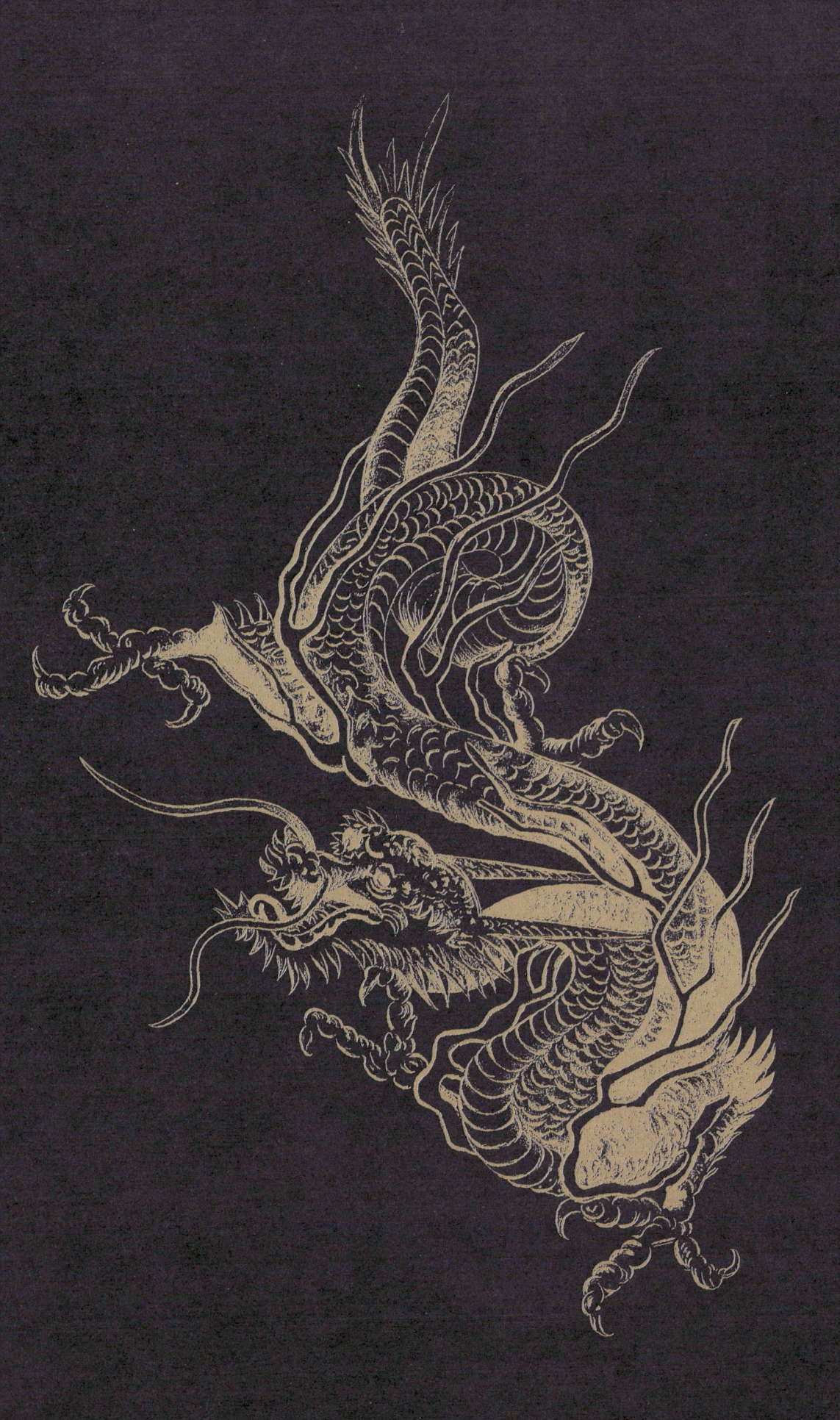

TATTOO GALLERY

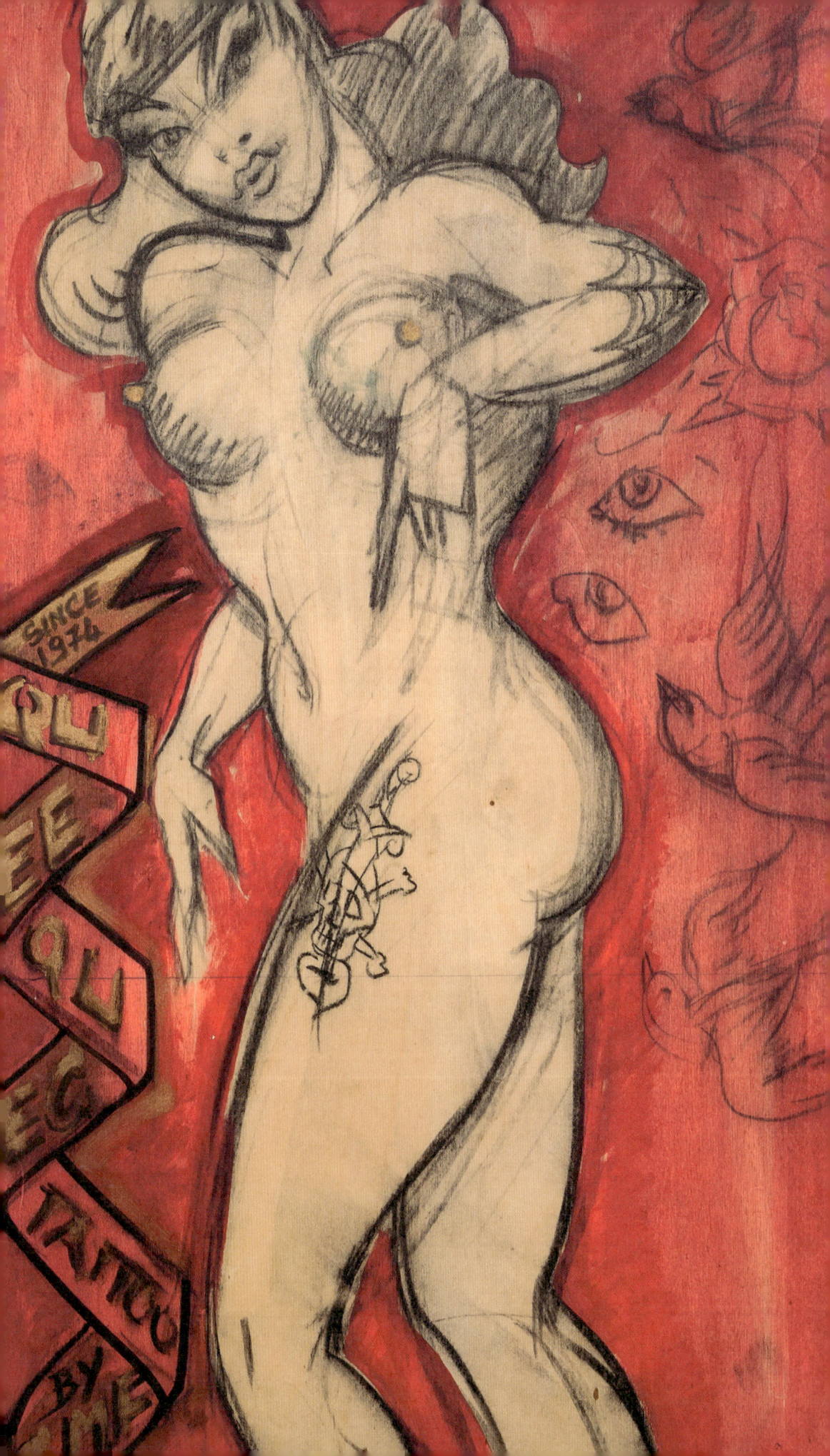

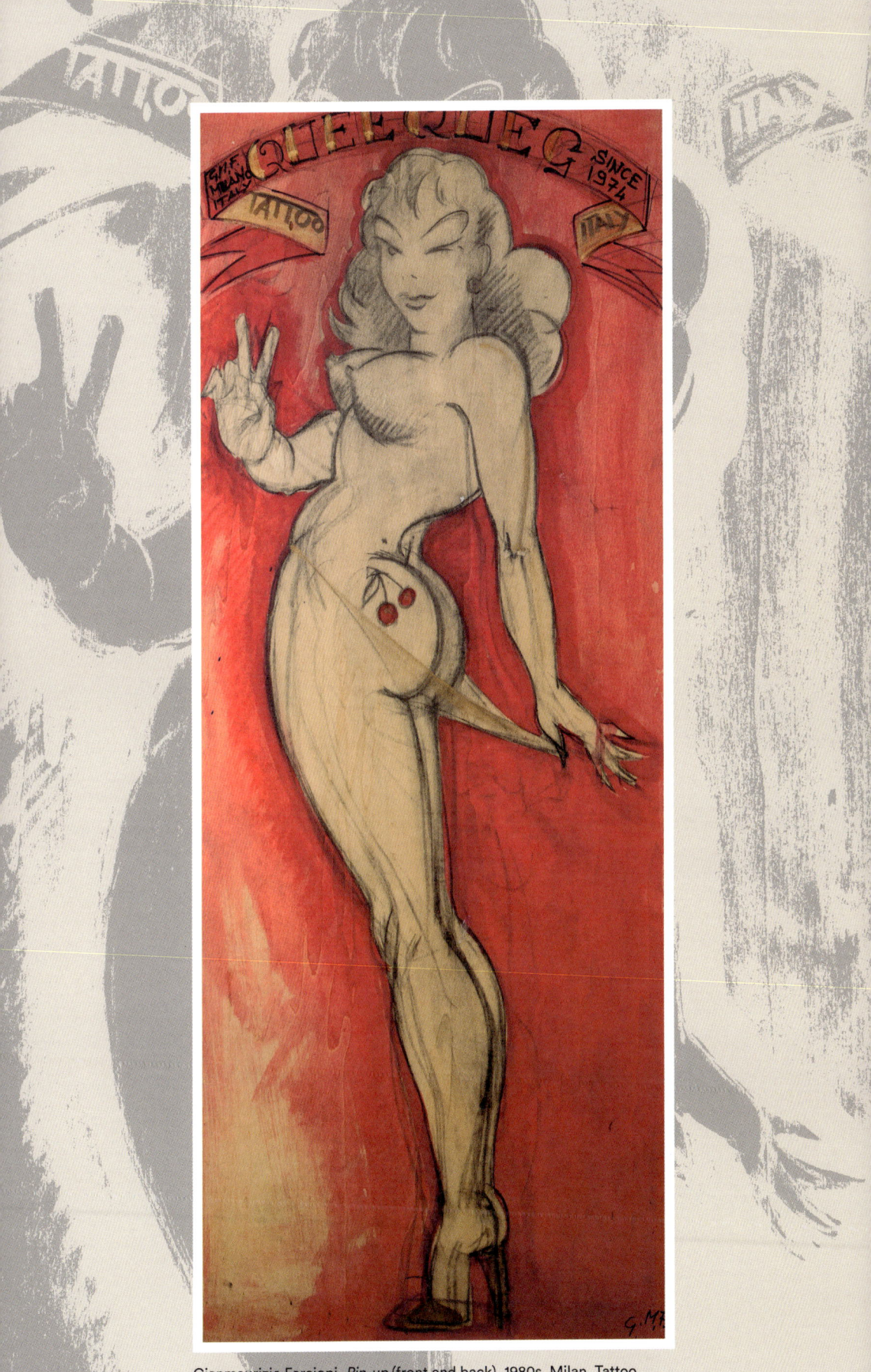

Gianmaurizio Fercioni, *Pin-up* (front and back), 1980s. Milan, Tattoo
Museo Gianmaurizio Fercioni.

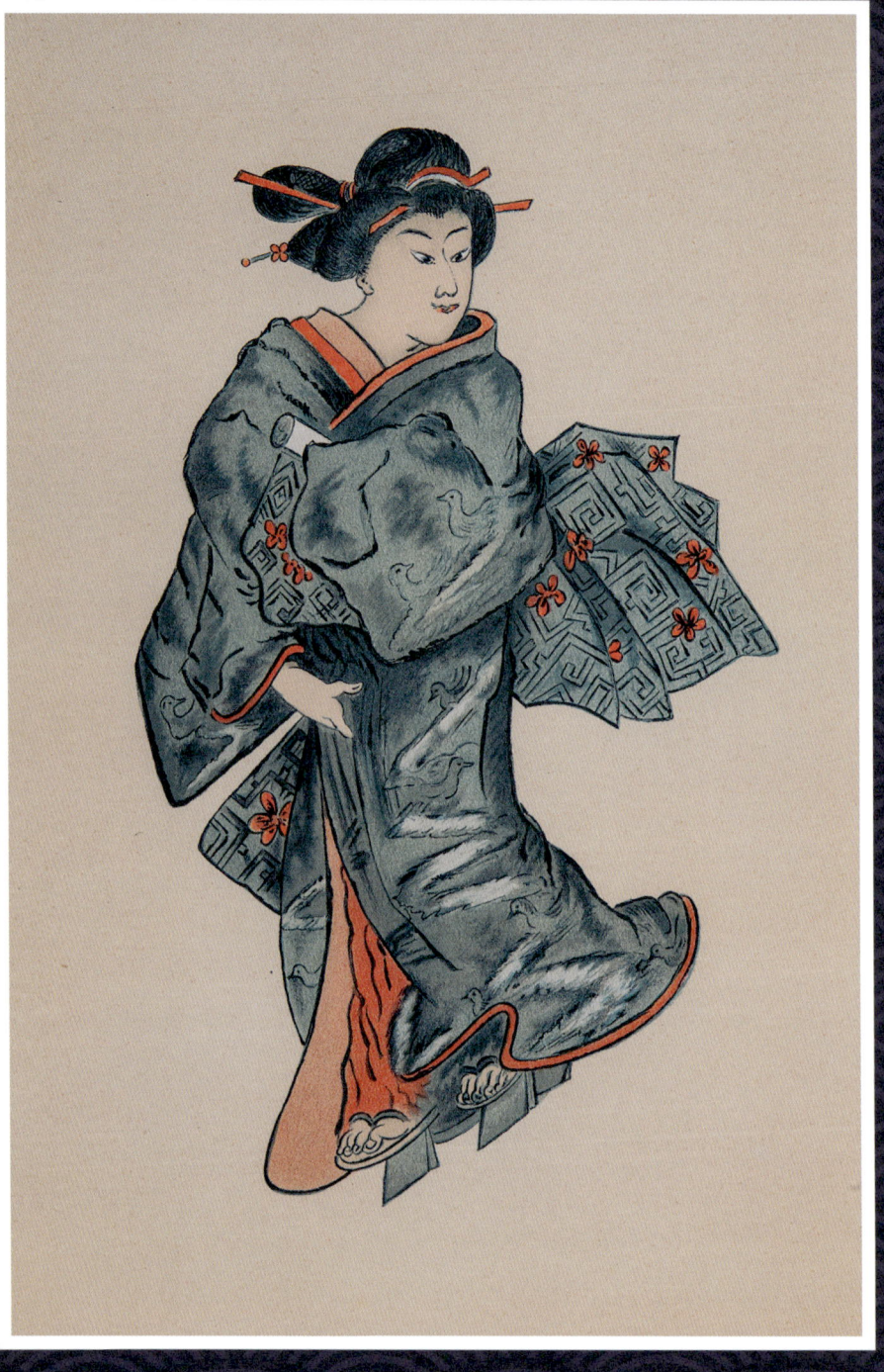

Drawings for Japanese tattoos, in *Wilhelm Joest, Tatowiren: Narbenzeichnen und Korperbemalen; Ein beittrag zur vergleichenden ethnologie* (Berlin: Asher, 1887). Milan, Tattoo Museo Gianmaurizio Fercioni.

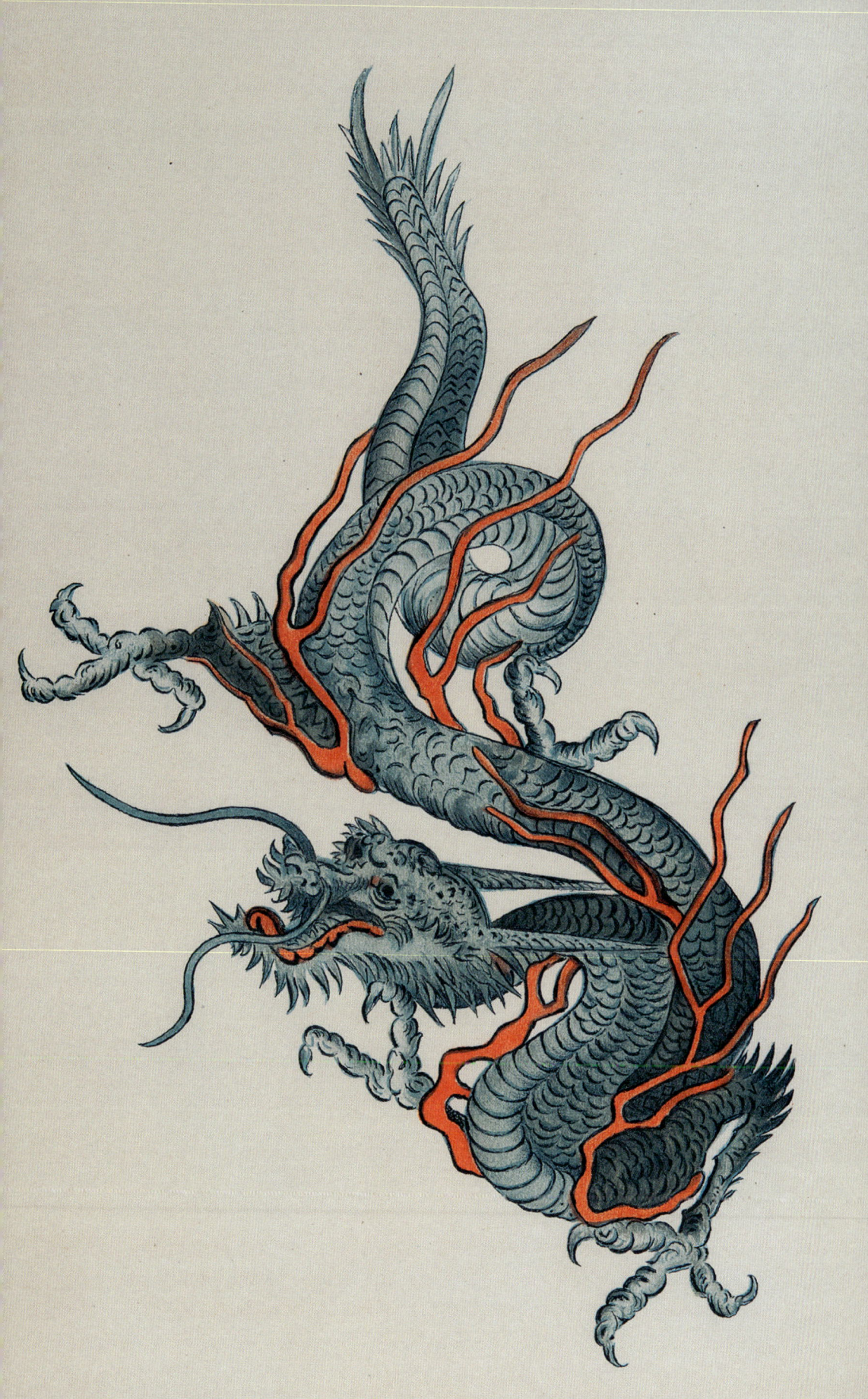

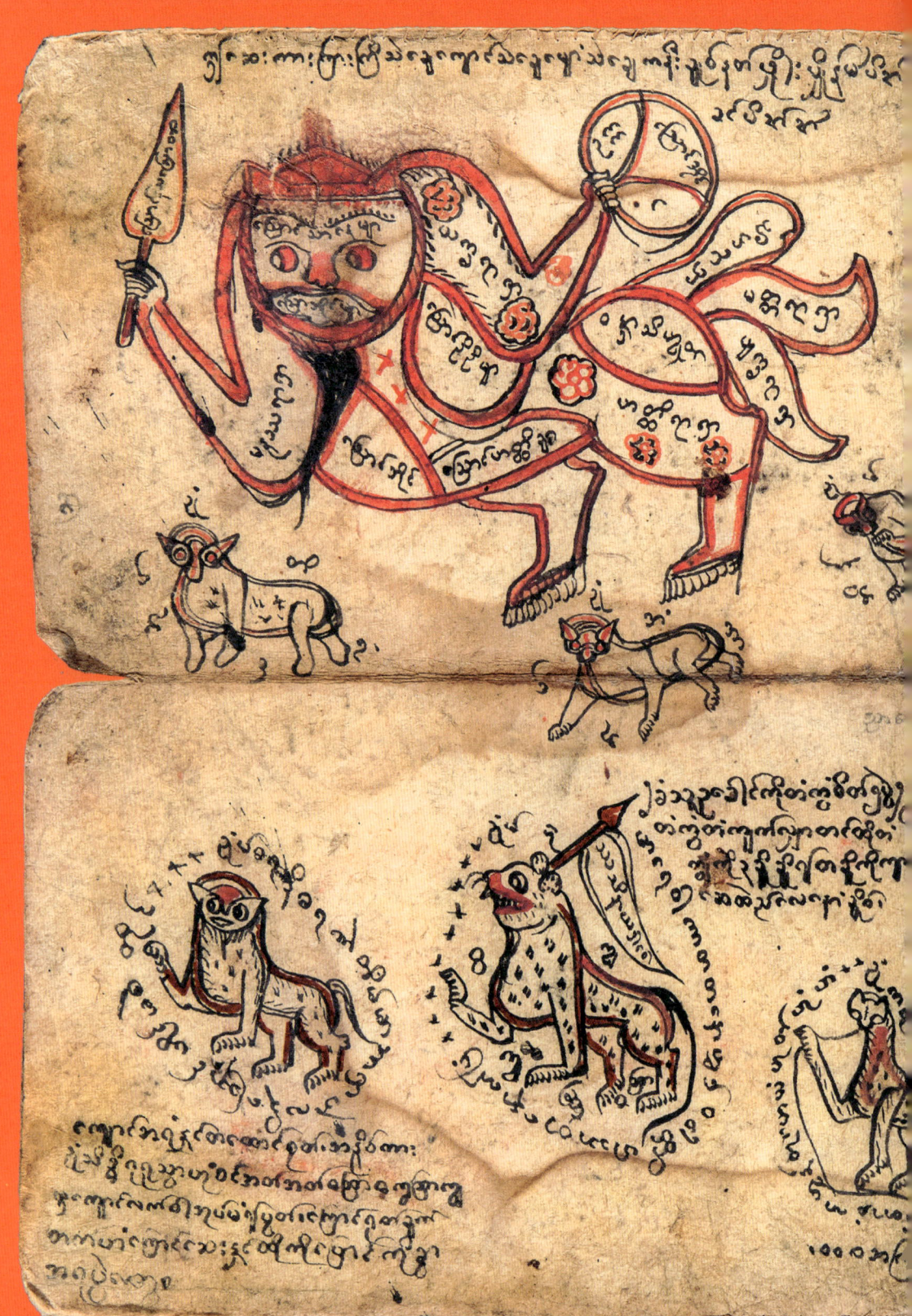

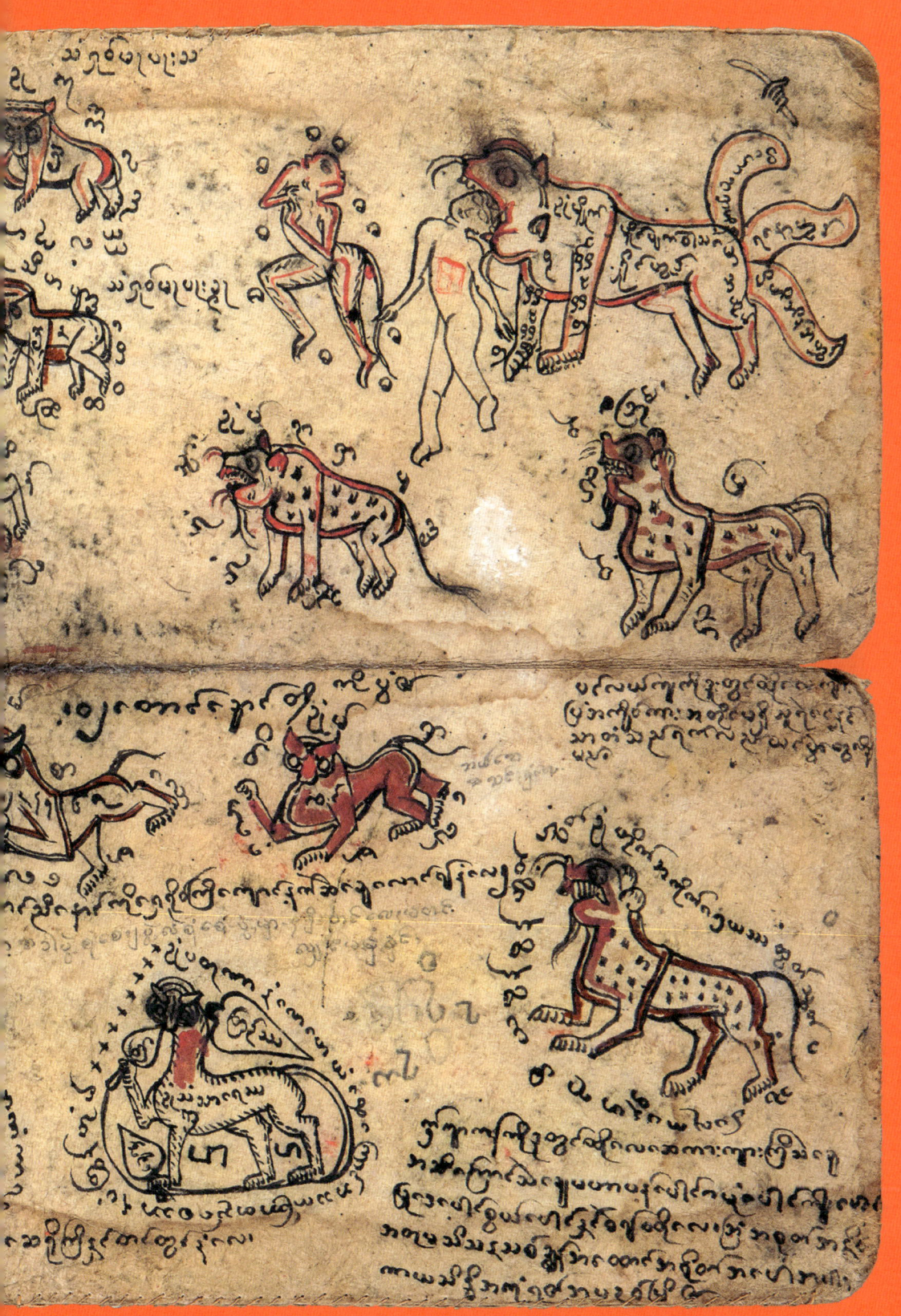

Index of tattoo designs, Burma, nineteenth century. Milan, Tattoo Museo Gianmaurizio Fercioni.

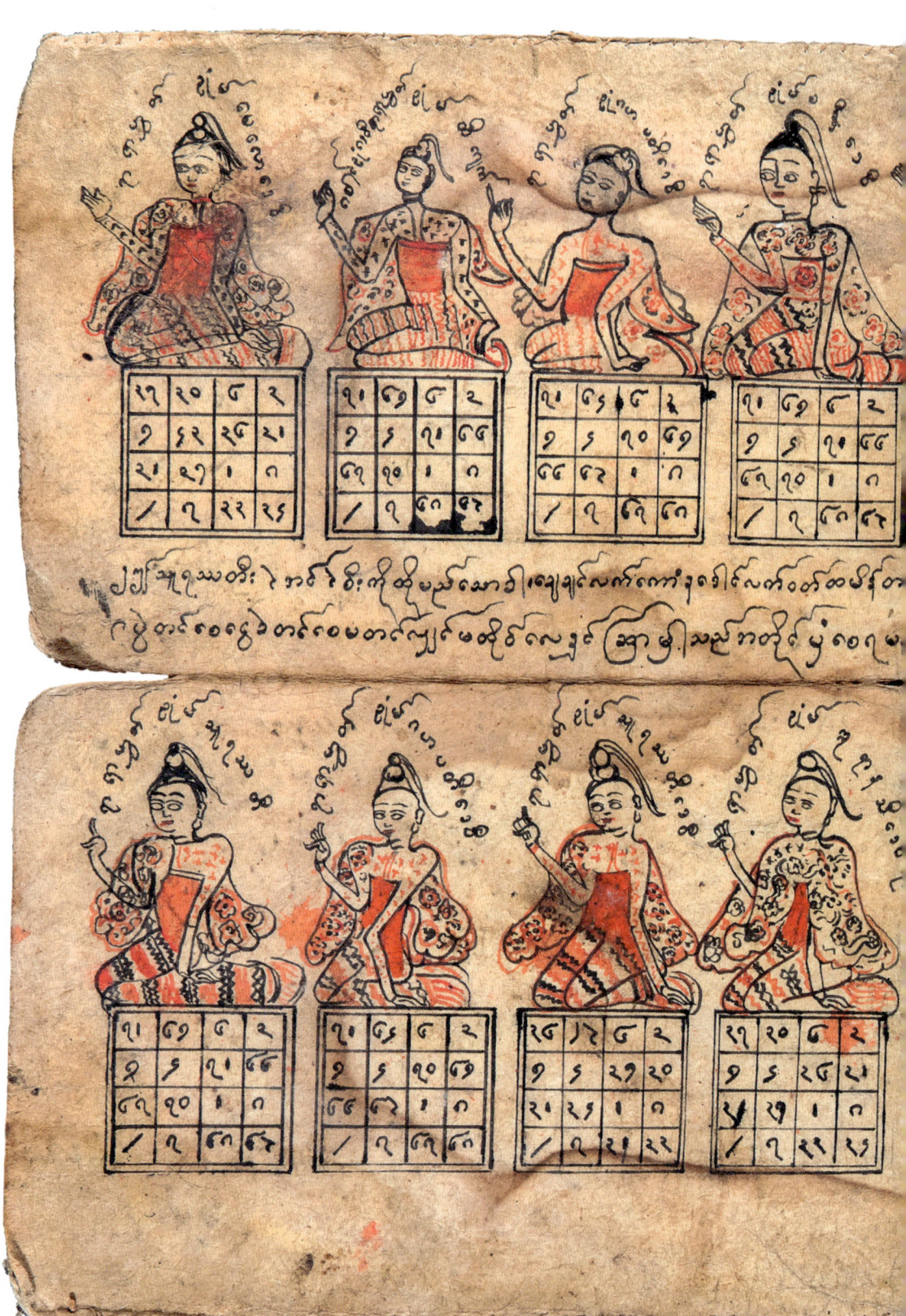

152

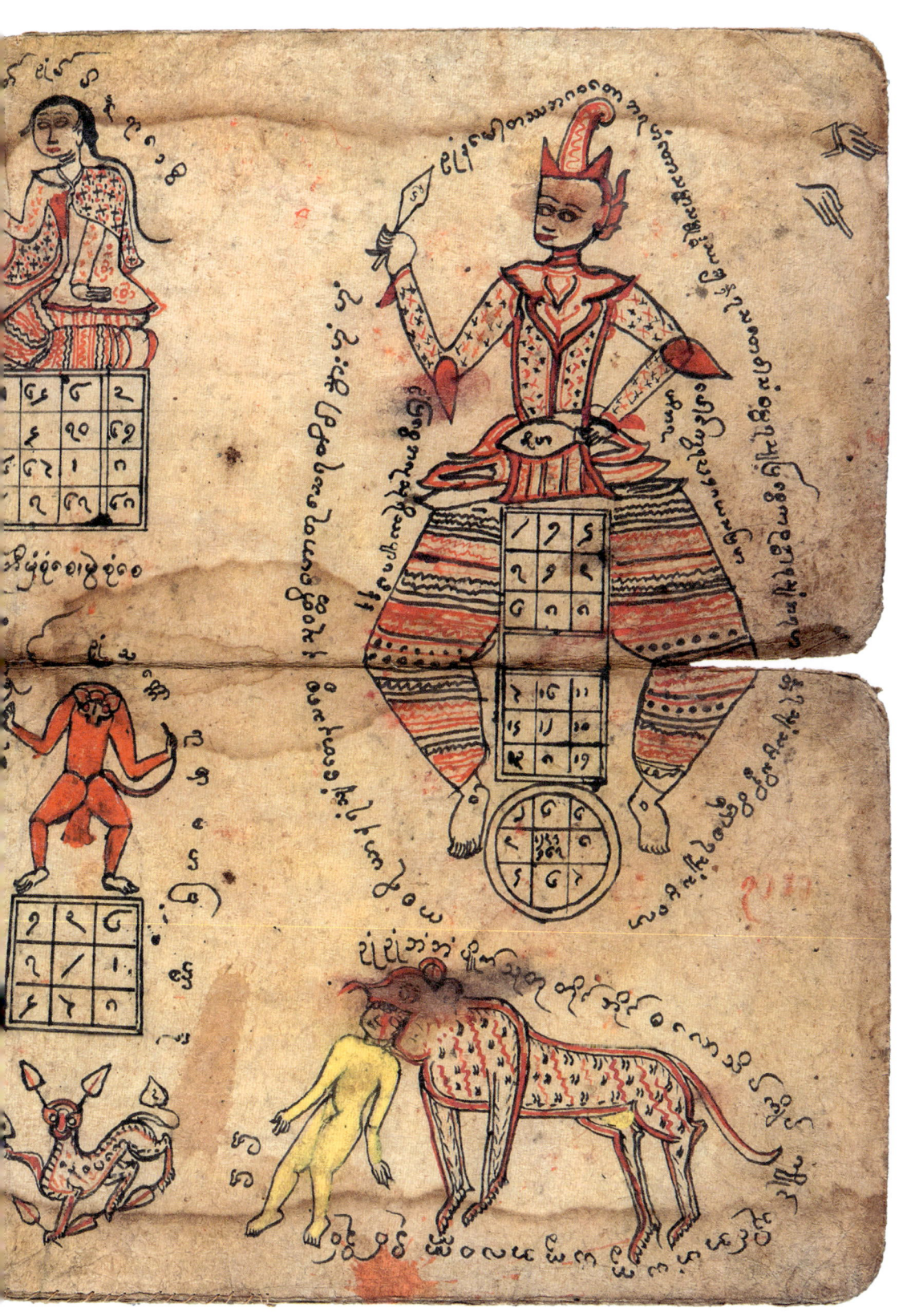

Index of tattoo designs, Burma, nineteenth century. Milan, Tattoo Museo Gianmaurizio Fercioni.

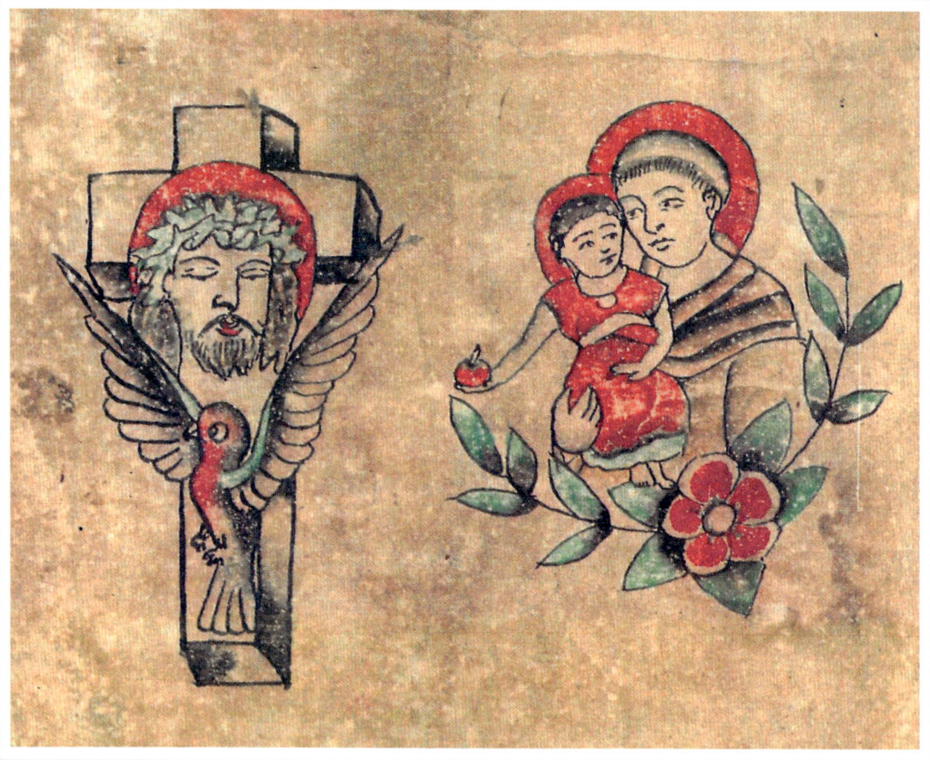

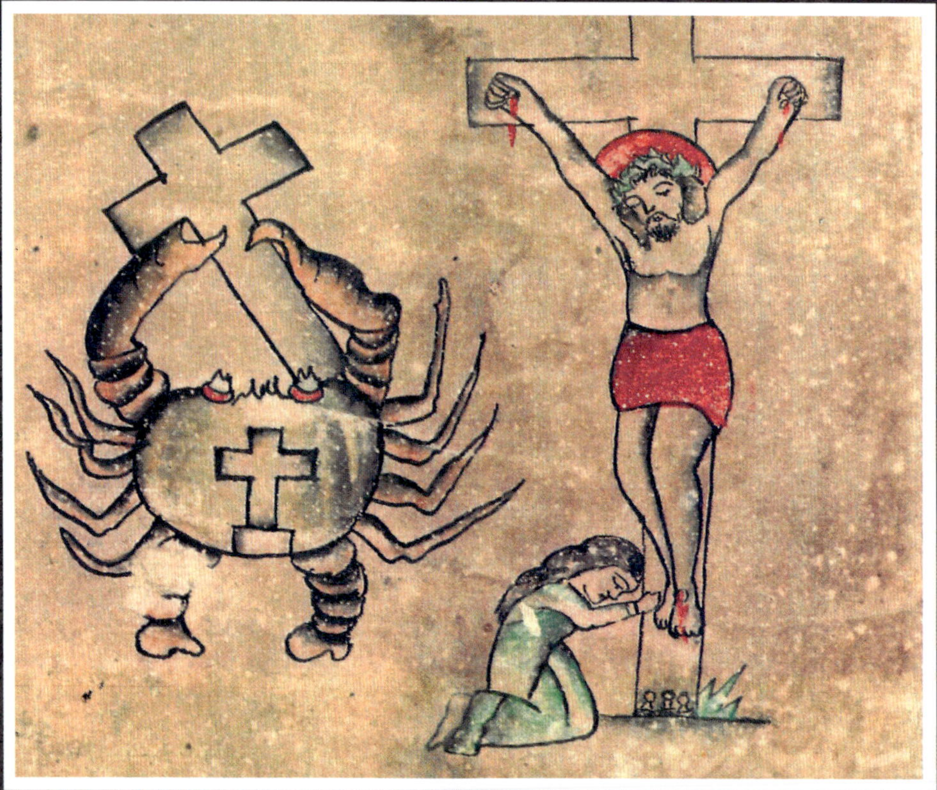

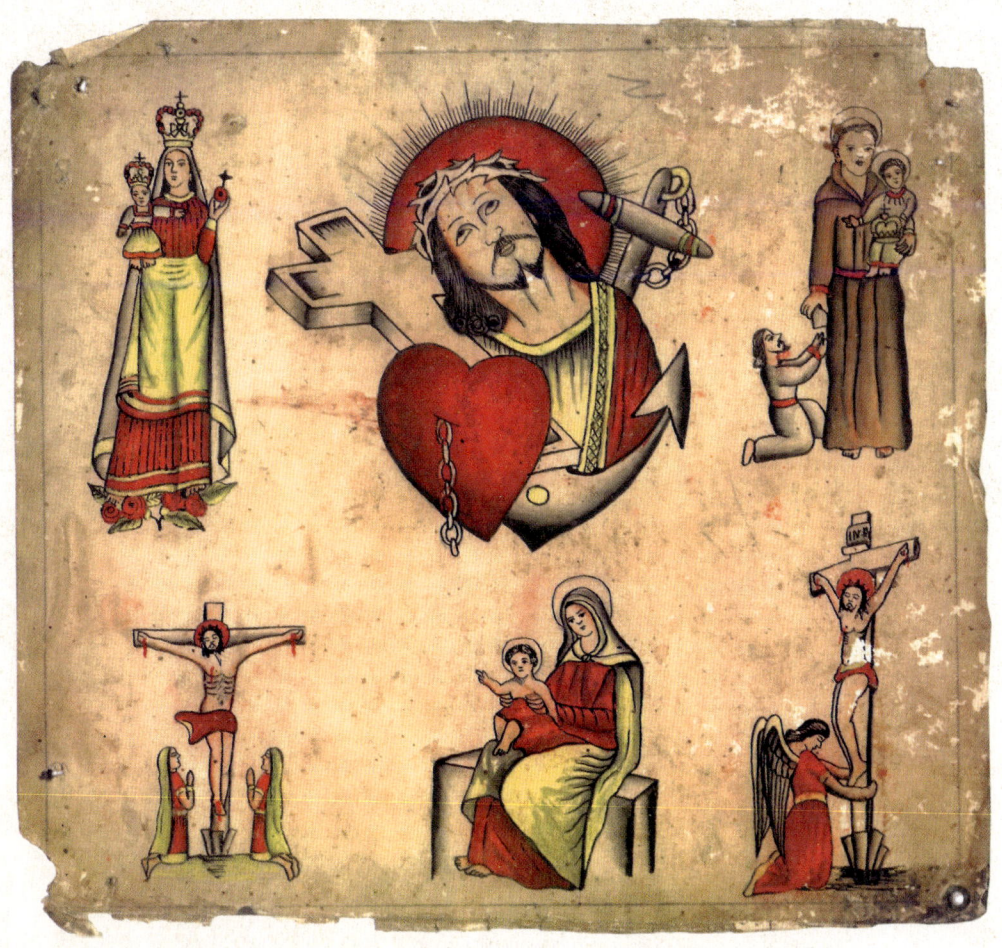

This and opposite page: Tattoo designs with subjects for western customers, India, twentieth century. Milan, Tattoo Museo Gianmaurizio Fercioni.

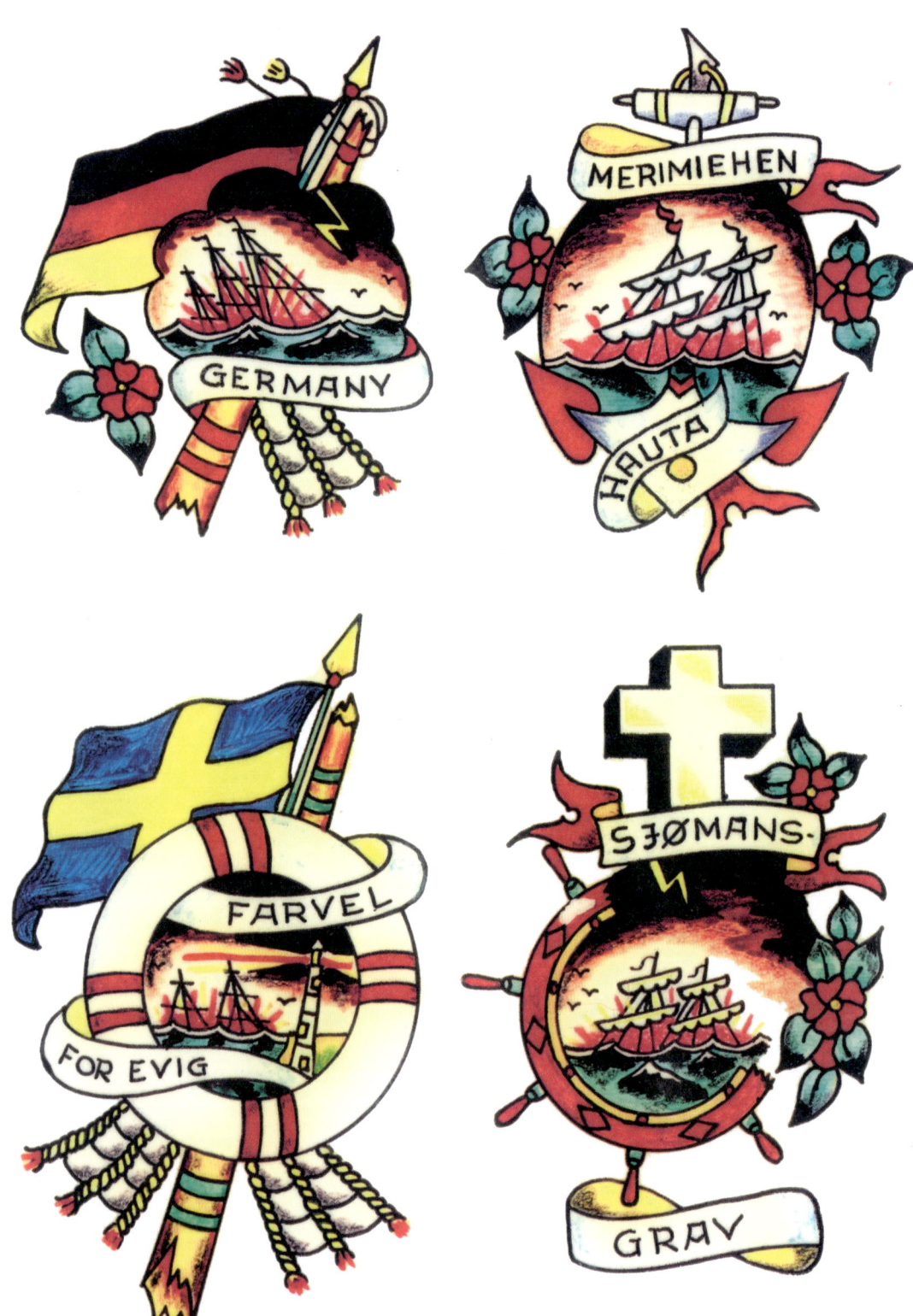

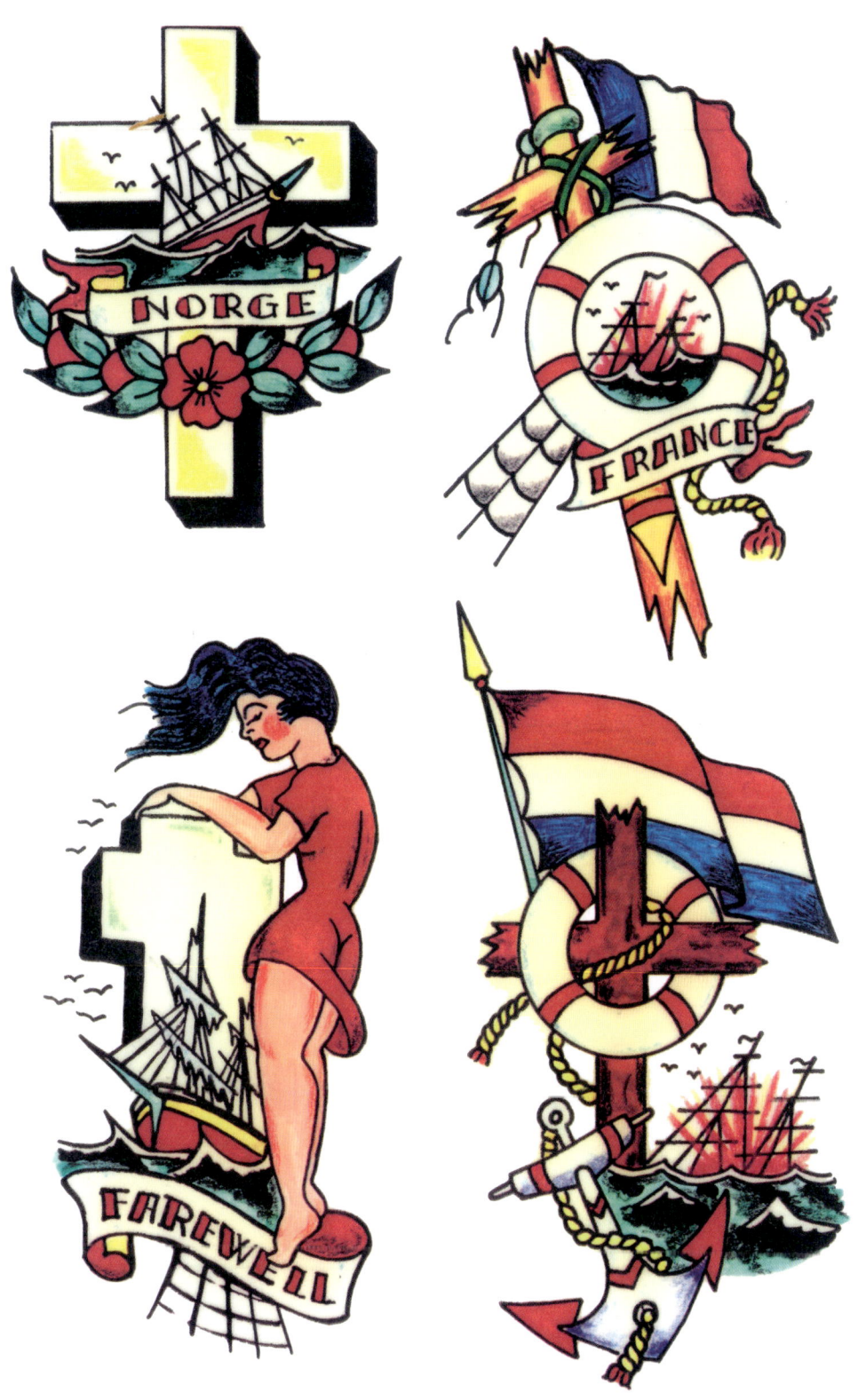

This and opposite page: Herbert Hoffmann, tattoo designs, 1950s. Milan, Tattoo Museo Gianmaurizio Fercioni.

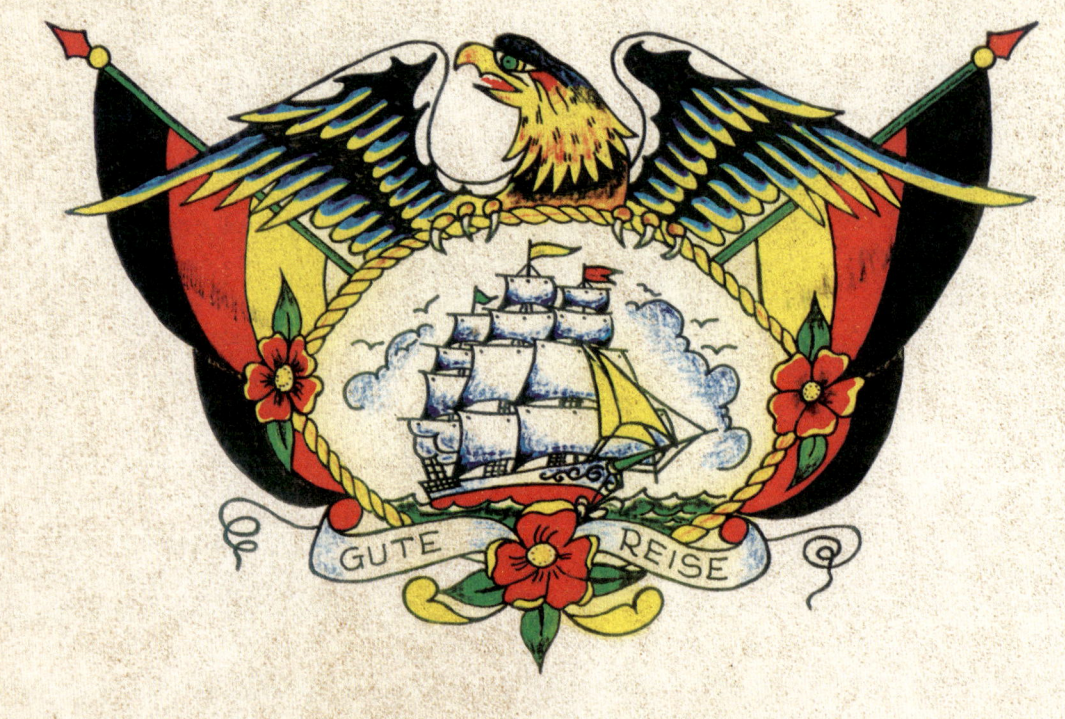

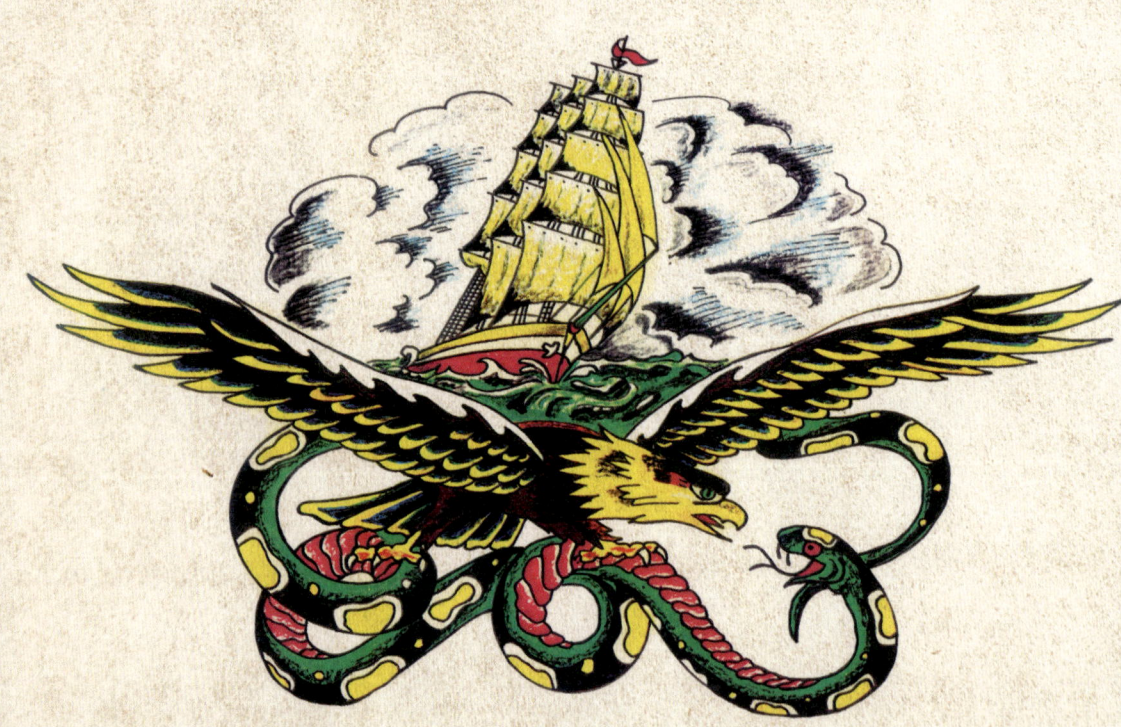

This and opposite page: Herbert Hoffmann, tattoo designs, 1950s. Milan, Tattoo Museo Gianmaurizio Fercioni.

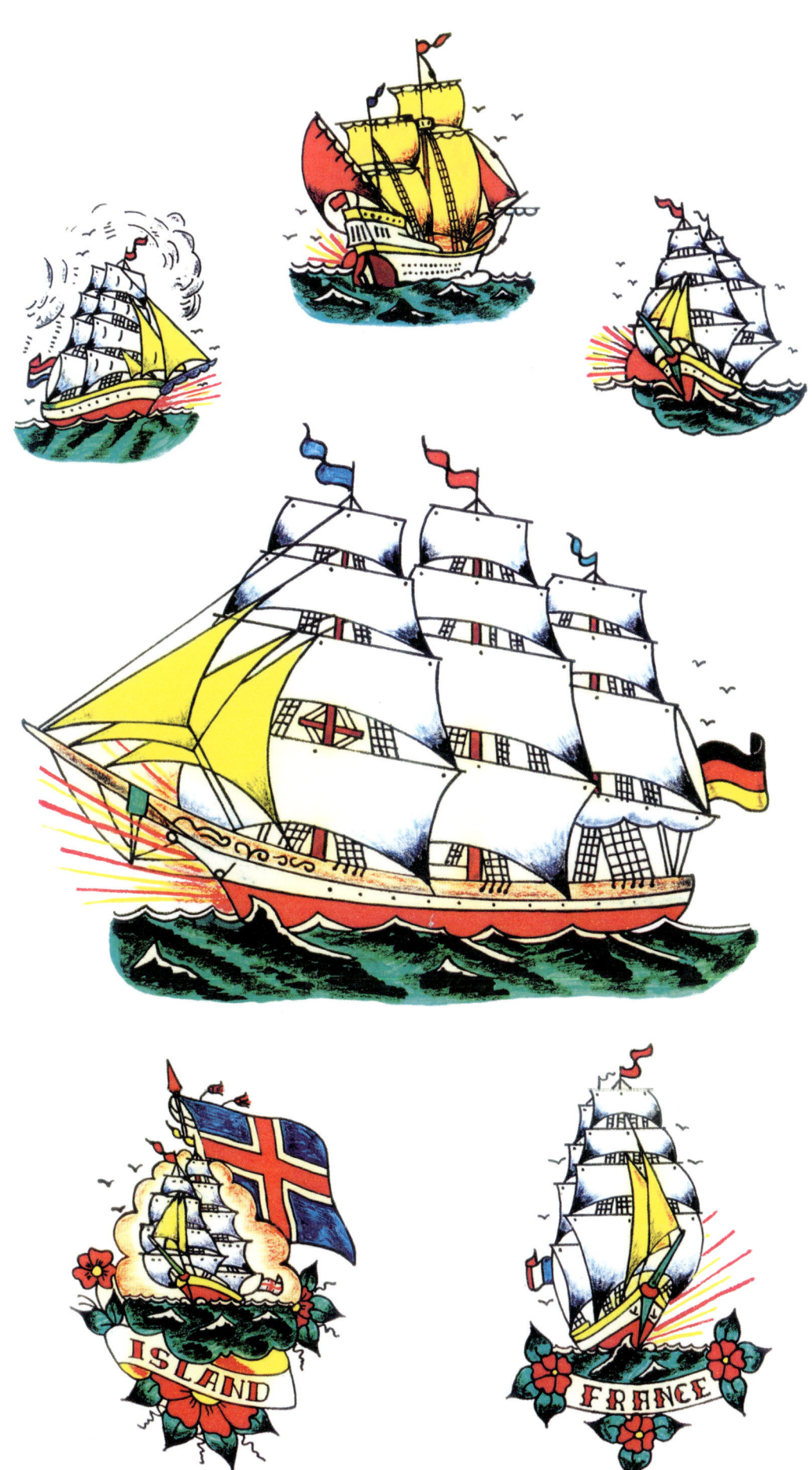

159

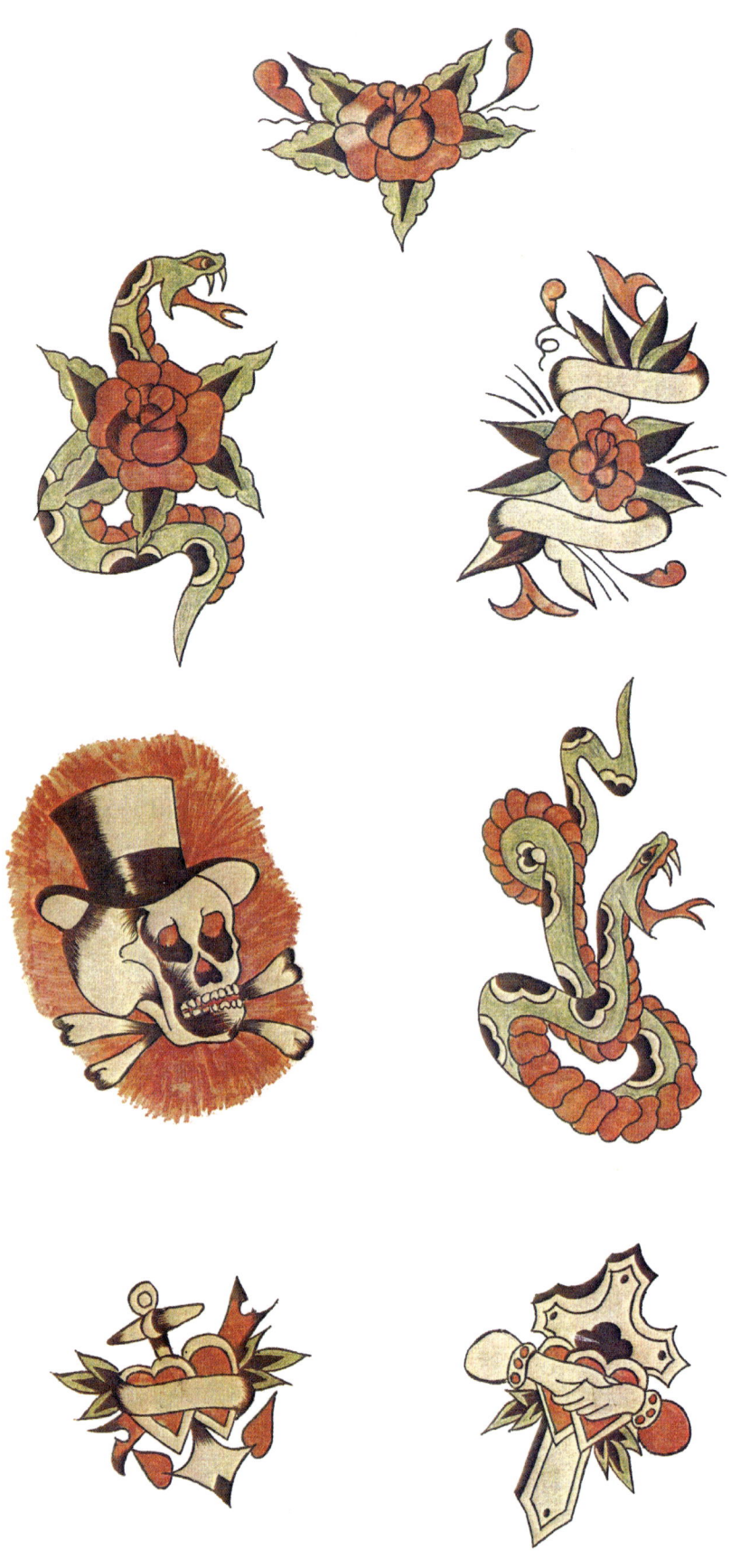

This and opposite page: Tattoo designs, United Kingdom, twentieth century. Milan, Tattoo Museo Gianmaurizio Fercioni.

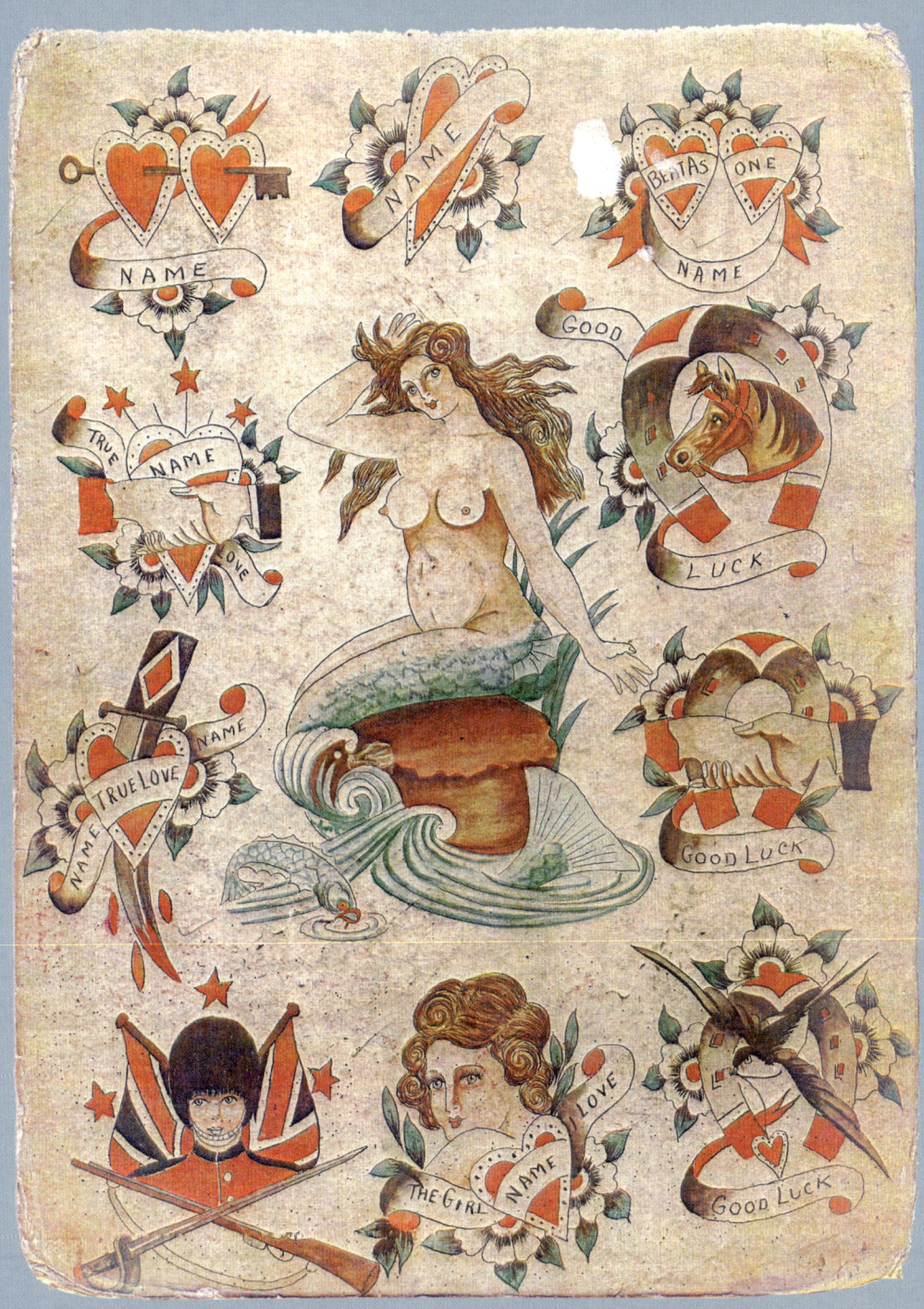

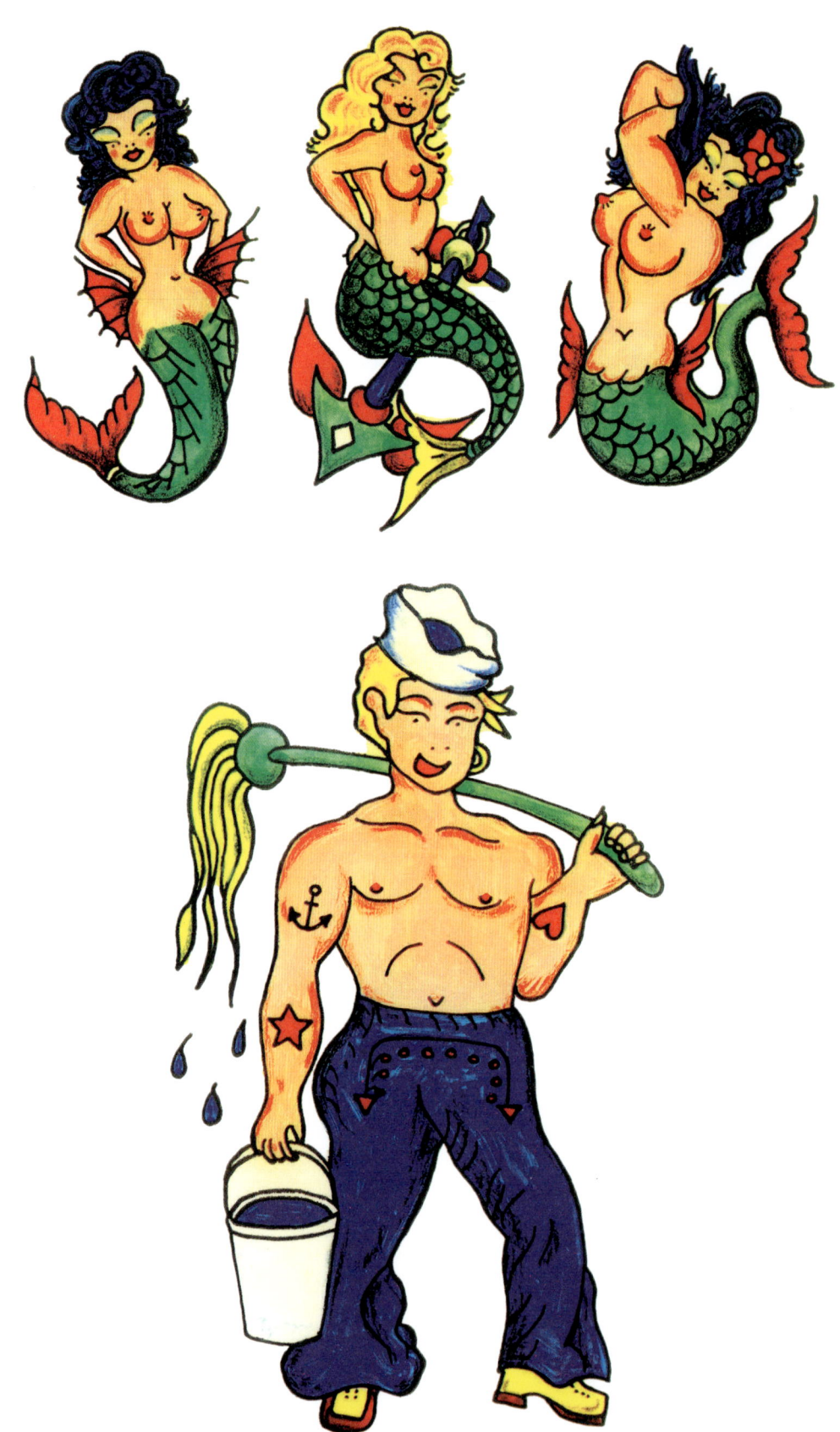

This page through page 173: Herbert Hoffmann, tattoo designs, 1950s. Milan, Tattoo Museo Gianmaurizio Fercioni.

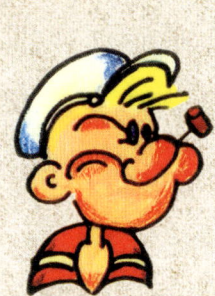
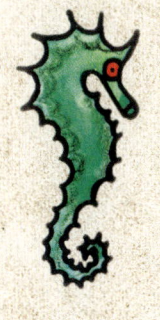
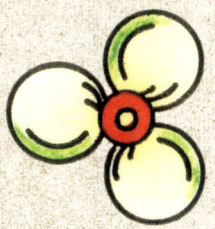
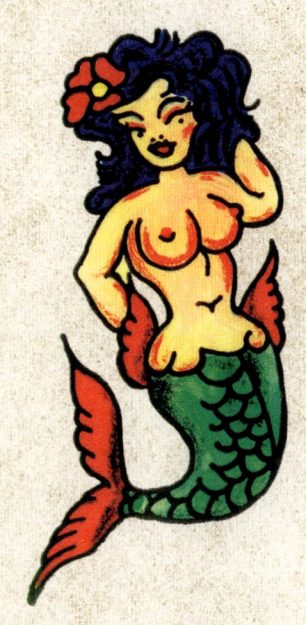
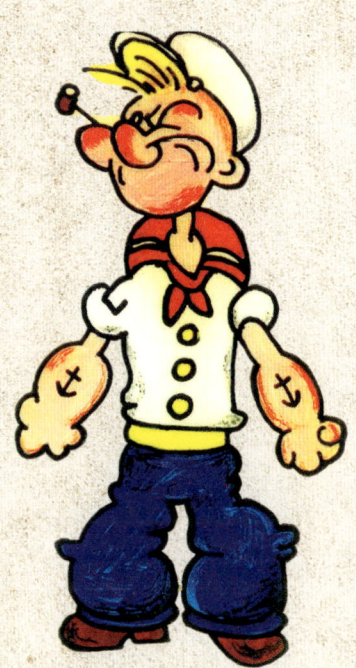
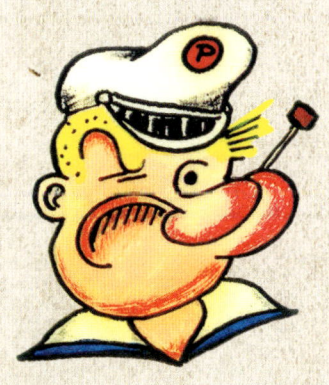
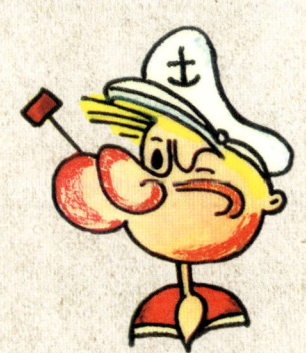

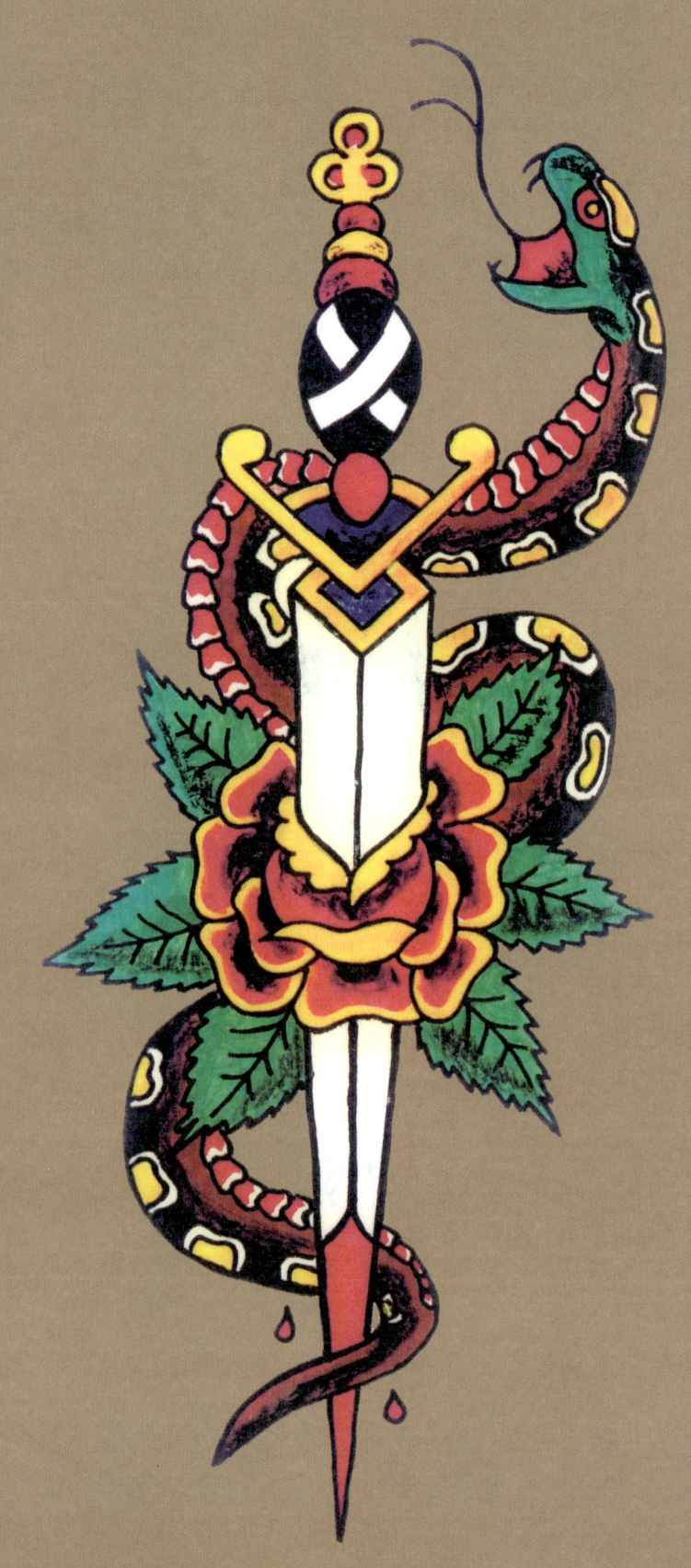

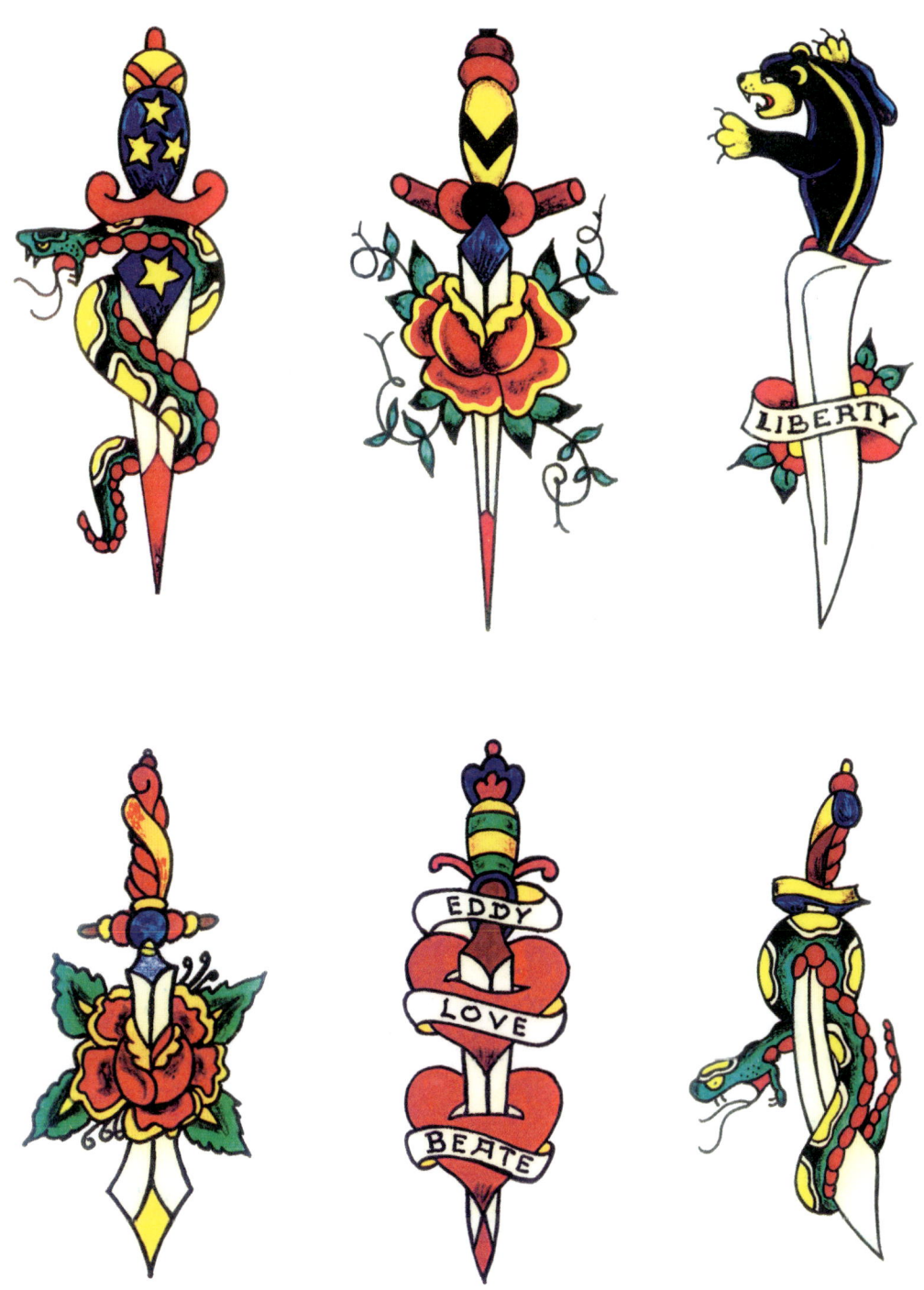

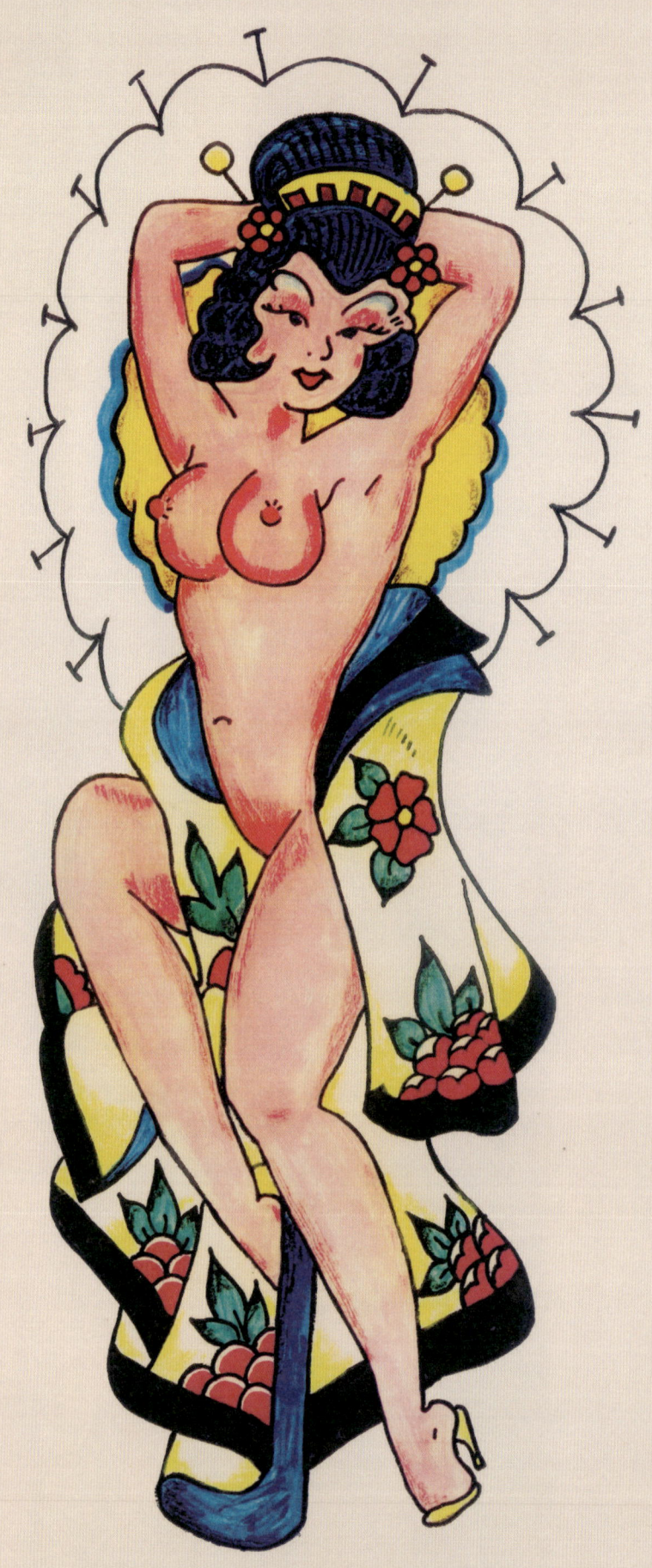

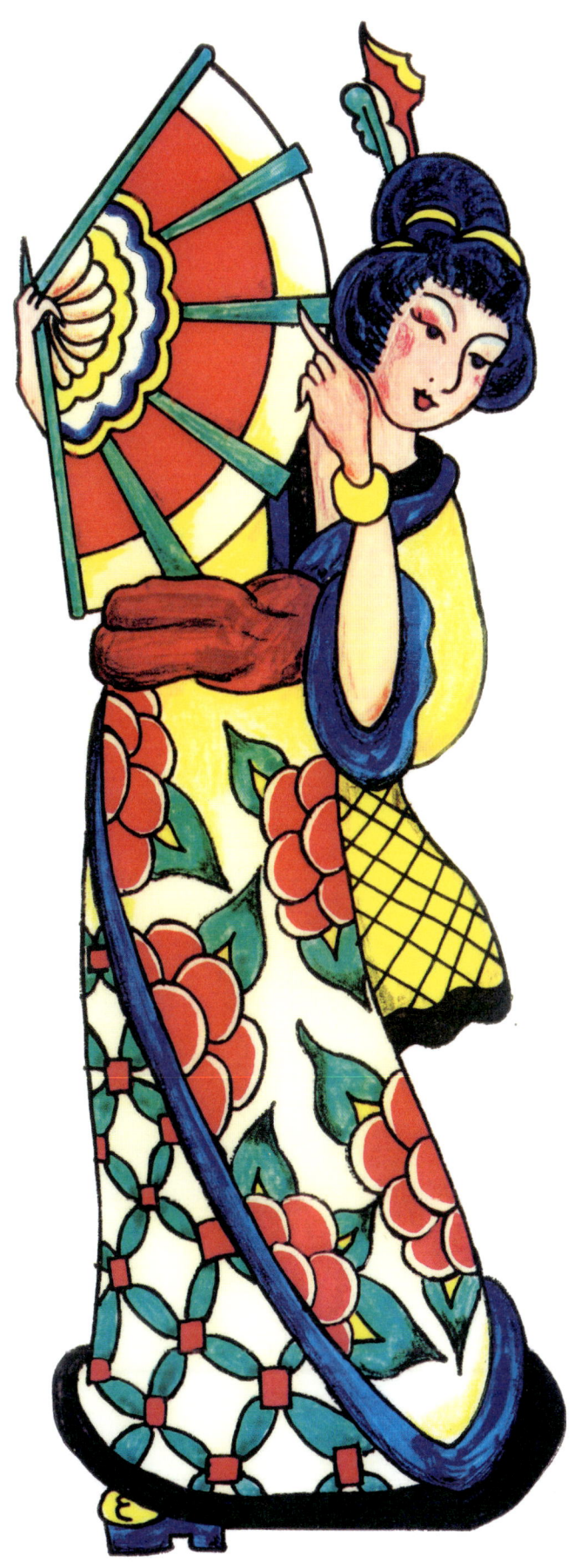

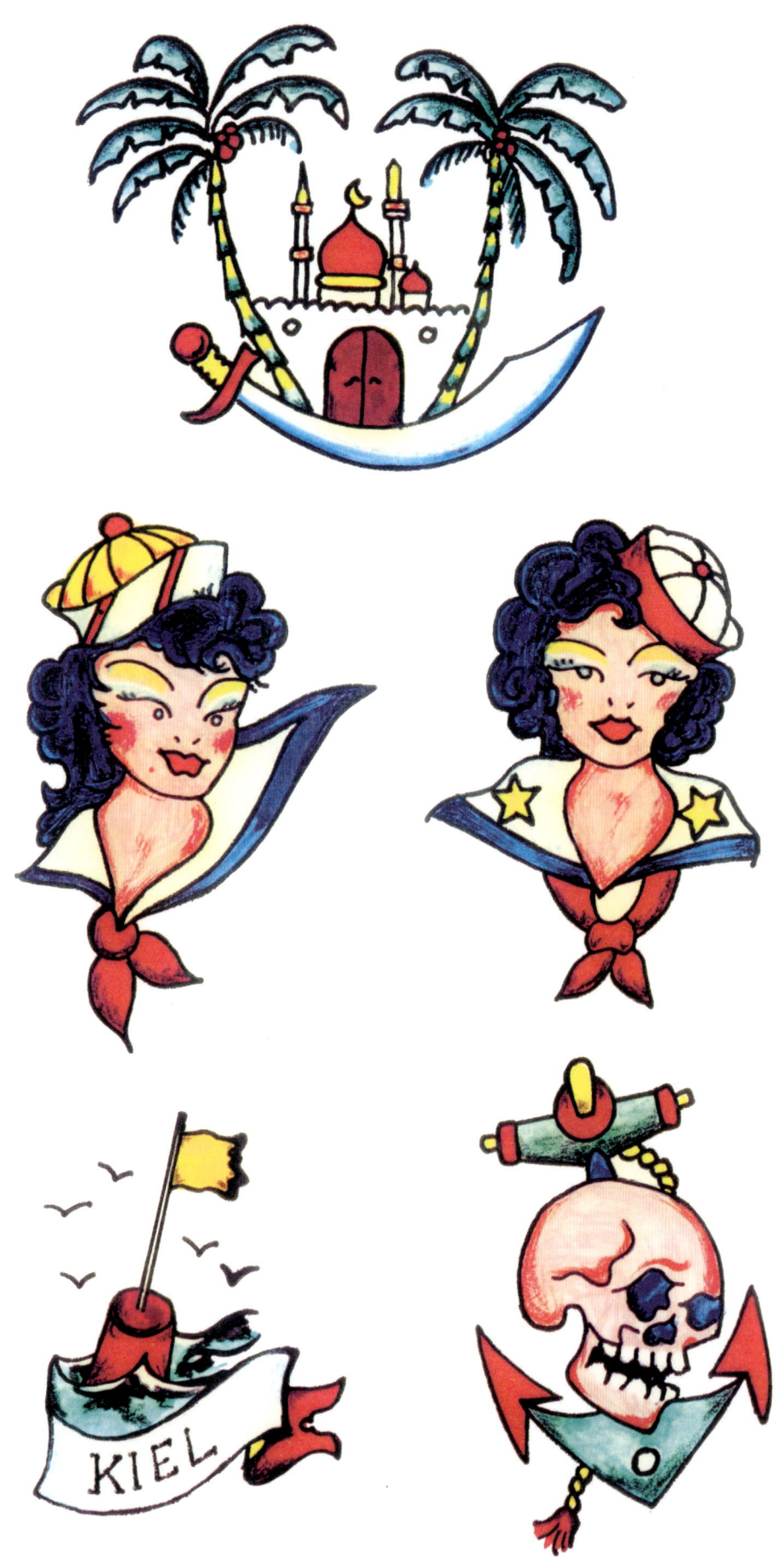

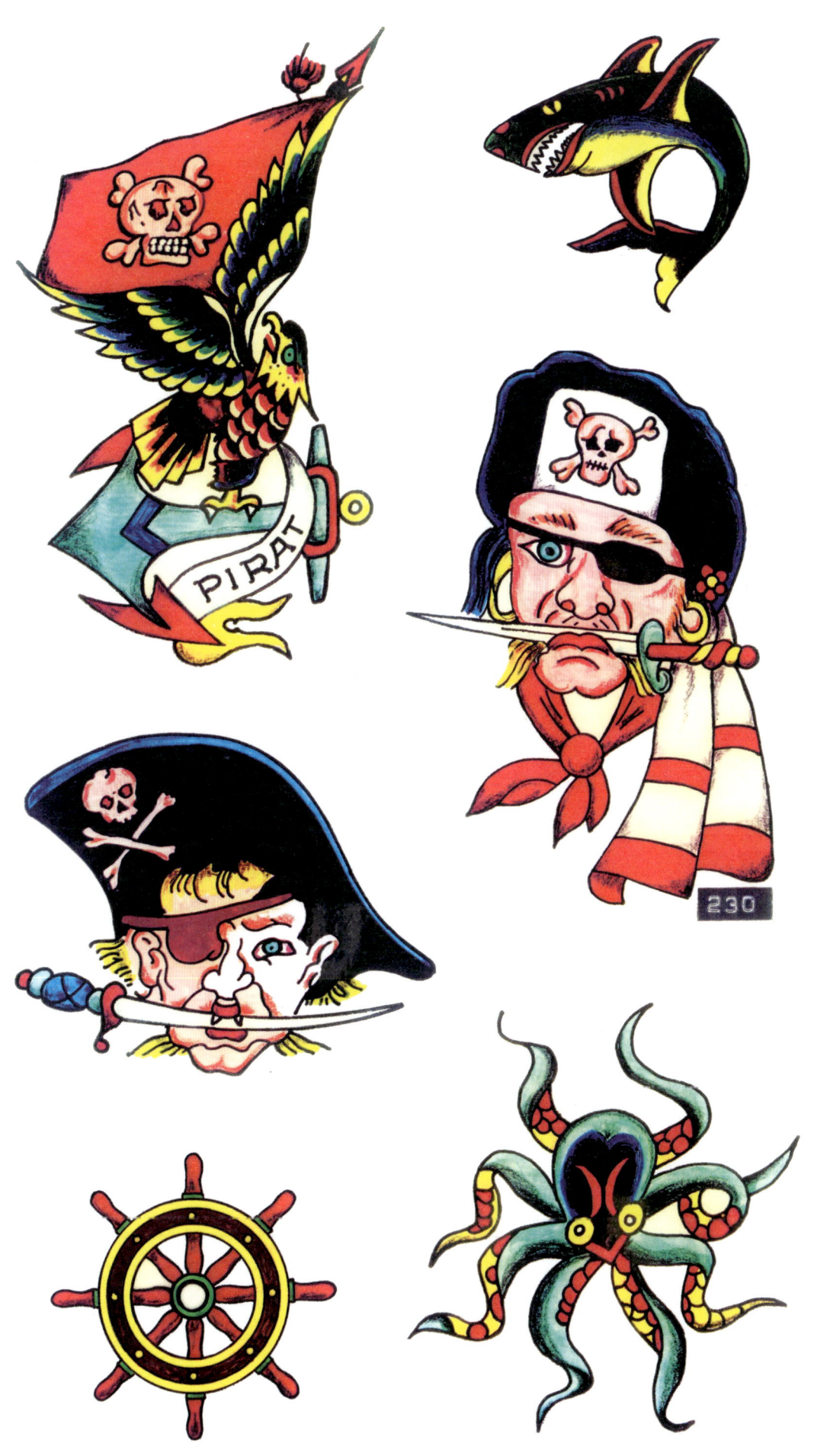

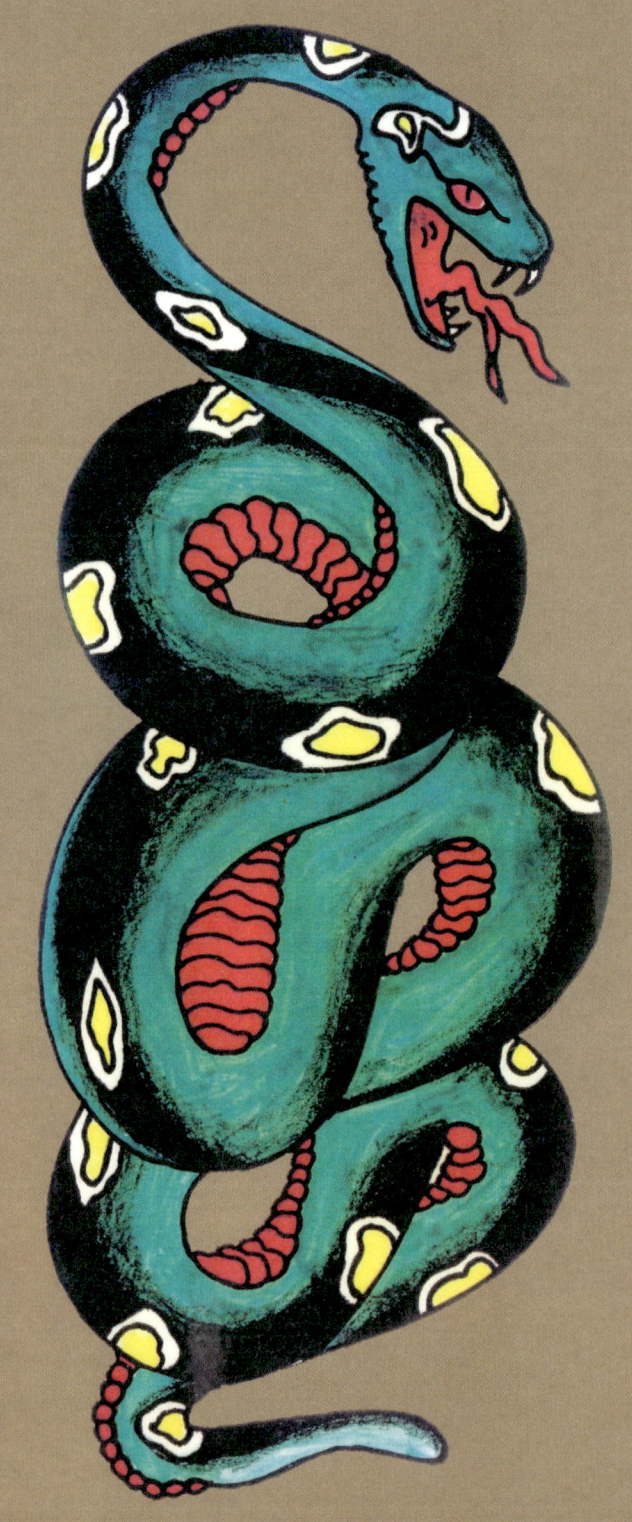

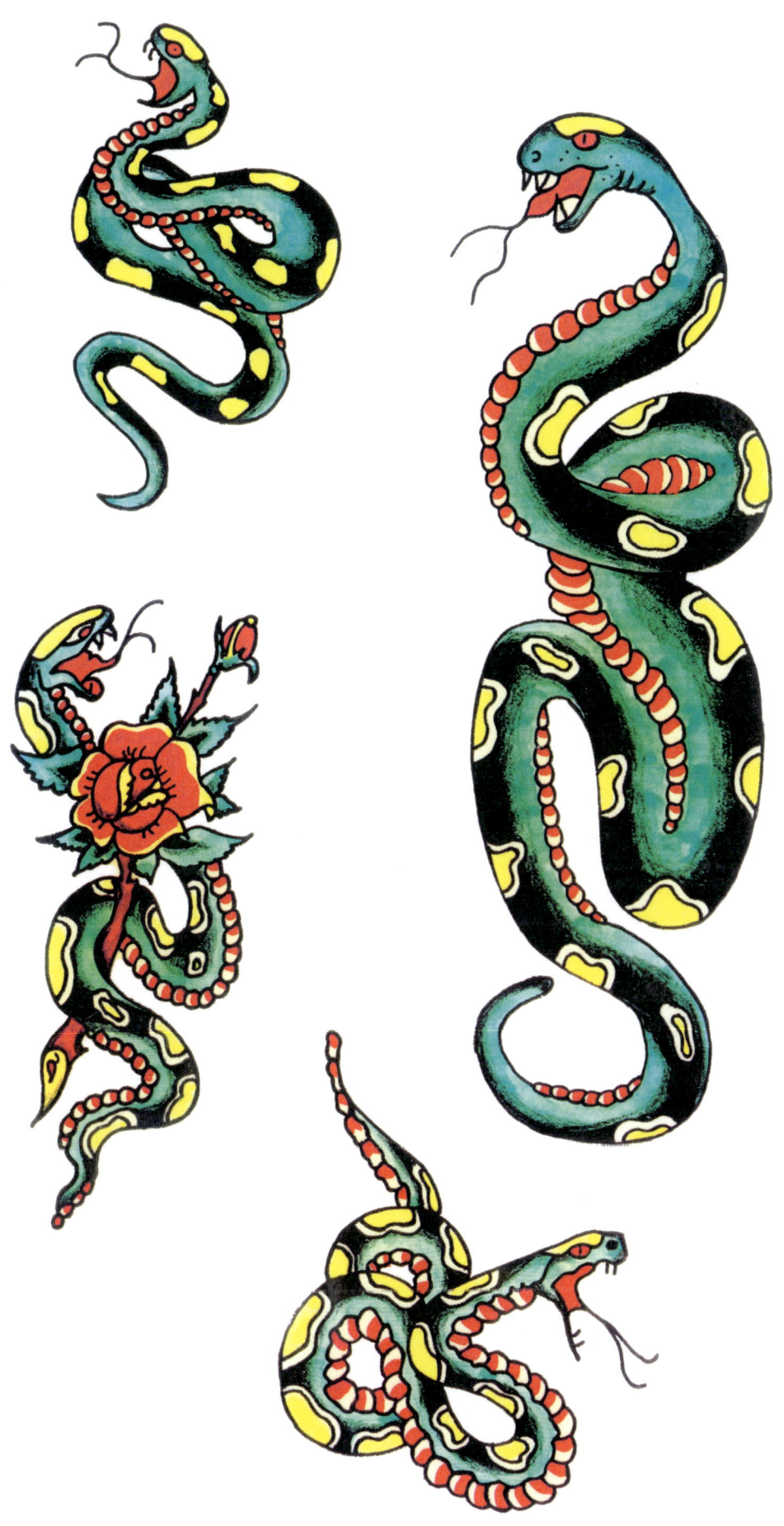

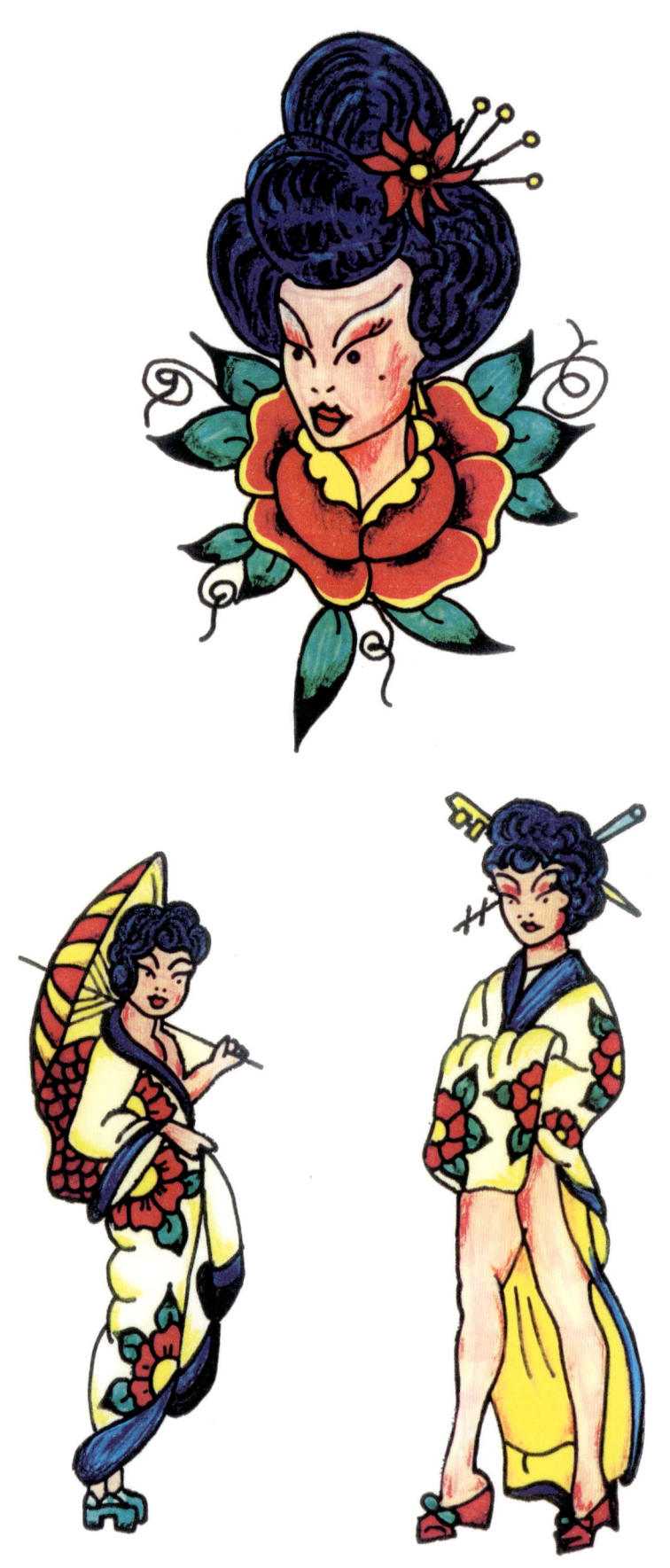

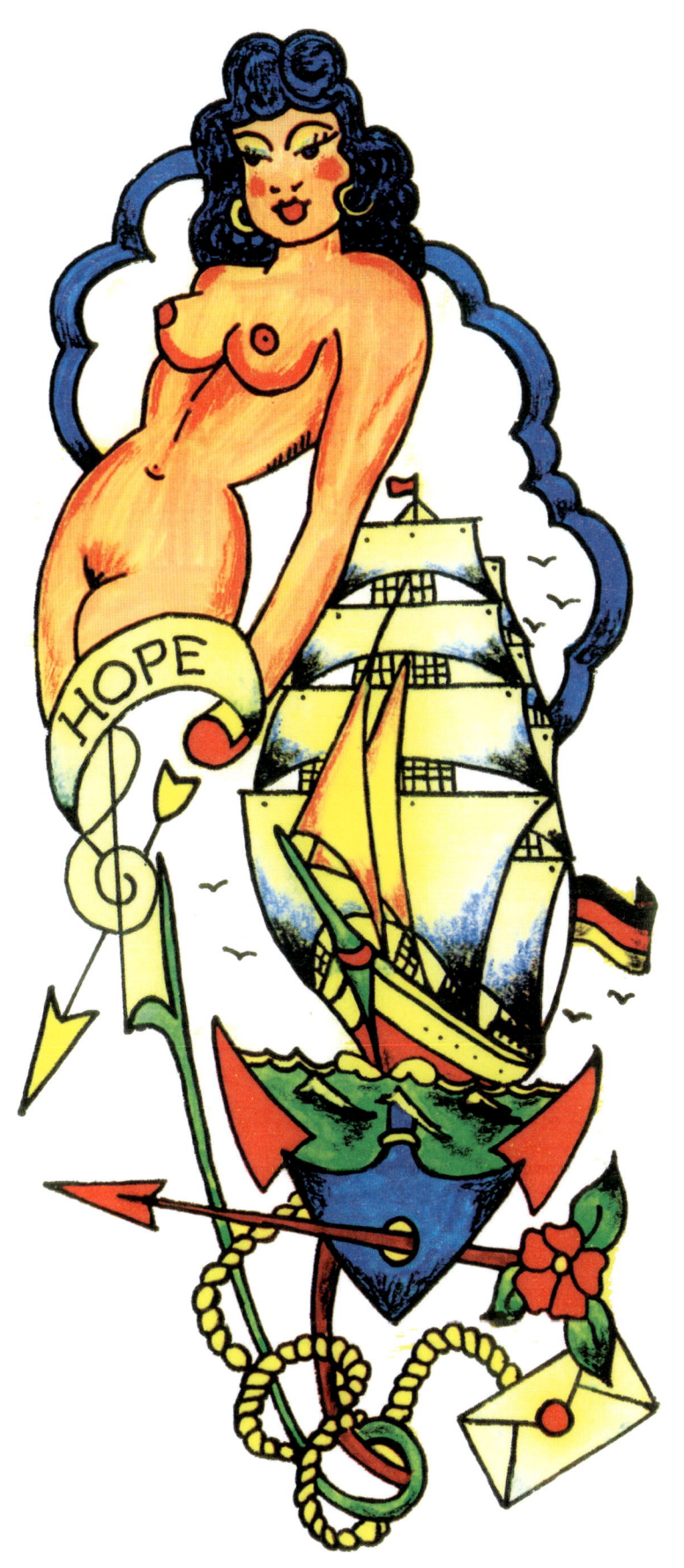

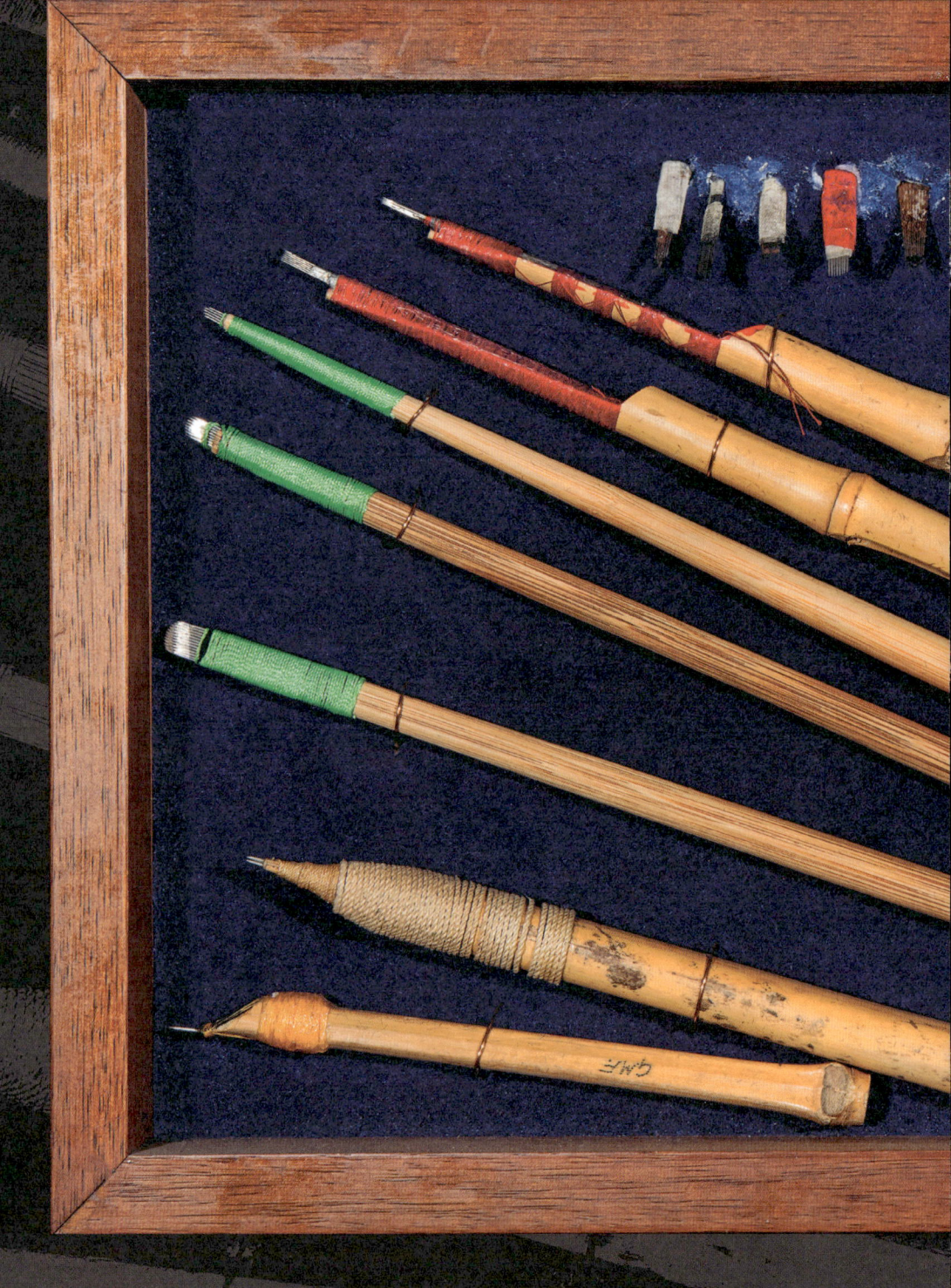

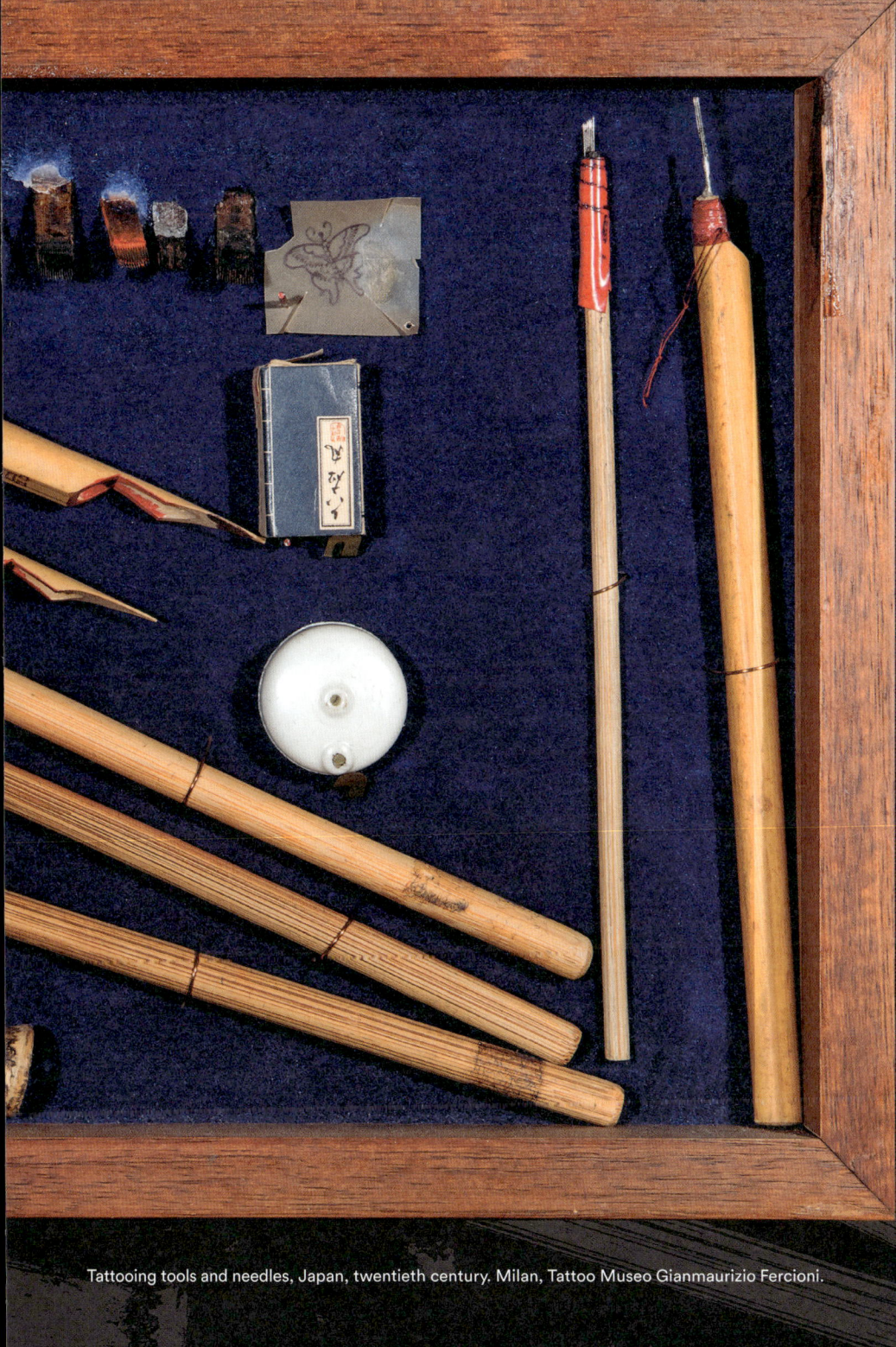

Tattooing tools and needles, Japan, twentieth century. Milan, Tattoo Museo Gianmaurizio Fercioni.

Photograph Credits

© Studio Fotografico Perotti / Diego Brambilla: pp. 22–23, 88, 89 top left, 89 top right, 89 bottom, 90 top left, 90 top right, 90 bottom left, 90 bottom right, 91 top, 91 bottom, 92 top left, 92 top right, 92 bottom left, 92 bottom right, 93, 95 top, 95 bottom, 114, 146, 147, 148, 149, 150–151, 152–153, 174–175

© DeAgostini Picture Library / Scala, Florence: pp. 24–25, 26–27 top, 26–27 bottom, 62

© Museo Archeologico dell'Alto Adige, Bolzano / Paul Hanny: p. 33 top

© Museo Archeologico dell'Alto Adige / Ospedale Regionale di Bolzano: p. 33 center

© Museo Archeologico dell'Alto Adige, Bolzano / Sara Welponer: p. 33 bottom

© Museo Archeologico dell'Alto Adige, Bolzano / Harald Wisthaler: pp. 34 top, 34 left, 34 right

© Museo Archeologico dell'Alto Adige, Bolzano / foto-dpi.co: p. 35

© Museo Archeologico dell'Alto Adige, Bolzano / EURAC / Marco Samadelli / Gregor Staschitz: pp. 36 top, 36 bottom, 37 top, 37 bottom, 38 top, 38 bottom

© The Trustees of the British Museum, London / Scala, Florence: pp. 39 bottom, 46 right

© Brooklyn Museum, New York: pp. 44, 46 left

© RMN-Grand Palais / Christian Dècamps / RMN-GP / Dist. Photo Scala, Florence: p. 45 left

© Museo Egizio, Turin: pp. 45 right

© The Metropolitan Museum of Art, New York: p. 47

© Anne Austin: pp. 48–49, 50–51

© Parco Archeologico di Cerveteri e Tarquinia–Museo Nazionale Archeologico Cerite, Cerveteri: p. 54

© Allard Pierson Museum, Amsterdam: p. 53

© Alamy Stock Photo / Jozef Sedmak: p. 65

© Alma Mater Studiorum Università di Bologna, Sistema Museale di Ateneo, Collezione delle cere anatomiche "Luigi Cattaneo / Photo Marco Pintacorona": pp. 76 top left, 76 top right, 76 bottom

© Museo delle Civiltà, Collezione Arti e Tradizioni Popolari, Rome / Photo Gaia Schiavinotto: pp. 77, 78 top, 78 left, 78 right, 82, 85

© Museo delle Civiltà, Collezione Arti e Tradizioni Popolari, Rome: pp. 79 top left, 79 top right, 79 bottom left, 79 bottom right, 80, 81 top left, 81 top right, 81 bottom left, 81 bottom right, 83, 84, 86, 87

© Gian Paolo Barbieri, courtesy of Fondazione Gian Paolo Barbieri: p. 94

© Archives of the Museo di Antropologia Criminale "Cesare Lombroso" of the University of Turin: pp. 100, 101, 102–103, 104–105, 106, 107, 108, 109 top left, 109 top right, 109 bottom, 110, 111 top, 111 left, 111 right, 112 top, 112 bottom, 113 top, 113 bottom

© Library of Congress, Washington, DC: p. 115 left

© State Library of Victoria, Melbourne: p. 115 right

© Yale University Library, Beinecke Rare Book and Manuscript Library, New Haven, Connecticut: p. 116

© Musée Carnavalet–Histoire de Paris, Paris: p. 119

© Nataša Ilinčic: pp. 129, 131 top left, 131 top right, 131 bottom left, 131 bottom right, 133

© Zohra Bensemra / Reuters / Contrasto: pp. 134–135, 136–137, 138–139

© Jodi Hilton: pp. 140, 141 left, 141 right, 142–143

Holders of the rights to any unspecified iconographic sources should contact the publisher.

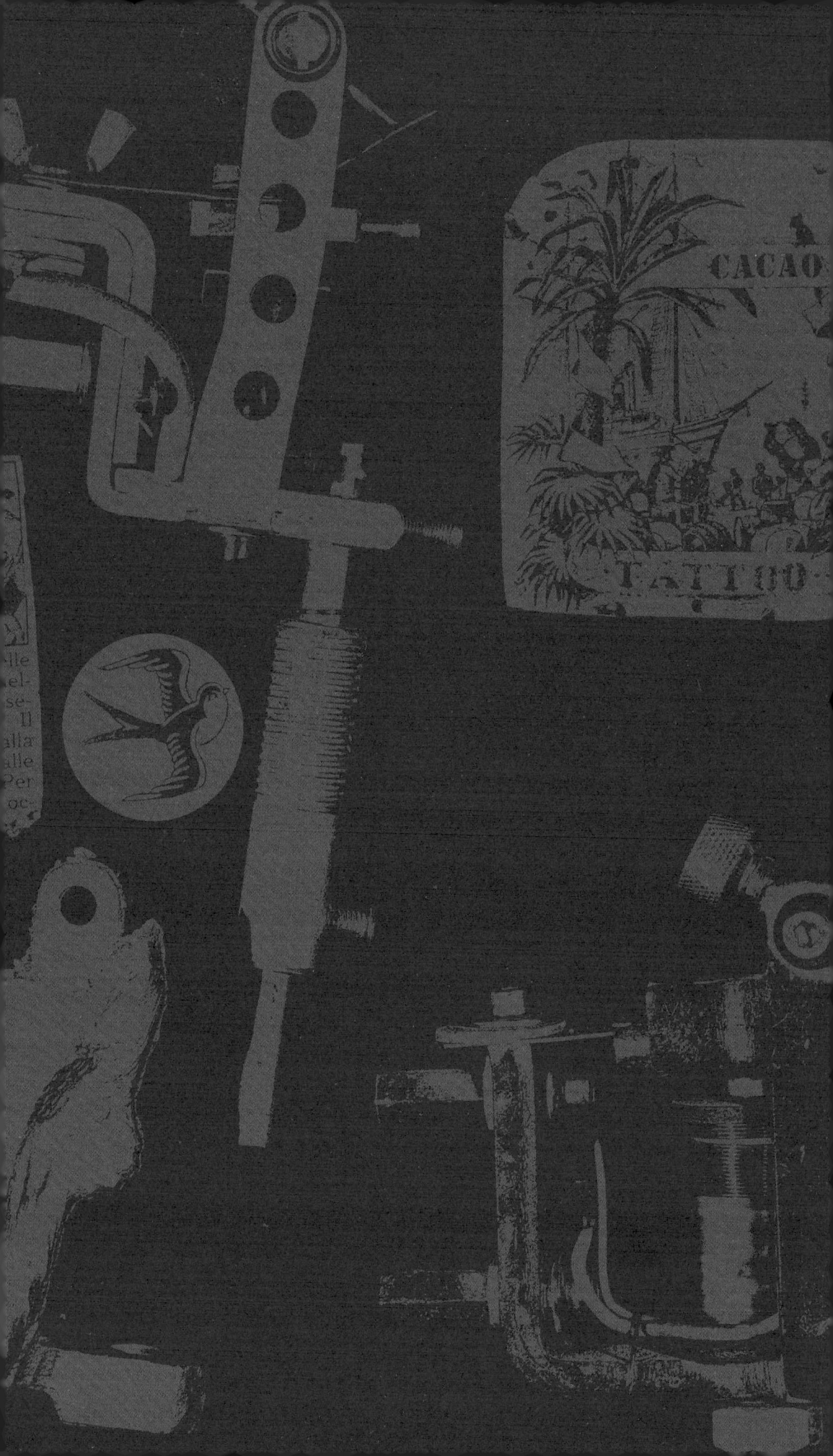